SOCIAL WORK AND SOCIAL POLICY
Concepts and Methods

SOCIAL WORK AND SOCIAL POLICY

Concepts and Methods

P.R. Gautam

R.S. Singh

CENTRUM PRESS

NEW DELHI-110002 (INDIA)

CENTRUM PRESS
H.O.: 4360/4, Ansari Road, Daryaganj,
New Delhi-110002 (India)
Tel: 23278000, 23261597, 23255577, 23286875
B.O.: No. 1015, Ist Main Road, BSK IIIrd Stage,
IIIrd Phase, IIIrd Block, Bangalore-560085 (INDIA)
Tel: 080-41723429
Email: centrumpress@gmail.com
Visit us at: www.centrumpress.com

Social Work and Social Policy: Concepts and Methods

First Edition, 2011

ISBN 978-93-80836-06-5

PRINTED IN INDIA

Printed at Balaji Offset, Delhi.

Contents

Preface

An understanding of social policy is vital for engaging practically with social work values, dealing with political and ethical questions about responsibility, rights, our understanding of 'the good society'. Social policy primarily refers to guidelines and interventions for the changing, maintenance or creation of living conditions that are conducive to human welfare. Thus, social policy is that part of public policy that has to do with social issues. The Malcolm Wiener Centre for Social Policy at Harvard University describes it as *"public policy and practice in the areas of health care, human services, criminal justice, inequality, education, and labour"* Social policy often deals with issues which Rittle & Webber (1973) called wicked problems.

Social Policy is also distinct as an academic field which focuses on the systematic evaluation of societies' responses to social need. London School of Economics professor Richard Titmuss is considered to have established Social Policy (or Social Administration) as an academic subject and many universities offer the subject for undergraduate and postgraduate study. Social Policy and Administration is an academic subject concerned with the study of social services and the welfare state. It developed in the early part of the 20th century as a complement to social work studies, aimed at people who would be professionally involved in the administration of welfare. In the course of the last forty years, the range and breadth of the subject has developed.

Social Policy is a subject area, not a discipline; it borrows from other social science disciplines in order to develop study in the area. The contributory disciplines include sociology, social work, psychology, economics, political science, management, history, philosophy and law. Social policy draws on sociology to explain the social context of welfare provision. If we are trying to improve people's welfare, it is helpful to try to understand something about the way that people are, and how welfare policies relate to their situation. Some writers have gone further, arguing that because welfare takes place in a social context, it can only be understood in that context. This has been particularly important for 'critical social policy', which begins from a view of social policy as underpinned by social inequality - particularly the inequalities of class, race and gender.

The book endeavours to provide all requirements of students, teachers, social workers, social work institutions to enable them to achieve success in social work and related activities.

—*Authors*

1

Introduction

Social Policy

The name 'social policy' is used to apply :

1. to the policies which governments use for welfare and social protection
2. to the ways in which welfare is developed in a society, and
3. to the academic study of the subject.

In the first sense, social policy is particularly concerned with social services and the welfare state. In the second, broader sense, it stands for a range of issues extending far beyond the actions of government-the means by which welfare is promoted, and the social and economic conditions which shape the development of welfare.

Social Policy and Administration

Social Policy and Administration is an academic subject concerned with the study of social services and the welfare state. It developed in the early part of the 20th century as a complement to social work studies, aimed at people who would be professionally involved in the administration of welfare. In the course of the last forty years, the range and breadth of the subject has developed. The principal areas relate to :

- policy and administrative practice in social services, including health administration, social security, education, employment services, community care and housing management;

- social problems, including crime, disability, unemployment, mental health, learning disability, and old age;
- issues relating to social disadvantage, including race, gender and poverty; and
- the range of collective social responses to these conditions.

Social Policy is a subject area, not a discipline; it borrows from other social science disciplines in order to develop study in the area. The contributory disciplines include sociology, social work, psychology, economics, political science, management, history, philosophy and law.

Welfare

Welfare is an ambiguous term, used in three main senses:

- Welfare commonly refers to 'well-being'. In welfare economics, welfare is understood in terms of 'utility'; people's well-being or interests consist of the things they choose to have.
- Welfare also refers to the range of services which are provided to protect people in a number of conditions, including childhood, sickness and old age. The idea of the 'welfare state' is an example. This is equivalent to the term 'social protection' in the European Union.
- In the United States, welfare refers specifically to financial assistance to poor people (e.g. Temporary Aid to Needy Families). This usage is not generally reflected elsewhere.

Welfare is often associated with needs, but it goes beyond what people need; to achieve well being, people must have choices, and the scope to choose personal goals and ambitions.

The idea of the "welfare state" is explained, along with models of welfare provision in several countries, in another page of this website. Choose this link to go there.

Arguments for Welfare

The basic arguments for collective provision are :

- *humanitarian.* Concerns about poverty and need have been central to many developments.
- *religious.* Several of the world's major religions make charity

a religious duty. Beyond charity, Catholicism recognises a duty of social solidarity (or mutual social responsibility); Judaism, Islam and Lutheran Christianity require collective responsibility for one's community.

- *mutual self-interest.* Many welfare systems have developed, not from state activity, but from a combination of mutualist activities, gradually reinforced by government.
- *democratic.* Social protection has developed in tandem with democratic rights.
- *practical.* Welfare provision has economic and social benefits. Countries with more extensive systems of social protection tend to be richer and have less poverty. (The main difficulty of evaluating this is knowing which comes first, wealth or welfare.)

There is scarcely a government in the world that does not recognise the force of these arguments and make some form of collective social provision. The real disputes are not about whether welfare should exist, but about how much provision there should be, and how it should be done. External link: A mediaeval argument for welfare provision: Jean Luis Vives, writing in 1526 .

Arguments Against Welfare

The main objections to the provision of welfare come from the 'radical right'. They are against welfare in principle, on the basis that it violates people's freedom. Redistribution is theft; taxation is forced labour.

These arguments rest on some questionable assumptions:

- *People have absolute rights to use property as they wish.* People in a society are interdependent, and the production of property depends on social arrangements. Rights to property are conventional. Liability to taxation is part of the conventions.
- *People do not consent to welfare provision; redis tributive arrangements are based in compulsion.* This is not necessarily true. Several countries have developed welfare systems, in whole or in part, on a voluntary, mutualist basis-Denmark, Finland and Sweden have moved to compulsion only recently.

- *The rights of the individual are paramount.* Property rights are certainly important, but few people would argue that property rights are more important than every other moral value. If one person owns all the food in a region while everybody else is starving, do the others have no moral claim on it?

The radical right also claim that the welfare state has undesirable effects in practice. *Economically*, it can be argued that economic development is more important for welfare than social provision. Dollar and Kraay, for the World Bank, have argued that property rights and a market economy are essential for growth and so for the protection of the poor. The other main argument is that the welfare state undermines economic performance. However, this position is not supported by the evidence. In *social* terms, the welfare state is accused of fostering dependency and trapping people in poverty. Evidence on the dynamics of poverty shows that poverty and dependency are not long-term, but affect people at different stages in the life cycle; the population of welfare claimants is constantly changing.

Where poor people are separated and excluded by welfare, this is mainly the product of the kinds of restricted, residual system the radical right has been arguing for.

Who is Welfare for?

Residual welfare : Welfare provision is often seen as being for the poor. This was the dominant model in English-speaking countries; the English Poor Law (1598-1948) was exported to many other countries. This has been taken as the model of a residual system of welfare, in which welfare is a safety net, confined to those who are unable to manage otherwise.

Solidarity : Welfare in much of Europe is based on the principle of solidarity, or mutual responsibility. The responsibilities which people have to each other depend on their relationships; people in society are part of solidaristic social networks. Many of the rights which people have are particular, rather than general-they depend on a person's circumstances, work record or family relationships, not on general rights protected by the state. Those who are not part of such networks are said to be 'excluded'.

Institutional welfare : An institutional system is one in which need is accepted as a normal part of social life. Welfare is provided for the population as a whole, in the same way as public services like roads or schools might be. In an institutional system, welfare is not just for the poor: it is for everyone.

Industrial achievement/performance : Welfare has often been seen as a 'hand maiden' to the economy. It helps employers, by preparing and servicing the capacity of the work force, and it acts as an economic regulator, stimulating demand when production is low.

Universality and Selectivity

Universal benefits and services are benefits available to everyone as a right, or at least to whole categories of people (like 'old people' or 'children'). Selective benefits and services are reserved for people in need. The arguments refer to the same issues as 'institutional' and 'residual' welfare, but there is an important difference. Institutional and residual welfare are principles: universality and selectivity are methods. A residual system might use a universal service where appropriate (e.g. a residual system of health care might be associated with universal public health); an institutional system needs some selective benefits to ensure that needs are met.

Universal services can reach everyone on the same terms. This is the argument for public services, like roads and sewers: it was extended in the 1940s to education and health services. The main objection to universal services is their cost. Selectivity is often presented as being more efficient: less money is spent to better effect. There are problems with selective services, however: because recipients have to be identified, the services can be administratively complex and expensive to run, and there are often boundary problems caused by trying to include some people while excluding others. Selective services sometimes fail to reach people in need.

Models of Welfare

Esping-Andersen has described three main types of welfare regime:

- *corporatist* regimes are work-oriented and based on individual contribution.

- *social democratic* regimes favour universalist values.
- *liberal* regimes tend to be residualist.

The grouping of particular countries tends to be unreliable, but the classification may help to understand some of the main patterns of provision. The blue bars show the proportions of poor people; the red bars the "poverty gap", how far those remaining fall below minimum standards. Social protection in the UK and Sweden is institutional; the UK covers less of its population, but the shortfall is not as great as in Sweden. France is solidaristic, but its performance has still secured coverage as good as the institutional welfare states. The German system is work oriented: it excludes some people who have not contributed, and it does not extend to those on the highest incomes. The system in the US has substantial residual elements, and social policy is often hostile to the poor.

Society and the Welfare of its Citizens

There are three main interpretations of the idea of a welfare state: For other uses, see Politics (disambiguation).... Social democracy is a political ideology emerging in the late 19th and early 20th centuries from supporters of Marxism who believed that the transition to a socialist society could be achieved through democratic evolutionary rather than revolutionary means.... The Enlightenment (French:; German:; Italian:; Portuguese:) was an eighteenth century movement in European and American philosophy some classifications also include 17th century philosophy (usually called the Age of Reason).... Utopian socialism is a term used to define the first currents of modern Socialist thought.... A trade union or labour union is an organization of workers.

The European Revolutions of 1848, known in some countries as the Spring of Nations or the Year of Revolution, were a revolutionary wave which erupted in Sicily and then, further triggered by the revolutions of 1848 in France, soon spread to the rest of Europe and as far afield as... Orthodox Marxism is the term used to describe the version of Marxism which emerged after the death of Karl Marx and acted as the official philosophy of the Second International up to the First World War and of the Third

International thereafter.... Representative democracy is a form of government founded on the principles of popular sovereignty by the peoples representatives.... Labour rights are laws created in order to always have fairness and keep peace between employees and employers.... Civil liberties is the name given to freedoms that protect the individual from government.... A mixed economy is an economy that has a mix of economic systems.... This article is about secularism.

For other uses, see Fair trade (disambiguation).... Environmental movement is a term often used for any social or political movement directed towards the preservation, restoration, or enhancement of the natural environment.... This is a list of parties in the world that consider themselves to be upholding the principles and values of social democracy.... The official symbol of Socialist International.... The Party of European Socialists (PES) is a European political party whose members are 33 social democratic, socialist and labour parties of the European Union member states as well as Norway.... The International Trade Union Confederation (ITUC) is the worlds largest trade union federation.... Eduard Bernstein Eduard Bernstein was a German social democratic theoretician and politician, member of the SPD, and founder of evolutionary socialism or reformism.

Etymology

The English term "welfare state" is believed to have been coined by Archbishop William Temple during the Second World War, contrasting wartime Britain with the "warfare state" of Nazi Germany. The English language is a West Germanic language that originates in England.... This article or section does not cite its references or sources.... Mushroom cloud from the nuclear explosion over Nagasaki rising 18 km into the air.... Nazi Germany, or the Third Reich, commonly refers to Germany in the years 1933–1945, when it was under the firm control of the totalitarian and fascist ideology of the Nazi Party, with the Fuhrer Adolf Hitler as dictator.

In German, a roughly equivalent term (*Sozialstaat*, "social state") had been in use since 1870. There had been earlier attempts to use the same phrase in English, for example in Munroe Smith's text "Four German Jurists", but the term did not enter common use until William Temple popularized it. The Italian term "Social state" (*Stato sociale*) has the same origin. (Edmund) Munroe Smith, (born 1854), was an American jurist and historian, born in Brooklyn....

The Swedish welfare state is called Folkhemmet and goes back to the 1936 compromise between the Union and big Corporate companies. It is a Mixed economy, build on strong unions and a strong system of Social security and universal health care. Swedish welfare refers to the Swedish variant of the mixed economy prevalent in much of the industrialized world.... Folkhemmet, meaning the Peoples Home, as the idea of the Social Democratic welfare state played an important part in Sweden during the 20th Century.... Union generally refers to two or more things joined into one, such as an organization of multiple people or organizations, multiple objects combined into one, and so on.... Corporate may refer to either A corporation, a type of legal entity, often formed to conduct business Corporate (film), a 2006 Bollywood film starring Bipasha Basu.... A company in the broadest sense is an aggregation of people who stay together for a common purpose.... A mixed economy is an economy that has a mix of economic systems.... Social security primarily refers to social welfare service concerned with social protection, or protection against socially recognized conditions, including poverty, old age, disability, unemployment and others.... Universal health care is a situation in which all residents of a geographic or political region have access to most types of health care....

In French, the synonymous term "providence state" was originally coined as a sarcastic pejorative remark used by opponents of welfare state policies during the Second Empire (1854-1870). It has been suggested that this article or section be merged with pejoration.... 1854 (MDCCCLIV) was a common year starting on Sunday.... 1870 (MDCCCLXX) was a common year starting on Saturday (link will display the full calendar) of the Gregorian calendar (or a common year starting on Monday of the 12-day slower Julian calendar).... In Spanish and many other languages, an analogous term is used: *estado del bienestar*; translated literally: "state of well-being". In Portuguese, a similar phrase exists: *Estado de Bem-Estar-Social*; which means "well-being-social state".

The Development of Welfare States

An early version of the welfare state appeared in China during the Song Dynasty in the 11th century. Prime Minister Wang Anshi believed that the state was responsible for providing its citizens the essentials for a decent living standard. Accordingly, under his direction the state initiated agricultural loans to relieve the farming peasants. He appointed boards to regulate wages and plan pensions for the aged and unemployed.

The development of social insurance in Germany under Bismarck was particularly influential. Some schemes, like those in Scandinavia, were based largely in the development of autonomous, mutualist provision of benefits. Others were founded on state provision. The term was not, however, applied to all states offering social protection. The sociologist T.H. Marshall identified the welfare state as a distinctive combination of democracy, welfare and capitalism. Alternative meaning:

Nineteenth Century (periodical) (18th century — 19th century — 20th century — more centuries) As a means of recording the passage of time, the 19th century was that century which lasted from 1801-1900 in the sense of the Gregorian calendar.... (19th century-20th century-21st century-more centuries) Decades: 1900s 1910s 1920s 1930s 1940s 1950s 1960s 1970s 1980s 1990s As a means of recording the passage of time, the 20th century was that century which lasted from 1901–2000 in the sense of the Gregorian calendar (1900–1999... For specific national programs, see Social Security (United States), National insurance (UK), Social Security (Sweden) Social security refers to a variety of government programs providing for social welfare and social protection and the alleviation of poverty among senior citizens and the disabled.... Bismarck redirects here.... For other uses, see Scandinavia (disambiguation).... Thomas Humphrey Marshall (1893-1981) is a British sociologist, most noted for his essays, such as the essay collection Citizenship and Social Class.

Examples of early welfare states in the modern world are Germany, all of the Nordic Countries, the Netherlands, Uruguay and New Zealand in the 1930s. Germany is generally held to be the first social welfare state. Changed attitudes in reaction to the Great Depression were instrumental in the move to the welfare state in many countries, a harbinger of new times where "cradle-to-grave" services became a reality after the poverty of the Depression. During the Great Depression, it was seen as an alternative "middle way" between communism and capitalism. In the period following the Second World War, many countries in Europe moved from partial or selective provision of social services to relatively comprehensive coverage of the population. Political map of the Nordic countries and associated territories.

The 1930s were described as an abrupt shift to more radical and conservative lifestyles, as countries were struggling to find a solution to the Great Depression, also known as the World Depression.... For other uses, see The Great Depression (disambiguation).... A boy from an East Cipinang trash dump slum in Jakarta, Indonesia shows what he found.... Communism is an ideology that seeks to establish a classless, stateless social organization based on common ownership of the means of production.... For other uses, see Capitalism (disambiguation).... Mushroom cloud from the nuclear explosion over Nagasaki rising 18 km into the air.... For other uses, see Europe (disambiguation).... A social worker is a person employed in the administration of charity, social service, welfare, and poverty agencies, advocacy, or religious outreach programs.

The activities of present-day welfare states extend to the provision of both cash welfare benefits (such as old-age pensions or unemployment benefits) and in-kind welfare services (such as health or childcare services). Through these provisions, welfare states can affect the distribution of wellbeing and personal autonomy among their citizens, as well as influencing how their citizens consume and how they spend their time.

After the discovery and inflow of the oil revenue, Saudi Arabia, Kuwait, Qatar, Bahrain, Oman and the United Arab Emirates all became welfare states. However, the services are strictly for citizens and these countries do not accept immigrants; those born in these countries do not qualify for citizenship unless they are of the parentage belonging to their respective countries.

In the United Kingdom, the beginning of the modern welfare state was in 1911 when David Lloyd George suggested everyone in work should pay national insurance contribution for unemployment and health benefits from work. David Lloyd George, 1st Earl Lloyd-George of Dwyfor, OM, PC was a British statesman who was Prime Minister throughout the latter half of World War I and the first four years of the subsequent peace....

In 1942, the 'Social Insurance and Allied Services' was created by Sir William Beveridge in order to aid those who were in need of help, or in poverty. Beveridge worked as a volunteer for the poor, and set up national insurance. He stated that 'All people of working age should pay a weekly national insurance contribution. In return, benefits would be paid to people who were sick, unemployed, retired or widowed.'

The basic assumptions of the report were the National Health Service, which provided free health care to the UK. The Universal Child Benefit was a scheme to give child benefits, which encouraged people to have children so they could afford to keep them alive and not for them to starve to death. This was particularly useful after the second world war, where the population in England declined, so encouragement for new babies was encouraged, which sparked the baby boom.

The impact of the report was huge and 600,000 copies were made. He recommended to the government that they should find ways of tackling the five giants, being Want, Disease, Ignorance, Squalor and Idleness. He argued to cure these problems, the government should provide adequate income to people, adequate health care, adequate education, adequate housing and adequate employment. Before 1939, health care had to be paid for, this was done through a vast network of friendly societies, trade unions and other insurance companies which counted the vast majority of the UK working population as members.

These friendly societies provided insurance for sickness, unemployment and invalidity, therefore providing people with an income when they were unable to work. But because of the 1942 Beveridge Report, in 5th July 1948, the National Insurance Act, National Assistance Act and National Health Service Act came into force, thus this is the day that the modern UK welfare state was founded. William Henry Beveridge was a British economist and social reformer.

Debating the Welfare State

The concept of the welfare state remains controversial, and there is continuing debate over governments' responsibility for their citizens' welfare. Here, it is crucial to clarify what exactly one means by welfare state. First, a welfare state is not a state run economy.

The welfare state refers to the programs paid by the government that provide basic temporary and conditional finacial help to those legally unable to provide to themselves because of their current economic situation due to health problems, mental diseases, etc. or because of a major natural disaster or terrorist attack.

Arguments in Favour

- humanitarian-the right to the basic necessities of life is a fundamental human right, and people should not be allowed to suffer unnecessarily through lack of provision.
- altruism-helping others is a moral obligation in most cultures; charity and support for people who cannot help themselves are also widely thought to be moral choices.
- utilitarian-the same amount of money will produce greater happiness in the hands of a less well-off person than if given to a well-off person; thus, redistributing wealth from the rich to the poor will increase the total happiness in society.
- religious-major world religions emphasize the importance of social organization rather than personal development alone. Religious obligations include the duty of charity and the obligation for solidarity. However, before the welfare state in the UK, charitable donations were normally 10% of a persons income and the number of charities in the UK was enormous as was the amount of support given by them to the paupers. Therefore although this is fulfilled by a welfare state, it is actually a concept of welfare, not necessarily welfare provided by the state.
- economic-social programs perform a range of economic functions, including e.g. the regulation of demand and structuring the labour market.

- social-social programs are used to promote objectives regarding education, family and work.
- market failure – in certain cases, the private sector fails to meet social objectives or to deliver efficient production, due to such things as monopolies, oligopolies, or asymmetric information.
- social justice-the money the state provides comes from the nation's labour and natural resources through universal taxation, the rich manages the wealth that is often inherited, and do not necessarily contribute more than the average worker, therefore it is a matter of justice to provide for the private individual who cannot legally provide to himself. Further, there will also be members of societies who through disability, health problems, or other causes out of the individual's control, are unable to provide for themselves.
- economies of scale-some services can be more efficiently paid for when bought "in bulk" by the government for the public, rather than purchased by individual consumers. The highway system, water distribution, the fire department, universal health, and national defence might be some examples anti-crime-people with low incomes do not need to resort to crime to stay alive, thus reducing the crime rate. Empirical evidence indicates that welfare programs reduce property crime.

Arguments against There are a number of meanings for humanitarianism: humanitarianism, humanism, the doctrine that peoples duty is to promote human welfare.... For the ethical doctrine, see Altruism (ethics).... This article discusses utilitarian ethical theory.... Various Religious symbols, including (first row) Christian, Jewish, Hindu, Bahai, (second row) Islamic, tribal, Taoist, Shinto (third row) Buddhist, Sikh, Hindu, Jain, (fourth row) Ayyavazhi, Triple Goddess, Maltese cross, pre-Christian Slavonic Religion is the adherence to codified beliefs and rituals that generally involve a faith in a spiritual.

In modern usage, the practice of charity means the giving of help to those in need.... Solidarity is a Polish trade union federation founded in September 1980 at the then Lenin Shipyards, and originally led by Lech. This article is about the human activity. Wage labour is the socioeconomic relationship between a worker and an employer in which the worker sells their labour under a contract (employment), and the employer buys it, often in a labour market.... Market failure is a term used by economists to describe the condition where the allocation of goods and services by a market is not efficient.... This article is about the economic term.... This article does not cite any references or sources.... In economics, information asymmetry occurs when one party to a transaction has more or better information than the other party.... Social justice refers to the concept of an unjust society that refers to more than just the administration of laws.... The increase in output from Q to Q2 causes a decrease in the average cost of each unit from C to C1.

- moral (compulsion) – libertarians believe that the "nanny state" infringes upon individual freedom, forcing the individual to subsidize the consumption of others. They argue that social spending reduces the right of individuals to transfer some of their wealth to others, and is tantamount to a seizure of private property.
- reduced morality – the introduction of the welfare state and benefits that support people who do not contribute to the national good, reduces the compulsion to contribute. Supporting single mothers with accommodation, benefits, rate rebates, etc.. slowly makes being a single mother a more acceptable life to lead despite the mounting evidence that it leads to depression in the mothers and children. Without a welfare state, families would be forced to support non-contributing members which would ensure children were given an upbringing which strongly discouraged this way of life.
- religious/paternalism – some Protestant Christians and an increasing number of Catholics also believe that only voluntary giving (through private charities) is virtuous. They hold personal responsibility to be a virtue, and they believe that a welfare state diminishes the capacity of individuals to develop this virtue.
- anti-regulatory-the welfare state is accused of imposing

greater burdens on private businesses, of potentially slowing growth and creating unemployment.

- efficiency-the free market leads to more efficient and effective production and service delivery than state-run welfare programs. They argue that high social spending is costly and must be funded out of higher levels of taxation. According to Friedrich Hayek, the market mechanism is much more efficient and able to respond to specific circumstances of a large number of individuals than when run by the state. An example of the inefficiency of the state is that in the UK, there is one non-teaching civil servant for every classroom in the country, whether they be administrators, managers, inspectors, etc.
- motivation and incentives-the welfare state may have undesirable effects on behaviour, fostering dependency, destroying incentives and sapping motivation to work.
- charitable-by the state assuming a larger burden for the financial care of people, individuals may feel it is no longer necessary for them to donate to charities or give to philanthropies.
- managerial statecraft-this paleoconservative view posits that the welfare state is part of an ongoing regime that remains in power, regardless of what political party holds a majority. It acts in the name of abstract goals, such as equality or positive rights, and uses its claim of moral superiority, power of taxation and wealth redistribution to keep itself in power.
- Crime-state provided welfare normally incurs high tax economy, this in turn leads to people feeling protective over their earnings and therefore looking for ways to cheat the tax system to pay less tax. This in turn reduces overall morality. People dependent on welfare have been found by surveys to be more depressed and have a lower self esteem than working people, this in turn often leads to them feeling rejected, hopeless and/or abandoned by the populace at large, therefore they have a lower self of national unity of community responsibility and may turn to crime to get back at society or just fill the time.

Statue of Liberty-Liberty is one meaning of freedom. Freedom may mean any of the following: the British newspaper, Freedom in music: the 1989 album by Neil Young, Freedom a song by Rage Against the Machine a song by Richie Havens geographically: a town in New York, USA; Freedom a... In economics, a subsidy is generally a monetary grant given by a government to lower the price faced by producers or consumers of a good, generally because it is considered to be in the public interest.... In economics, consumption refers to the final use of goods and services to provide utility.

Religious is a term with both a technical definition and folk use.... Image of traditional cultural paternalism: Father Junipero Serra in a modern portrayal at Mission San Juan Capistrano, California Paternalism refers usually to an attitude or a policy stemming from the hierarchic pattern of a family based on patriarchy, that is, there is a figurehead (the father, pater in Latin) that... Protestantism encompasses the forms of Christian faith and practice that originated with the doctrines of the Reformation.

This article does not cite any references or sources.... Friedrich August von Hayek, CH (May 8, 1899 in Vienna March 23, 1992 in Freiburg) was an Austrian-born British economist and political philosopher known for his defence of liberal democracy and free-market capitalism against socialist and collectivist thought in the mid-20th century.... Managerial State is a paleoconservative concept used in critiquing modern social democracy in Western countries.... The term paleoconservative (sometimes shortened to paleo or paleocon when the context is clear) refers to an American branch of conservative Old Right thought that is frequently at odds with the current of conservative thought as espoused by the Republican Party elite....

Some criticism of welfare states concern the idea that a welfare state makes citizens dependent and less inclined to work. Certain studies indicate there is no association between economic performance and welfare expenditure in developed countries and that there is no evidence for the contention that welfare states impede progressive social development. R. E. Goodin et al, in *The Real Worlds of Welfare Capitalism* (Cambridge University Press, 1999), show that on some economic and social indicators the

United States performs worse than the Netherlands, which has a high commitment to welfare provision. However, the United States leads most welfare states on certain economic indicators, such as GDP per capita (although in 2006 it had a lower GDP per capita than Norway).

The United States also has a low unemployment rate (although not as low as Denmark, Norway) and a high GDP growth rate, at least in comparison to other developed countries (its growth rate, however, is lower than Finland's and Sweden's, two nations with relatively small populations but comparatively high commitments to welfare provision; the United States' growth rate is also lower than the world's overall). The United States also leads most welfare states in the ownership of consumer goods. For example, it has more TV's per capita, more personal computers per capita, and more radios per capita than what people would call welfare states. Wage labour is the socioeconomic relationship between a worker and an employer in which the worker sells their labour under a contract (employment), and the employer buys it, often in a labour market....

Another criticism comes from Classical Liberalism. Namely, that Welfare is theft of Property or Labour. This criticism is based upon classical liberalist ideals, wherein a citizen owns his body, and owns the product of his body's labour (i.e. goods, services, or money). Note that in this definition property that is inherited is not included. So to remove money through legal mechanisms set by a democratically elected assembly from the working or non-working citizen and give it to a non-working or handicapped citizen or to a child is argued to be theft of the worker's property and/or labour and a violation of his property rights.

A third criticism is that the welfare state allegedly provides its dependents with a similar level of income to the minimum wage. Critics argue that fraud and economic inactivity are apparently quite common now in the United Kingdom and France. Some conservatives in the UK claim that the welfare state has produced a generation of dependents who rely solely upon the state for income and support instead of working even though assistance is only given to those unable to work so that actually being able to work and instead relying on the state for income is a criminal offence. The welfare state in the UK was created to provide a carefully selected number of people with a subsistence level of benefits in order to alleviate poverty, but that as a matter of opinion has been overly expanded to provide a large number of people indiscriminately with more money than the country can afford.

On the other hand, benefits handed-out in the U.S. often exceed $10 an hour (varying state-to-state), when one accounts for *all* the free services provided (free housing, free food, free welfare checks), such that it's wiser economically not to work, rather than to accept $6 at the local retail store. One must not forget that even working families may be eligible for benefits when even when working their income does not cover their or their children's basic needs. This article deals with conservatism as a political philosophy.

A fourth criticism of the welfare state is that it results in high taxes. This is usually true, as evidenced by places like Denmark (tax level at 50.4% of GDP in 2002) and Sweden (tax level at 50.2% of GDP in 2002). Such high taxes do not necessarily mean less income for the nation overall, since the state taxes go directly to the people it is taxed from. The real issue is that they result in a major redistribution of that income from the citizens on the productive side of the equation to the citizens on the welfare state side. Thus the productive, self-reliant citizens subsidise the lifestyle of others.

A fifth criticism of the welfare state is the belief that welfare services provided by the state are more expensive and less efficient than the same services would be if provided by private businesses. In 2000, Professors Louis Kaplow and Steven Shafell published two papers, arguing that any social policy based on such concepts as justice or fairness would result in an economy which is Pareto inefficient. Anything which is supplied free at the point of consumption would be subject to artificially high demand, whereas resources would be more properly allocated if provision reflected the cost. However it is not clear how this would apply to services such as health and education, where individuals are unlikely to demand more services that are actually required where the benefits of providing the service flow through to all levels of society (by reducing disease, and increasing the wealth-creation abilities of the population). Pareto efficiency, or Pareto optimality, is an important notion in neoclassical economics with broad applications in game theory, engineering and the social sciences....

The most extreme criticisms of states and governments, are from anarchists, who believe that all states and governments are undesirable and/or unnecessary. Most anarchists believe that while social welfare gives a certain level of independecy from the market and individual capitalists, it creates dependence to the state, which is the institution that, according to this view, supports and protects capitalism in the first place. Nonetheless, according to Noam Chomsky, "social democrats and anarchists always agreed, fairly generally, on so-called 'welfare state measures'" and "Anarchists propose other measures to deal with these problems, without recourse to state authority." Anarchists believe in stopping welfare programs only if it means abolishing government and capitalism as well.

The Welfare State and Social Expenditure

Welfare provision in the contemporary world tends to be more advanced in the countries with stronger and more developed economies. Poor countries, on the other hand, tend to have limited social services. Within developed economies, however, there is very little correlation between economic performance and welfare expenditure. Image File history File links No higher resolution available.... Image File history File links No higher resolution available.... The Organization for Economic Cooperation and Development (OECD) is an international organization of those developed countries that accept the principles of representative democracy and a free market economy.... Year 2001 (MMI) was a common year starting on Monday (link displays the 2001 Gregorian calendar).... Image File history File links No higher resolution available.... Image File history File links No higher resolution available.... Image File history File links No higher resolution available.... Image File history File links No higher resolution available....

There are individual exceptions on both sides, the higher levels of social expenditure in the European Union are not associated with lower growth, lower productivity or higher unemployment, nor with higher growth, higher productivity or lower unemployment.

Nation	*Welfare expenditure(% of GDP)*	*GDP per capita (PPP US$)*
Denmark	29.2	$29,000
Sweden	28.9	$24,180
France	28.5	$23,990
Germany	27.4	$25,350
Belgium	27.2	$25,520
Switzerland	26.4	$28,100
Austria	26.0	$26,730
Finland	24.8	$24,430
Netherlands	24.3	$27,190
Italy	24.4	$24,670
Greece	24.3	$17,440
Norway	23.9	$29,620
Poland	23.0	$9,450
United Kingdom	21.8	$24,160
Portugal	21.1	$18,150
Luxembourg	20.8	$53,780
Czech Republic	20.1	$14,720
Hungary	20.1	$12,340
Iceland	19.8	$29,990
Spain	19.6	$20,150
New Zealand	18.5	$19,160
Australia	18.0	$25,370
Slovak Republic	17.9	$11,960
Canada	17.8	$27,130
Japan	16.9	$25,130
United States	14.8	$34,320
Ireland	13.8	$32,410
Mexico	11.8	$8,430
South Korea	6.1	$15,090

Note: *no data for China, India, Indonesia, Brazil, Russia, and Pakistan, who are not members of the OECD.*

Likewise, the pursuit of free market policies leads neither to guaranteed prosperity nor to social collapse. The table shows that countries with more limited expenditure, like Australia, Canada and Japan, do no better or worse economically than countries with high social expenditure, like Belgium, Germany and Denmark. The table does not show the effect of expenditure on income inequalities, and does not encompass some other forms of welfare provision (such as occupational welfare). Overall, there is a slight positive correlation between increased spending on social services and higher GDP per capita as well as higher HDI rating. World map indicating Human Development Index (2006)....

The table below shows, first, welfare expenditure as a percentage of GDP for some (selected) OECD member states, and second, GDP per capita (PPP US$) in 2001: The Organization for Economic Cooperation and Development (OECD) is an international organization of those developed countries that accept the principles of representative democracy and a free market economy....

Human Welfare, Economic Development and Civilized Society

Since the recent communal conflagrations in Gujarat, many concerned Indians have been extremely disturbed by the failure of the state administration to conduct itself according to the Indian constitution-i.e. without discriminating on the basis of religion. They have repeatedly attacked the state government for failing to follow the "rule of law", and have expressed considerable concern for Muslim refugees, some of who still languish in makeshift refugee camps. By and large, the English-language media has not shirked from publicizing the frustration of such Indians, who feel that the safety and well-being of India's religious minorities cannot be taken lightly. On the other hand, critics of the English-language media have accused most English-speaking journalists of having a *'pseudo-secular'* bias since they have rarely shown the same concern for Hindus expelled from the Srinagar valley, the vast majority of whom are yet to be rehabilitated. They also note how even though 30% of the riot-refugees in Gujarat were Hindus, this was almost never acknowledged.

They further allude to how Islamic separatist terrorists are made to seem respectable-they are referred to as "alienated from the centre", as "aggrieved parties", as being "defenders of a 'unique' Kashmiri identity" but never as communal "fascists"-a term routinely used to describe Hindutvadi supporters of the VHP or the Bajrang Dal.

While it is doubtlessly true that the mainstream Indian media has deeply-internalized double standards on the issue of secular fairness and justice, the issue of media insensitivity, and selective reporting goes much deeper. For instance, even though there were almost daily stories concerning the communal crisis in Gujarat, crimes against Dalits and Adivasis are seldom reported as frequently. A recent study (as reported in the Deccan Herald) revealed that as many as 30,000 Adivasis and Dalits died as a result of caste-related crimes in 2001. In many instances, law enforcement authorities either looked the other way, or collaborated with the perpetrators. But these violations of the Indian constitution, this breakdown in the 'rule of law' does not appear to excite the same level of outrage. Even those who claim to be "radical" or "progressive" rarely pay sufficient attention to unpunished crimes against Dalits. It is little wonder that Dalit leaders such as Mayawati and Kanshi Ram have accused the Indian political and media elite of being biased and "Manuwadi".

This raises a very troubling question. Is the Indian media only going to report about constitutional violations when they pertain to religious and communal tensions? Are they going to shut their eyes to crimes against other oppressed groups? Do other victims count for less? Shouldn't crimes that result from caste or gender differences, sexual or marriage preferences, or property conflicts, also concern us just as deeply?

Although the Indian constitution is quite specific in outlining certain types of protections, there are other areas where it is quite vague in it's support of basic human rights. It is particularly weak in defending economic rights, or the right to employment, for instance.

Homeless children, widows, the elderly, or the disabled (who can be the most destitute people in India) do not have any explicit protection in the constitution, and not enough demand that any government-(whether local, state or national) take care of them, because there is no specific group or person to blame for their plight, and no Indian law has been explicitly violated. They are simply victims of harsh circumstances.

Yet, this chronic failure of Indian society to take care of it's most vulnerable and helpless citizens rarely draws media attention. In fact, any serious discussion of "refugees" ought to at least acknowledge that the millions of Indians who live in slums are also "refugees"-they are refugees of a peculiar economic situation where jobs are plentiful only where land prices are high, and affordable housing is scarce. Although anarchic growth is not a uniquely Indian problem, being so densely populated, the consequences of unplanned capitalist growth are much more intensely felt. But these victims of India's anarchic development cannot point a finger at any government body and say: "you have failed us-you must rehabilitate us too". They are rehabilitated only when the land they occupy is needed for something else, and they have enough political clout to resist being moved without compensation.

The truth is that since the collapse of the Soviet Union, there has been a conspiracy of silence concerning such fundamental human rights-those that are essential to a life of hope and dignity for all. Rarely does the subject of human welfare, of the duties of the state in ensuring a minimum standard of human existence enter the public discourse in India. And when a brave individual attempts to lead a discussion on the social responsibilities of the state, there is often a chorus of detractors, and the debate is quickly squelched by anti-communist baiters or market fundamentalists who wish to see the state retreat from all it's obligations except those pertaining to law and order and national defence.

Even those who might sympathize with the need for greater attention to public welfare give up-either because they conclude that there is no money for it in India, or because they have a concern that if the government can't even manage the PDS properly, how could it ever be expected to efficiently implement more expansive social security measures. They accept the rationalization that if socialism "failed" in Russia, how could such "socialist" measures work in much poorer India.

However, it is important to note that the manner in which the Indian government has implemented the PDS, it has been neither socialist, nor driven by free-market concerns. On the one hand, it has stepped in to procure and store grains from individual farmers (many of whom are not poor)-on the other hand, it has left the distribution of this grain to petty traders. But a truly socialist approach would require that the government not only procure and store the grain, it would also require that the government take charge of distribution-not leave it in the hands of corrupt and unscrupulous private traders. A genuinely socialist approach would also entail active government intervention in the production of grain, allocating land and resources in a way so as to ensure proper soil and water management, that a variety of grains in the right proportions were produced-not simply allow the anarchic over-production of wheat and rice (to the detriment of other crops-such as pulses and oil seeds).

To further compound things, the government has been pampering a small section of Indian farmers by constantly raising the minimum purchase price over and above the rate of inflation, making it inevitable that PDS and open-market prices will also have to rise in proportion. It should be noted that such an artificial increase in price is tantamount to an annual tax increase, which hurts the poorest Indians the most.

To describe this policy-which Favours an army of petty traders, and only a minority of farmers (many of whom need no governmental help), but hurts the interests of the majority of the Indian masses as a "socialist" policy is simply absurd, and makes a mockery of socialist principles that are intended to uplift those who suffer from a lack of means and resources.

The truth is that the Indian government allows the Indian consumers of grain neither to profit from free-market practices that might at least result in lower prices during years of good harvests, nor to fully benefit from it's generous procurement policies.

In fact, it may be noted that India's medieval Rajput rulers followed more intelligent policies in this regard. During good harvest years, the Rajput kings procured only as much grain as was necessary to build buffer stocks for the bad years. Beyond that, grain was freely traded and sold in the 'mandis'. In the bad years, the state intervened in the distribution process to ensure that there was no starvation. In all years, there was strict monitoring of the traders to prevent hoarding and price-gauging.

Given India's geography and climate, state intervention in the procurement and distribution of grain has always been necessary, but clearly there are many ways of doing it-some more effective than others. But there could also be other means to ensure food security.

For instance, throughout the world, even unabashedly capitalist governments provide more social security options to their citizens than does the Indian government. Take just the US, as an example: there are food stamps for the poor, free schooling and public libraries, annual budget allocations for low-income housing, unemployment compensation for six months (extendible to nine months during a recession), social security for the elderly, as well as additional allocations for child safety and welfare. Although inadequate, such welfare measures have played a vital role in keeping poverty rates well below India's. Those who argue that India is too poor to afford such measures might note that India's GNP has grown considerably since independence. It is much more capable of meeting the needs of it's poorest citizens today than it was in 1947.

The problem of social security in India is no longer just a question of money, but how certain administrative practices prevent optimal use of resources, and blatantly Favour special interest groups (such as politically influential grain traders and self-Centreed farmer's lobbies). If there was adequate concern, will and commitment to solve the problem, innovative and workable solutions could always be found.

It might be especially useful to note that the Mauryan state under Emperor Ashoka took special pride in it's welfare policies. Ashokan edicts and reports from visiting chroniclers attest to this concern for public welfare. Surviving chronicles from the Gupta period suggest that the state had a formula for calculating pensions-that all those who had performed some service to society may have been entitled to a pension. Chinese travellers like Huen Tsang also made note of welfare measures undertaken during the

Harsha reign in Kannauj. If pre-industrial India could provide pensions and other welfare measures to it's citizens, it seems astounding that a nation that is much more developed, and can now launch it's own satellites can't afford to be more charitable towards it's weakest citizens. Clearly, it is a question of priorities, and also a question of being enlightened enough to realize that attention to the social welfare needs of the poor and unfortunate can also lead to benefits for the rich.

Those who admire the successes China has enjoyed since it's economic "liberalization" might wish to consider how China's "liberalization" took place after 90% of the population was already well-schooled, and at least had some shelter. To this date, the Chinese government requires most new enterprises to build workers hostels in the special enterprise zones-so that growth in industry doesn't lead to a concomitant growth in slums. This has ensured that China's new urban areas look much more attractive-they are neat and clean, virtually free of the chaotic squatter settlements-of irregular markets and residential colonies, or unsightly slums that seem to proliferate throughout urban India.

Indians may have become inured to India's unseemly squalor-but many foreign investors aren't as tolerant. Time and time again, serious investors have been dissuaded from investing in India because India's cities appear ugly and uninviting. On the other hand, China's new enterprise zones gleam with attractively designed modern buildings situated along wide tree-lined boulevards. It's best cities now boast well-paved sidewalks with pleasingly maintained flower beds, separate bike lanes and a work force that appears competent and well-dressed. Concern for public welfare is translating into much higher rates of international investment as well.

This is not to unconditionally or uncritically endorse the economic policies of the Chinese government (which are clearly leading to very lop-sided development and putting a severe strain on China's environment), but rather to point out how concern for public well-being and social welfare is not necessarily incompatible with economic development. Greater attention to housing and schooling, and improved public infrastructure are not just concessions to the poor-they can attract new entrepreneurs and industrialists as well. This has been the case with every other advanced economy-whether it be Korea or Japan, Sweden or Germany, or Singapore, or Hong Kong.

It is high time India's industrialists realize this, especially if they wish to seriously compete for international investment in any quantity. India is not like the US where land is plentiful, and there are no shortages of power or water. Rather than chafe at all regulations, Indian industry ought to be more open-minded to those that lead to better management of the country's scarce resources, and help raise living standards across the board, thus improving India's general investment climate.

Consider how today, land is allocated for industrial use without due concern for low-cost housing or availability of essential resources. Initially, this may not pose a problem, but soon enough the slums and the accompanying squalor develops. This then puts off new international investors.

However, with their powers to regulate and manage industry, state and local governments have all the tools to ensure that when industrial areas are developed, a certain amount of land is kept aside for low-cost housing, for transport arteries, for public parks and other essential facilities. State governments and the Centre can also be more proactive in steering new investment to smaller towns and cities where housing and other costs may be lower, rather than permit reckless new development in already crowded metros.

Instead of resisting such sensible trends, India's industry leaders should actively intervene to ensure that industrial growth occurs in a thoughtful and balanced way-so that scarce resources are not stressed-so that India's cities and industrial areas present a picture that is not only pleasant for India's citizens, it is also irresistible for any foreign investor. Citizens welfare and economic development need not always be contradictory goals.

It is imperative to recognize that economic development and social welfare are both essential pillars of a civilized society. Haphazard economic growth that does not raise the living standards of the vast majority cannot be an end in itself. The hallmark of any civilized society is the welfare of it's people. That must always be at the forefront of any discussion concerning India's future progress. Globalization, welfare reform and the social economy: developing an alternative approach to analyzing social welfare systems in the post-industrial era.

Our understanding of the relationship between globalization and contemporary social welfare systems is heavily influenced by three conventional approaches to studying welfare reform: the political economy, moral economy, and mixed economy approaches. In addition to analyzing the strengths and weaknesses of each of these approaches, a central aim of this article is to introduce the social economy approach as an emergent alternative. Drawing from a growing body of work on institutional innovation within the European third sector, I argue that the social economy approach makes a valuable contribution to understanding the role of welfare networks in reconfiguring globalizations' impact on the character and quality of social provision so as to better reconcile social efficacy with social justice.

Increasing market integration, changing demographics, and shrinking public budgets have fuelled a pervasive redefinition of the state's role in providing for the social welfare of citizens. In addition to challenging public administration's dominance over the production and distribution of social services, policy makers and politicians from across the political spectrum have called into question the once pervasive belief that the state is exclusively entitled to guarantee the collective well being of its citizenry. Together, these developments have produced a climate favourable to the expanding role of the third sector, not only in the delivery of social services, but in the formulation and stipulation of social welfare policy as well.

Despite third sector organizations' increasing centrality in the development of contemporary social welfare systems, the two dominant approaches to studying welfare reform have downplayed, if not ignored, their importance as an interface between globalization and social wellbeing. Locked into a dichotomous state-society framework, the political economy and moral economy approaches have had a polarizing effect on the way we understand globalization and its consequences for welfare. Whereas the former adopts the 'welfare state' as its central analytic unit and focuses on the degree to which globalization is undermining states' capacity to protect their citizens social rights, the latter concentrates on the societal dynamics of the 'welfare society', underscoring the key role of societal actors in responding to societal need and the extent to which the state has become the chief impediment to achieving social justice. As a result of this dualism, the salience of the third sector for transforming the structural and cultural foundation of social welfare systems, and thus its capacity to mediate the effects of globalization, has not been fully appreciated.

The so-called mixed economy approach emerged more recently to underscore the inherent pluralism of social welfare systems and the role of the third sector as a vital intermediary between state, society and economy (Anheier and Seibel, 1990; Gidron, Kramer, Salamon, 1992; Salamon & Anheier, 1996; Salamon, 2002). Stemming primarily from professionals and practioners involved in the implementation and delivery of social and human services, this approach illuminates the black box that separates policy formation from societal outcomes by underscoring the productivist underpinnings of the social welfare systems. Although it has made significant advances in connecting the micro-level institutional dynamics involved in service provision to broader economic and sociopolitical processes underlying contemporary welfare reform, in focusing somewhat narrowly on the organization and management of welfare production, it fails to explore the broader structural implications of welfare reform and does not take sufficient account of the social consequences that emerging welfare mixes have on both users and citizens more broadly defined.

Given the shortcomings of these conventional approaches to welfare reform, there is a particular need to identify and develop new approaches to understanding the capacity of contemporary social welfare systems to meet the formidable challenges posed by globalization. A central aim of this paper is to introduce such an approach. Based on a detailed analysis of the strengths and weakness of the three conventional approaches mentioned above, I establish the foundation for what I identify as a social economy approach to welfare. Drawing from a growing body of work on institutional innovation within the European third sector, I argue that this emergent alternative makes a valuable contribution to understanding the role of welfare networks in reconfiguring globalizations' impact on the character and quality of social provision so as to better reconcile social efficacy with social justice.

Conventional Approaches to Analyzing the Development of Contemporary Social Welfare Systems

Each of the three conventional approaches to studying the development of contemporary social welfare systems—the political economy approach, the moral economy approach and the mixed economic approach—is based on a distinctive analytical model, each with its own conceptual frameworks, theoretical preferences, and normative commitments. While each approach has contributed significantly to our understanding of how and why social welfare systems develop, disciplinary boundaries and distinctive research agendas have tended to thwart cross fertilization among them.

Thus, looking more closely at how they compare to one another is important not only for identifying the social economy perspective as an emergent alternative, but also for generating a more integrated, informed understanding of the impact of globalization on social development in the twenty-first century.

The Political Economy Approach

Emerging during a period of profound faith in the state as the key to prosperity and progress, the political economy approach reflects the social ideals of the post-war era: universalism, equality, and the power of the state to provide an unprecedented quality of life for its citizens. The welfare state, its key unit of analysis, is conceptualized as a form of embedded liberalism—a reformist compromise capable of compensating for, if not correcting, the most deleterious affects of the capitalist economy.

Although initially focused on the political engineering of social protection vis-a-vis social rights and regulations, with the end of the so-called Golden Age of the welfare state, the political economy approach has focused on questions and issues pertaining to welfare retrenchment and the respective role of politics and economics in driving welfare reform. Although long a concern within liberal welfare states like the United States, more recent debates about an emerging global "third way" (Giddens, 2001) and the transformation of "vice into virtue" among conservative, christian democratic welfare states have drawn attention to the ways in which welfare states are 'recalibrating' and the relevant degree of freedom they have in dealing effectively with the cultural and economic challenges of globalization.

Within the political economy framework, the key point of contention focuses on the extent to which there has been greater convergence or persistent divergence among historically distinctive models of welfare state development. The convergence thesis holds that welfare states, particularly those characterized by comprehensive, national social programs and public services, face growing external constraints to their ability to maintain generous, publicly financed social protections. According to this thesis, shifting patterns in international trade and finance increase competitive pressures within the global economy, thus restricting government's maneuverability in crafting policy to meet domestic social and economic objectives.

As traditional macro-economic policy tools become harder to manage and labour and total production costs rise due to the diversification of demand and the increasing use of technology, governments must rely heavily on non-payroll taxes to finance welfare expenditures. Yet high rates of inflation combined with shrinking tax bases make substantial tax increases both economically and politically unpopular. Combined with significant pressures to reduce budget deficits, this situation places critical limits to the expansion of social spending and thus the ability and willingness of governments to provide wide-ranging, long term public benefits. In addition to scaling back cash-based subsidies and increasing eligibility requirements, devolving competencies to lower levels of government and off-loading services to private providers are seen as the logical product of welfare states' increasing vulnerability to the vagaries of market forces.

The divergence thesis, by contrast, is advanced by those who see the link between economic imperatives and policy choices as over determined. From this perspective, political preferences, policy legacies, and institutional arrangements are conditioned by historically driven, path-dependent processes which mitigate if not compel differential responses to common challenges. Because powerful structural, political and cultural forces are seen as mediating both policy makers perception of the challenges arising from globalization as well as their responses to them, different types of welfare states are seen as posing unique constraints and opportunities for reform.

And because social reform reflects tensions generated by existing sociopolitical cleavages, cultural values, and strategic maneuvering by relevant political actors, the divergence thesis expects that reform will reflect the adoption of a wide range of policy tools. Thus, while decentralization and privatization may be standard policy proposals across a variety of welfare states, the specific policies formulated and implemented will vary. Thus, whereas the introduction of new technology systems aimed at maximizing choice and increasing economic efficiency is expected in Liberal welfare states like the United States and Great Britain, it is less likely in continental European countries where the legacies of familialism and paternalism are stronger and budget control is a higher priority.

While the political economy approach to welfare reform offers an important contribution to our understanding of the constraints and opportunities facing governments as they attempt to craft solutions to the challenges raised by globalization, one of its key drawbacks is that by emphasizing convergence vs. divergence, it is of limited utility in helping us to better understand the more nuanced dynamics of welfare reform. While the state is imbued with responsibility and control over welfare, society is seen primarily as the passive recipient of state-generated policies and prescriptions. Thus, arguments about the positive or negative effect of reforms on social welfare tend to be based almost exclusively on their implications for the state. Either they are increasing the state's capacity to effectively and fairly respond to social needs or undermining its efforts to maintain its commitments to reasonable, equitable and/or just social benefits.

A second, yet related problem with the political economy approach is that in focusing on the nation-state as its primary, and in most cases exclusive, level of analysis, the space between policy making and policy outcomes remains a black box. In confining the analysis of globalization and its subsequent affects on welfare reform to "high politics," understood as elite-level policy formation, the political economy approach underestimates or leaves out important dynamics that operate in the realm of "low politics," as well as a variety of cross cutting territorial and sector-based considerations that profoundly impact the inter-play between policy making and policy implementation and thus the substantive impact that welfare reform has on users and citizens.

The Moral Economy Approach

Whereas the political economy approach is fuelled by a profound skepticism about the ability of society to meet the collective social needs of citizens, the moral economy approach embraces community as the primary guardian of social well being. Grounded in a conception of welfare provision as the natural extension of voluntary, mutualistic forms of self-help, the moral economy approach offers an alternative framework for conceptualizing and analyzing social welfare systems as a product of the so-called welfare society, a model for organizing social welfare on the basis of interlocking individual sanctions and rewards emanating from local communities.

The moral economy approach can be further separated into a progressive and a conservative version based on distinctive interpretations of the social fabric of society. The conservative version of the welfare society is profoundly skeptical of the governments' ability to gauge social needs and harness capitalism to fulfil these needs. Emerging as a reaction to the state's perceived colonization of civil society, this version of the moral economy perspective underscores the dangers of publicly provided, state-regulated welfare. Conceptualized as a paternalistic bureaucracy, the state is seen as creating harmful 'welfare dependencies,' which erode personal responsibility and weaken the ability of people to help themselves by undermining community-based social and ethnical norms. By contrast, the welfare society, which is viewed as complementing, rather than competing with market-based exchange mechanisms, is seen as strengthening the social fabric of society by reinforcing traditional values such as family loyalty and social obligation. A more progressive version of the moral economy approach embraces the welfare society not as the locus of cultural preservation, but rather as part of a broader movement toward social solidarity and associative democracy. Emphasizing participation and connectedness to local community as a principle legitimating factor in empowering and assisting people in need, this perspective sees reciprocity as a necessary precursor to developing healthy and productive societies. Less a reaction to the state than a response to the commerciahzation and alienation that has accompanied the process of modernization, this version of the moral economy approach sees communities as critical to actively reconstituting society by reconstructing identities and extending affective bonds between groups of people that increasingly lack a shared moral culture. From this perspective, the welfare society embodies a realm of fluid, multi-faceted relationships which counteract individualism and narrow self interest by fostering trust, mutual respect, and collective participation.

Regardless of their distinctive under standings of the social fabric of the welfare society, both versions of the moral economy approach underscore the importance of social actors, emotive ideas, and the non-rationality of culture in the development of social welfare systems. Challenging the authority of the state as legitimate arbitrator of welfare reform, they expand the scope of inquiry beyond the political economy approach's relatively narrow focus on poverty rates, social security, and income-transfers to encompass a broader array of social arrangements and processes, from more traditional conceptions of self-help to community care and the creation of alternative consciousness.

Despite this noteworthy advantage, the moral economy approach suffers from several shortcomings. First, by ignoring, by and large, the distributional aspects of social welfare systems, it obscures the important role that societal stratification and inequality play in welfare reform. Because the most marginalised segments of the population usually lack the capacity to voice their concerns and press their needs effectively, they tend to be disadvantaged by a welfare society which relies predominately if not exclusively on self identification of need and voluntary responses to those needs. Second, the moral economy approach reproduces the state-society dualism of the political economy approach, thus obscuring rather than clarifying the relationship between the two realms. By viewing he welfare society as an autonomous locus of proactive community engagement, responsive to both individual want and collective need, the moral economy approach portrays the state as outside of, and thus largely irrelevant to, society.

Where the state is considered, however, the focus of the moral economy approach is almost exclusively on its coercive power. As a result, it tends to underestimate the state's role in establishing the foundation for effective responses to a variety of welfare dilemmas, including stimulating the welfare enhancing properties of community activism by, for example, outlawing discriminatory practices, redistributing scarce resources, and guaranteeing social rights. A third problem with the moral economy approach is that it does not pay adequate attention to the multiplicity of institutional configurations involved in the day-to-day operation of social welfare systems. Consequently, it fails to appreciate the extent to which the distinctive juridical and legal status of private and non-profit organizations is critical to the success of welfare reform.

The Mixed Economy Approach

The growing complexity of the inter-organizational linkages connecting social organizations to one another and to public institutions, and the recognition of this development as critical to determining the consequences of welfare reform, has led to the development of a third approach, frequently defined as the mixed economy of welfare. While those who employ this approach come from a wide array of disciplines, principally economics, but also social welfare, public administration, and non-profit management, they ground their analysis in a concept of the welfare mix which is distinctive from both that of the welfare society the welfare state.

The concept of the welfare mix emphasizes institutional plurality and shared responsibility for welfare. Inevitably, social welfare systems draw on a variety of organizational resources, all of which are embedded within a broader set of exchange and production relationships. As the guarantor of citizen's legal entitlements and a key source of power, the state, understood more broadly as the public sector, is recognized as playing a vital role in the creation of social markets, understood as quasi-markets for social goods and services which separate purchasers, usually government agencies, from providers. The public sector is balanced, however, by two equally important sectors, the private and non-profit sectors, each of which operates according to a unique set of norms and principles. Thus, within the mixed economy approach, it is the relationship between the public, private and non-profit sectors that determines temporal and spatial variation in the output of social welfare systems.

Emphasizing institutional plurality, the mixed economy approach to welfare offers an analytic framework in which the output of welfare systems varies both temporally and spatially according to the relationship between the public, private and non-profit sectors. Thus, in addition to identifying a third sector, distinct from both the state and society, the mixed economy approach has contributed to our understanding of social welfare systems by paving the way for more sophisticated longitudinal and comparative empirical analysis of welfare systems across a variety of local and national contexts.

While paving the way for a more sophisticated comparative analysis of welfare systems and their capacity to mediate pressures for reform, the mixed economy approach has two significant limitations.

First, by assuming a difference in kind between organizations according to the presence or absence of certain sector-based properties and functions, the welfare mix approach falls into the same dilemma of the previous two approaches.

It fails to fully appreciate the breadth and depth of organizational variation within each sector, thus divorcing pertinent issues relating to social production (i.e. contracting, management, participation) from core issues of policy reform (i.e. cost effectiveness, marginalization, entitlement issues).

Second, in focusing on the technical and economic aspects of institutional performance, it obscures the social and political relevance of reform. By failing to link institutional outputs to the types of system-wide properties that give them meaning for those that they affect most directly, such as marginalised citizens and welfare users, the mixed economy approach does little to improve our understanding of the issues related to social justice.

An Emerging Paradigm: The Social Economy Approach to Welfare Reform

More recently, a growing body of work emerging from the social economy literature has established the basis for a new approach to welfare reform. Motivated by a shared set of theoretical and empirical concerns about the role of the third sector in mediating the relationship between state, society, and economy, this social economy approach is distinct from conventional approaches in that it offers an alternative conceptual understanding of social welfare systems as dynamic, open systems, grounded in complex institutional networks. In addition, it seeks to accumulate knowledge about collective forms of entrepreneurship and the extent to which they act as catalysts of change within emerging welfare networks.

Like political economy and moral economy approaches, the social economy approach is concerned about macro-level developments in the economy and society. Yet, it links these changes to questions and concerns relating to the social and administrative underpinnings of social welfare. As such, it introduces greater dynamism by exploring the micro foundations of institutional change, thus avoiding the political and moral economy approaches' over-emphasis on the degree to which macro-level structural and cultural forces Favour continuity over change within social welfare systems. Although recognizing that third sector organizations may rarely determine social and economic outcomes on their own, the social economy approach underscores their critical role in establishing the context and meaning that determine how every day people perceive of and experience social welfare.

While overlapping with the mixed economy approach in its attention to the third sector, the social economy approach encompasses a broader understanding of the third sector as a highly differentiated and interpenetrated institutional realm neither derivative of, nor inherently in competition with, the public and private sectors. In proposing a more fluid conceptualization of the third sector as an important nexus of interaction between different principles (i.e. exchange, redistribution, and reciprocity) otherwise seen as distinctive characteristics of either economy, state, or community, the social economy approach moves beyond conventional under standings of market values and interests and social values and interests as inherently conflicting. Embedded in both society and the economy, third sector organizations create, reconstruct and maintain social relationships as well as the universe of practices and forms of mobilizing economic resources, which, as Saucier and Thivierge (2003) observe, are key to combating poverty, generating social solidarity, and satisfying human needs.

The Rise of Welfare Networks

The social economy approach takes for granted that the processes of globalization and modernization have fundamentally altered the parameters of contemporary welfare systems, and thus its principle concern is in understanding the capacity of third sector organizations to serve as a socially efficacious response to these twin challenges.

Although identifying and explaining the causes of broader structural change is not a central component of the social economy approach, its analysis of the third sector's role in responding to change is informed by an understanding of globalization and modernization as symptomatic of a fundamental shift in the productive infrastructure of society from one which was industrial to one which is predominately informational and service based.

By impacting employment opportunities and family dynamics, this structural shift in the economy significantly impacts the demographic composition of society, which in turn fuels greater pressures toward administrative, political and economic decentralization. While these processes significantly increase the complexity of welfare systems, the capacity of national public administrators to manage social welfare systems diminishes as greater policy responsibility is transferred to the subnational level, shifting the locus of public intervention away from the central government to lower levels of government.

In tandem with a pervasive post-materialist shift in values post-in-dustrialism entails a transition away from both the state and society as dominant organizing infrastructures of the social welfare systems toward more amorphous welfare networks. This reconstitution of welfare systems into welfare networks motivates three key developments:

1) The potential for constructing more efficacious responses to new and old social and economic risks, and
2) The emergence of a more complex and differentiated third sector, and
3) A more fluid process of reform facilitated by the proliferation of new organizational forms and strategies utilized in social welfare provision.

Social Risk and Emerging Welfare Networks

The key characteristics defining the new post-industrial era—the blurring of boundaries between sectors, the increasing specialization and volatility of social and economic relations, and the institutionalization of continual change—both exacerbate pre-existing risks and create new ones. They restrict the relevant degree of freedom afforded to governments to adopt and implement social policies that can harness the benefits and compensate for the losses incurred by globalization and modernization, thus contributing to what Beck (1998) identifies as the 'democratization of vulnerability' as risk becomes more fluid. Greater instability and increasing differentiation in citizens' needs and preferences make it increasingly difficult for public officials to guarantee a fair and equitable allocation of social and economic resources and a high standard of living to all citizens while the combination of diminishing public resources, increasing ethnic and cultural diversity (and with it the proliferation of social customs, norms, and practices) increase the threat of various forms of discrimination.

In tandem with these developments, welfare networks offer the potential for constructing more efficacious responses to risk, particularly those related to social exclusion and economic dependency. In much the same way that the creation of the market economy during the nineteenth century gave rise to what economic historian Karl Polanyi (1944) describes as a double movement, the social and economic processes set in motion by the current post-industrial shift has engendered a countermovement.

This countermovement, stimulated by the impulse to re-embed the economy in social relations, creates a new role for third sector organizations as the source of alternative social constructions capable of generating a collective response to social need. Although not intrinsically a promoter of social justice, in a context in which globalization, combined with a maturation of government commitments increases citizens' vulnerability to social dislocation while simultaneously undermining the capacity and legitimacy of the state to provide social protection, the third sector represents a force within local communities that works to make them more livable, and in many ways, more socially just. By creating new forms of connectivity and solidarity, covering new forms of social need, and mobilizing citizen awareness of and reaction to factors which undermine the public good, third sector organizations alleviate social marginalization, negotiate greater fairness...

The Civil Society in the Welfare State

This report on the civil society in the Swedish welfare state is based on 2,749 telephone interviews conducted with a random sample from the population register of persons 16-89 years of age throughout Sweden. The interviews were conducted in the Spring of 1994, at the bottom of a deep recession. The fieldwork was carried out by Demoskop AB from its telephone interviewing facilities in Stockholm. The analysis was done at Value Scope AB in Stockholm.

The Civil Society

In Sweden, with its focus on state-run welfare, the role of the civil society has long been ignored in public and political discourse. We find, however, that it not only is flourishing but also constitutes an essential part of the social fabric and represents the most meaningful aspect of life for the citizens of the Swedish welfare state.

The civil society includes family life, neighbourhood and community life, social activities, activities in voluntary associations, and religious and cultural activities. Our focus on the role of the civil society in welfare questions indicates that we need to complement the political scientist's view of Swedish civil society by bringing in family and community life.

Family Life

The general discourse in the media can convey the impression that the end of the 1910s finds the Swedish family weak and fairly insignificant. A review of our statistical data provides a different picture, one of stronger family bonds and responsibilities. The representation of a weak family in the general discourse is true of a minority, not of the majority.

In the 1910s most adults continue to live with others (77%) and thereby have daily contact with the most prevalent form of community life in the civil society. Single parents are not common: 6 percent of all women aged 16-44 years are mothers with children 14 years of age or younger who live without a spouse or partner; the figure for fathers who live alone with minor children is 0.4 percent.

In older age groups it is usual that one's children have moved from the parental home and that one has grandchildren. Among persons under 64 years of age, almost all have parents or parents-in-law who are living. Practically all individuals who live in Sweden thus have some close relative.

The nuclear family has changed significantly during recent generations. A half century ago, when a person moved from his parental home, both parents were usually still living in the home; if one of them was not in the home it was because he or she was deceased. Even today's youth usually have both parents living at home when he or she moves; only one out of five young people say that one parent had moved before he or she did so. Although the divorce rate has risen, three out of four young people have *not* experienced divorce or death among their parents. The idea that today's family is in dissolution and has ceased to function is thus not true for a majority of young people.

The civil society also comprises social life and activities in voluntary associations. With few exceptions, all those interviewed mix at least some of the time with both relatives and friends.

The most Meaningful Part of Life

Our interview dealt among other things with the family, work, helpfulness, and subsidies from the welfare state. At the end of the 30-minute long interview, the respondent was asked: "When you look back, what has given you the most in life? Is it your work, family life, social life, participation in voluntary associations, or your life as a citizen in a welfare state?" When it comes down to it, it is family life, social life, and participation in voluntary associations-that is, the civil society-which most people have experienced as most meaningful. Of all those interviewed, 60 percent were of this opinion. Every fourth person (28%) reported that work had been the most meaningful area in their life. Every tenth person (10%) answered that life as a citizen in a welfare state had been most meaningful to them. The media and the public discourse are filled with discussions about the problems of the economy and working life and with the problems of the welfare state. However, life in the civil society is most meaningful to the man on the street.

A Plurality of Income Sources

Of all adults 16-89 years of age in 1994, 84 percent live on income from the labour market in the form of employment, extra jobs, or pensions from previous employment.

By comparison, the proportion with income derived from the civil society is low-31 percent. One out of 20 persons receives cash contributions from family and relatives. As many have received some inheritance. Every fourth person has his own savings, income from capital or property, the sale of stocks or other assets.

Routinely distributed benefits from the state which the recipient need not apply for are provided to 43 percent of the population. Old-age pensions and child allowances constitute the largest share of such benefits.

Of the total population, 28 percent live entirely or partly on benefits that the recipients must apply for, such as housing allowances, student allowances, unemployment compensation, and disability pensions.

One and the same person can receive income from different sources and our figures represent percentages of people, not percentages of income in crowns.

The transition of industrial society to a non-industrial society-an information society with a great deal of knowledge imbedded in products and services-is changing the salaried form of work that was the cornerstone of social structure in the 1900s. The old view of salaried work as durable full-time employment with normal working hours for a stable employer is now disintegrating into an increasingly fragmented reality. We will discuss six ways of acquiring a livelihood in Sweden today:

Two-thirds of the general public 16-89 years of age are gainfully employed:

- 28 percent are employed in the public sector
- 26 percent are employed in the private sector
- 8 percent are self-employed
- 4 percent work "on a free basis".

One-third of the Swedes 16-89 years of age are not gainfully employed:

- 14.5 percent are 64 years of age or younger (looking for work, 7%, students, 3%, early or partial retirees, 3%, other, 2%)
- 20 percent are 65 years of age or older.

The very high number employed in public service is a reflection of the extensive nature of the Swedish welfare state in which the government not only finances welfare programs but also runs them as public bureaucracies.

Our classification is conventional, with the exception of the category "work on a free basis," an answer that was given by one out of 25 people. They do not consider themselves to be employed or to be self-employed. We have here a modern category of free-lancers. They are "engaged" rather than "employed."

One can read data about well-known phenomena such as employment and the length and disposition of working hours from the point of view of the civil society rather than from that of economics. We can then see how much is left over for the civil society once gainful employment has taken its share.

Work Hours

Involvement in the civil society on the part of the gainfully employed is limited by the length of their working hours. The combination of a high degree of employment and a large proportion of people with normal working hours restrains the activities of the civil society, This means that the lion's share of those gainfully employed are pulled out of the civil society at the same hours of the day and away from activities such as child care and care of the aged. In Sweden the dilemma has been resolved by moving much of the care of children and of the aged to public institutions. What has not been fully recognized is that the dilemma has also been resolved by departing from the usual work week and work hours.

Gainful employment is not limited to daytime hours Monday to Friday. It is true that 73 percent of those gainfully employed state that they work "normal working hours, that is Monday through Friday, sometime between 7 am and 6 pm", but four out of ten work on weekends or nights or late in the evening, and every fourth works early morning hours.

There is a stunning contrast between our findings and that which legislators, union negotiators, social planners and others assume to be normal and universally applicable-namely, full-time employment between 8 and 5, Monday through Friday.

When we examined the percentage of people who work only "normal" work hours (which, in our question, were extended to between 7 am and 6 pm) Monday through Friday, and who have a normal work week of 35 or 40 hours, we found that only every fourth person with gainful employment (27%) fitted this category (27% of blue collar workers, 37 percent of white collar workers and 7% of the self-employed).

Despite the many arrangements of work hours, the full need for flexibility has not been fulfilled. Every other person with normal work hours and preschool children wants to change his/her work hours in order to spend more time during the day with the children.

There is a conservatism in the view of work hours entertained by the authorities, the unions, and parliament. The Swedish civil society struggles successfully for its existence against these powers in regard to the question of work hours.

Job Hunters and The Unemployed

The interviews contain questions about occupation and about how one acquires a livelihood. In answer to the question about occupation, 9 percent (183 persons) between the ages of 16 and 64 said that they lack gainful employment but are looking for work; they are below retirement age and state that they have no gainful employment, no work from which they have sick leave or other forms of leave, and no other paid work.

In answer to the question about how one gains a livelihood, 7 percent (136 persons) stated that they receive unemployment compensation or labour market assistance. These categories-the jobless and those who receive unemployment compensation-overlap only partially.

Of the 136 persons interviewed who receive unemployment compensation, about one-half (55%) said that they were job hunting. According to their own statements given in our interviews, the other half (45%) are not looking for work.

We find that 3 percent of the population between the ages of 16 and 64 practice that which sociologists term "institutionalized evasion of institutional rules". Those who receive unemployment compensation are obliged to look for work, but not all do so. The unions and the authorities evidently look the other way. The old, formally accepted rules are stretc..hed to accomodate them to new, informally accepted norms.

Of those who have received unemployment compensation, 36 percent had some paid work the days just preceding the interview. Here we can detect yet another example of the bending of rules.

Job hunters and the unemployed have several different sources of income. Students' assistance, which in Sweden is part subsidy and part loan, is the most usual income source for those without a job who are looking for work but do not receive unemployment compensation.

Job hunters who receive unemployment compensation get along mainly on that income. The third category receives unemployment compensation at the same time as s/he has a job; in addition, some receive welfare and housing allowances and/or financial help from parents or other relatives.

On the whole, Sweden's social safety net managed to do its job during 1994, a year of deep recession and record high unemployment. This was not only the result of Sweden's special labour market policies. It was also due to that fact that almost all the unemployed are involved in a number of contexts in the private, public, and civil sectors which provide them with means of subsistence. In addition, in some cases the official rules for granting benefits have been reinterpreted to follow a new, informal praxis.

Several Sources of Income

The chapter concludes with a review of the income sources in the different population segments. One-third of the self-employed (34%) receive automatic state benefits, usually child allowances, as a supplement to their income from their own business.

Those who work on a free basis do not support themselves solely from such work; all of 48 percent also applied for benefits, usually in the form of student assistance, advance payments on maintenance allowances for children, child support, and housing allowances.

Every sixth person who was employed in the private sector also moonlighted (16%); 26 percent received child allowances and 6 percent received housing allowances. The income sources of those employed in the public sector resembled those of people employed in the private sector: 16 percent moonlighted, 32 percent received child allowances, and 6 percent received housing allowances.

Those without gainful employment of some kind who were below retirement age lived mainly on state benefits for which one must apply: student assistance (36%), disability pensions (22%), unemployment compensation, (23%), housing allowances (15%). Many-more than any other group-also receive income from the civil society, primarily in the form of assistance from family and/or relatives (19%).

Many old-age pensioners who were not gainfully employed had their own savings with which to supplement other income sources (39%). This group also had the highest incidence of recipients of housing allowances (16%).

One must be careful with claims such as x percent live on the market economy, y percent live off relatives, and z percent live off the state. Most people have more than one source of income, and this applies to all segments in society. In all of Sweden, for example, only 16 percent of people between the ages of 16 and 89 have neither a job in the public sector nor receive any benefits or pensions from it. Furthermore, the odds are small that these 16 percent do not have a wife/husband, parents or children who receive some form of payments from the public sector.

Private Transfers

Togetherness, personal contacts, and the ideal of helping one another characterize the civil society. In our research, these features were illuminated in questions asking how children and parents help one another, and how people generally offer time, goods, and money to assist others.

This chapter discusses three types of private transfers: (1) transfers in material goods, (2) financial assistance, and (3) assistance rendered in the form of time. Public discourse about welfare in Sweden has seldom paid attention to such transfers; it has instead been predicated on the assumption that all transfers are achieved through political decisions.

"Transfers" is a term used in the state bureaucracy; we did not use it in our interviews. The term is not to be found in the vocabulary of the civil society. Here one speaks of gifts and services and reciprocity, of consideration, love, help, and solicitude. This theme has many variations, and we can present here only a few examples, not the whole picture.

Of all those interviewed, 79 percent reported that they have provided or received assistance in kind in one or more of the ways which we exemplified in our survey, namely, by receiving house guests or being afforded such hospitality, or by showing generosity to relatives and friends by giving away garden products, a catch of fish or game.

Altogether 81 percent have given financial assistance to children, parents, parents-in-law, husband, wife, or partner, or have made donations to charitable organizations. Many help children and grandchildren financially. Every third parent with children who have moved from the parental home has at some time vouched for their bank loans.

A considerable portion of leisure time is spent caring for and helping others. Children help their parents, and many people have relatives who are sick, handicapped, or old and who require care and attention.

A total of 84 percent help others by contributing their time or efforts. Younger people help others significantly more by contributing their time, while older people help others significantly more through financial contributions.

Interestingly enough, work hours do not have much bearing on how one helps others. It is true that people with short work hours have more time to devote to gardening, fishing, and hunting, and can contribute material goods more than those with long work hours, while they also have fewer resources to help others financially. Yet people with long work hours also devote a great deal of time-more than the average-to assisting those close to them.

In smaller communities and on the countryside is above the average for help in the form of material goods. However, the degree of urbanization of residential area does not affect the extent to which assistance is rendered in terms of time or money.

Those who own their own business-often a small family firm-constitute a group with a high degree of social responsibility. They represent the highest percentages of assistance rendered in respect to both caring activities and private transfers. They have one foot in the civil society, the other in the marketplace.

People with the lowest household incomes are naturally less able to help others financially. However, the index for them lies under the average even in respect to assistance rendered in time or in material goods. Many older people belong to this income group.

A review of private transfers in Sweden shows that they are prodigious. I shall not attempt to translate their value into crowns. Any attempt at such a translation on the basis of the available data would require too many arbitrary assumptions. It should be noted, however, that it will be difficult to present these transfers as a percentage of the GNP since most of them do not enter into the basis for calculating the GNP.

An objection to the thought of calculating the transfers of the civil society is the idea that gifts, services, and reciprocal acts belong to a category that should not carry a price tag, according to the ethos of the civil society. But everyone, even an economist, removes the price tag before s/he gives away a gift. The behaviour of researchers follows other rules that those of private individuals, and we consider that such calculations represent a legitimate project for future research.

The simple conclusion that I wish to emphasize is that welfare in Sweden is by no means synonymous with welfare under public auspices. The network of mutual assistance of the civil society can be found in all segments of society. Other questions for future research could concern the interpretation of the renown success of Swedish welfare.

To what extent do the private activities of the civil society actually constitute a silent and hidden prerequisite for public welfare undertakings? To what extent are private transfers dependent on the existence of a base of public transfers? And-the most important research project-has Swedish welfare legislation been in harmony with the transfers of the civil society or has it staunched the flow of generosity of the civil society?

Caring in The Civil Society

It has been said that care giving functions in Sweden are socialized, that is, they are administered and carried out by the public sector. But many private individuals care for someone who is sick, handicapped, or elderly. In this chapter we wish to draw attention to such informal caring as a central function in the civil society.

One of the fundamental norms of the civil society holds that we must not fail those close to us when they are in need. International research on caring discusses both *nursing* and *caring*. Our concern here is with caring, not with nursing.

Slightly more than every fifth adult 16-89 years of age (22%) is a care in the civil society: five percent of all adults in Sweden look after a member of the household who is sick, handicapped, or elderly, and 18 percent regularly tend to someone who does not live in the household; one percent tend to someone in the household as well as to someone who does not share the same domicile. This totals to approximately 1,6 million individuals who are careers. The Swedish percentage of the population who are careers is slightly higher than the corresponding figure in the United Kingdom; some years ago that figure was 15 percent: four percent tended to someone in the same household and 12 percent tended to someone who did not live in the same household.

Many perhaps envisage careers as middle-aged women, but our results show that both men and women and persons of all ages are careers in the civil society: 23 percent of the women and 20 percent of the men in Sweden look after someone in or outside of their households.

There is hardly any difference in respect to caring between those who are gainfully employed and those who are not. Of all those gainfully employed, every fourth individual (23%) looks after or helps someone who is sick, handicapped or elderly; the corresponding figure for those not gainfully employed is 21 percent, and for pensioners, 20 percent.

In some cases municipalities provide caretaking that runs parallel to that provided by the civil society. Some of this is in the form of financial support to relatives who act as careers, and some in the form of public domestic assistance. As we saw, 22 percent of all adults in Sweden are careers. Of these, 8 percent assume their tasks with some financial support from public treasuries, but 14 percent do so without any public financial support. These figures indicate that there are approximately 450,000 men and 560,000 women who are careers without receiving any assistance from municipalities either in the form of public domestic assistance to the care recipient or payments to the care.

In the 2,749 interviews carried out, we found 601 persons who look after someone at home or in another household. Careers in the civil society primarily tend to family members (77%). Every third care in the home looks after a husband or wife, every fourth looks after children, and as many tend to parents or parents-in-law.

The picture is different for those who tend to someone who does not live in the same household: 37 percent look after parents or parents-in-law, and 28 percent help some other relative, 21 percent of careers help a friend or neighbour, 9 percent help an acquaintance, and 5 percent help someone with whom they have come in contact through an association, church, or the like.

Some of the care ministered in the home is quite demanding physically. Many careers assist others by lifting them and physically supporting them in, for example, getting in and out of bed and walking, and help them with their personal hygiene. Their duties may include responsibility for administering medication, injections, and for bandaging, and may thus border on nursing. Careers who look after others outside of the home rarely have duties of this kind.

Most careers, both within and outside of the home, help with practical tasks such as shopping, cooking, doing the laundry, and reparations. They keep the care recipient company, take him or her on excursions, walks, or visits to others, and generally see to it that all is well.

Giving care is normal in the civil society. Its occurrence in the civil society should not be interpreted as a sign that the publicly operated social system in Sweden has failed or is lacking in resources. Nor should it be seen as a sign that the commercial market for care giving in Sweden is underdeveloped or has failed. For those cases which the civil society cannot assist, care provided by public agencies or purchased on the commercial market are necessary options.

As we see, the care giving aspect of the civil society exists even in the most developed welfare state. Its norms are basically particularistic, and it embraces mainly those near and dear, not one and all, as in the public welfare system, whose norms are universalistic in principle. Universalistic norms are general and neutral. In cases governed by particularistic norms the relationships between individuals are all-encompassing (Parsons says "diffuse"): people help one another irrespective of what the assistance entails.

An interesting question for research is how responsibility between particularistic and universalistic institutions is distributed in modern welfare states. It is not certain that Sweden has arrived at the optimal distribution.

Cases

The civil society can in the main provide caretaking of the type described above, not professional nursing or medical cures. Of the cases considered, 82 percent involve chronic problems for which no cure is in sight; care will be required for the remainder of their lives. It is noteworthy against this background that, on the whole, the careers in the civil society consider themselves capable of coping with their tasks.

The million careers in today's Sweden would get more recognition for their contribution. Their work is hidden, and it is often lonely and unappreciated. One suspects that many need relief in the form of replacements some time during the week in order to see to their own daily needs. Many no doubt need a vacation. They also need understanding from their employers when they sometimes need to take time off from work or go home to handle a crisis situation that has arisen.

2

Implementing Social Policy

Social Policy

Social policy primarily refers to guidelines and interventions for the changing, maintenance or creation of living conditions that are conducive to human welfare.

Thus, social policy is that part of public policy that has to do with social issues. The Malcolm Wiener Centre for Social Policy at Harvard University describes it as *"public policy and practice in the areas of health care, human services, criminal justice, inequality, education, and labour"* Social policy often deals with issues which Rittle & Webber (1973) called wicked problems.

Social Policy is also distinct as an academic field which focuses on the systematic evaluation of societies' responses to social need. London School of Economics professor Richard Titmuss is considered to have established Social Policy (or Social Administration) as an academic subject and many universities offer the subject for undergraduate and postgraduate study.

History of Social Policy

Early proponents of scientific social planning, such as the sociologist Auguste Comte, and social researchers, such as Charles Booth, contributed to the emergence of social policy. Surveys of poverty that exposed the brutal conditions that existed, such as in the urban slum conurbations of Victorian Britain, pressured changes such as the reform of the Poor Law and welfare reforms by the British Liberal Party. Other significant examples of social policy are the social security policies introduced by the New Deal in the United States between 1933 and 1935 and health reforms in the UK following the Beveridge Report of 1942.

Types of Social Policy

Social policy aims to improve human welfare and to meet human needs for education, health, housing and social security. Social policies will be approached in vastly different ways depending on the ideological leanings of the governing power.

Important areas of social policy are:

- The welfare state
- Social security
- Unemployment insurance
- Pensions
- Healthcare
- Family Policy
- Social housing
- Social care
- Social exclusion
- Education policy
- Crime and Criminal justice
- Labour regulation.

The term 'social policy' can also refer to policies which govern human behaviour. 'Social policy' may refer to the following issues:

- abortion and the regulation of its practice
- the legal status of euthanasia
- the legal status of homosexuality
- the rules surrounding issues of marriage, divorce, and adoption
- poverty, welfare, and homelessness and how it is to deal with these issues
- the legal status of recreational drugs
- the legal status of prostitution.

Process of Policy-Making in India Since Independence

Policy process in India is done at many levels. The goals of the policy are determined by the vision of the leader of the political party in the ruling. Then these policies are detailed at the secretariat and passed down the ladder for the implementation. By the trickle down effect, these policies are reached to the grass root level. Following are the broad stages of the policy determination.

Policy Structure

Parliament is the supreme legislative body of a country. Our Parliament comprises of the President and the two Houses, Lok Sabha (House of the People) and Rajya Sabha (Council of States). The President has the power to summon and prorogue either House of Parliament or to dissolve Lok Sabha. The Constitution of India came into force on January 26, 1950. The first general elections under the new Constitution were held during the year 1951-52 and the first elected Parliament came into being in April, 1952.

But the Parliament has to follow certain procedure to decide any policy. The Fundamental Rights, Directive Principles of State Policy and Fundamental Duties are sections of the Constitution of India that prescribe the fundamental obligations of the State° to its citizens and the duties of the citizens to the State.

These sections comprise a constitutional bill of rights and guidelines for government policy-making and the behaviour and conduct of citizens. These sections are considered vital elements of the constitution, which was developed between 1947 and 1949 by the Constituent Assembly of India.

The Directive Principles of State Policy are guidelines for the framing of laws by the government. These provisions are not enforceable by the courts, but the principles on which they are based are fundamental guidelines for governance that the State is expected to apply in framing and passing laws.

The Fundamental Duties are defined as the moral obligations of all citizens to help promote a spirit of patriotism and to uphold the unity of India. These duties concern individuals and the nation. Like the Directive Principles, they are not legally enforceable.

Economical Policy

Nehru was fascinated by Soviet Union's Piatiletka or 5-year plan and tried implementing the same for the Indian Economy. He wanted India to have the best combination of Socialism and Capitalism and tried to implement Democratic Socialism in India. He wanted the state to be a principal entrepreneur and all its citizens to be equal share holders. He strengthened the democratic pillars of nation immensely by creating proper wealth distribution systems at all levels.

Nehru's economic policies are often confused by critics with those of his daughter, Indira Gandhi, who was more left-wing. Nehru's economics of state intervention and investment were conceived at a time when transfers of capital and technology important to India were not easily forthcoming from the developed world (which incidentally also had plenty of state-sponsored capital controls.) Nehru is often criticised by ill-informed commentators of the present-day, when transfers of capital are unhindered, easily channelled by recipient nations, and even encouraged for their high returns in emerging markets.

The Soviet Union was the only major power to allow India to develop independent capabilities in many spheres of heavy industry, engineering, and cutting-edge technologies. India's combination of internal political freedom, economic and political independence throughout its existence can be favourably compared with many client-states of the United States and the Soviet Union.

Till 1991, India followed more or less the same policy, and then it followed the policy of the liberalisation. This opened up the economy and brought in more FDI.

Foreign Policy

The foundations of India's foreign policy were laid during the freedom movement when our leaders, even when fighting for independence, were engaged with the great causes of the time. The principles of India's foreign policy, that emerged then, have stood the test of time: a belief in friendly relations with all countries of the world, the resolution of conflicts by peaceful means, the sovereign equality of all states, independence of thought and action as manifested in the principles of Non-alignment, and equity in the conduct of international relations. Under the leadership of Jawaharlal Nehru, India was the founder member of the Non-aligned Movement. India has also been in the forefront of the world community in the struggle against colonialism.

A notable feature of Indian foreign policy has been its strong advocacy of general and complete disarmament, with nuclear disarmament being accorded the highest priority. As a founder member of the United Nations, India has been firmly committed to the purposes and principles of the United Nations and has made significant contributions to its various activities, including peace-keeping operations. India's foreign policy has always regarded the concept of neighbourhood as one of widening concentric circles, around a central axis of historical and cultural commonalties. From this point of view, it has always given due priority to the development of relations with South East Asia.

Development Policy

The social problems of contemporary India are the result of a complex nexus between the factors of exclusion and inclusion rooted in history, values, and cultural ethos. Many of these problems based on the policy of segregation have not been addressed by the development strategy launched since Independence. Recent policies of globalization have further undermined the role of larger societal norms as well as the state apparatus that could counter exclusionary forces. The agenda of social development has remained unfinished, keeping social tensions simmering. Today, however, in the policy debate, orthodox economic liberalism is giving way to concerns regarding social consequences of globalization, as it affects the poorest and the marginalised sections of the population.

Thus, a number of highly important and far-reaching social policy measures have been brought on to the development agenda, in the form of the Right to Information Act, Rural Employment Guarantee Act, the Rural Health Mission among others. This unique volume argues the need to harness the energy of the nation to ensure their effective implementation through an overview of trends and patterns of development along with policies and programmes. It identifies key concerns and proposes measures of possible intervention.

Conclusion

Issues of sustainable livelihood and social and political participation of the vulnerable groups exists as the major problem in the India. They have least participation and access in the social, economic, political and cultural sector. They have been marginalised from the mainstream State system and the development process. Governments have failed to guarantee people's rights in the implementation level. People of the vulnerable groups are unable to acquire and use their rights. This has caused very insignificant access of this groups in the State system and the resources. They do not have adequate access to justice and equity.

Though the States have incorporated equality in their policy, the vulnerable groups have not been able to feel it in reality. They have been facing many challenges in enjoying their right to sustainable livelihood and social and political participation due to lack of priority of the States in protection and promotion of the interests of the vulnerable groups. Governments and elites of the region back up State terrorism and militarization in the name of national or internal security, resulting in violation of the civil and political rights of those who struggle for economic, social and cultural rights.

Human rights violation is supported by the unjust structure of society. There are many structures in the Indian societies that have to dismantled – unjust economic social and cultural structures. We can take the case of peasants for instance. If the peasants do not own and control the productive resources such as land, financial capital and technology, we cannot imagine human rights for them. As long as workers are laid off, or if they receive unjust, very low wages because of policies dictated by the International Monetary Fund (IMF), World Bank and World Trade Organization (WTO) and carried out by respective governments, there will never be improvement in economic, social and cultural rights or the right to development, nor will there be improvement in the realization of the civil and political rights of our peoples. This arises because the policies of such international organizations always influence the policies of India. To conclude, the government has to retrospect the basic policy making process which it is using for the last 60 years. This will help greatly in the development of the people.

Social Accountability in India

Moving from Mechanisms to Outcomes and Institutionalization in Large Scale Public Programs

Strengthening accountability relationships between policy makers, service providers and citizens is at the core of the public accountability effort. In the South Asia region, *"demand side"* approaches – the strengthening the voice and capacity of citizens to directly demand greater accountability and responsiveness from public officials and service providers – are increasingly gaining traction. These approaches often involve social accountability processes which rely on citizens, service users and civil society organizations to exact accountability and have been implemented by government and civil society alike in South Asia.

Since 2005, the World Bank has also led an effort to initiate and mainstream social accountability initiatives in the region. The first stage of this effort involved 6 projects in various service delivery contexts throughout India and Sri Lanka that integrated participatory data collection and tools of analysis with enhanced spaces for citizen with the state. These initiatives have lead to a new generation of social accountability practices that emphasize a solid evidence base and direct interaction between citizens and government functionaries.

Democracy and Well Being in India

India; the country holds an enviable record in institutionalising democracy in the form of Constitutionalism, a competitive party system, regular elections, rule of law, codification of political and civil rights, and guarantees of free press and a vibrant civil society. But even as India satisfies conditions that permit it to claim the label of democracy with some justification; a majority of the people continue to suffer from unimagined hardship, with the most vulnerable among them-the poor among the scheduled castes and tribes, hill people, forest dwellers, tribals, and women particularly the girl child-at tremendous risk in matters of both lives and livelihoods.

It is true that the decade of the 1990s which heralded the onset of economic reforms also brought a decline in poverty figures. In

1973-74, 55 percent of India's population fell below the poverty line; this was reduced to 36 percent in 1993-94, to further fall to 26 percent of a one billion population in 1999-2000. In absolute terms the number of poor declined from 323 million in 1983 to 260 million in 1999-2000. The fall in poverty figures has been accompanied by a great deal of improvement in the basic parameters of human development. According to the 2003-2004 Report of the Ministry of Health and Family Welfare, infant mortality has declined significantly from 110 deaths per 1000 live births in 1981 to 66 deaths per 1000 live births in 2001. Correspondingly, life expectancy has increased from 54 years in 1981 to 64.6 years in 2000. According to the 2001 Census, the literacy rate for the population above the age of seven stands at 65.4 percent, compared to 52.21 percent in 1991.

Four factors need to be noted in this connection. Firstly, poverty is unevenly spread across regions with Uttar Pradesh, Bihar, Madhya Pradesh, West Bengal, and Orissa accounting for 69 percent of the poor in 1999-2000. Equally striking are rural urban disparities: 75 percent of the 260 million poor live in rural areas with no access to land, productive resources or employment. Secondly, different states have differing records of human development. Whereas Kerala has a literacy rate of 92 percent which is comparable to that of Vietnam; Bihar-a backward state-continues to have a literacy rate of only 47.5 percent. Equally, whereas the literacy rate in urban areas is 80.30 percent, the corresponding literacy rate for rural areas is only 59.40 percent. Thirdly, human development has little to do with economic development.

Although the sex ratio according to the 2001 Census has improved slightly for the country in the decade of the 1990s, and is now 933 women per 1000 men compared to 927 women per 1000 men in the 1991 census, the situation has actually worsened in Himachal Pradesh, Gujarat, Haryana, Punjab, and Delhi which rank high on the scale of economic development. Fourthly we find a contradiction between human development indicators within a state. Take Himachal Pradesh, at the very time the state has witnessed a dramatic expansion of literacy levels; the sex ratio in the state has declined from 976 females per 1000 males in 1991, to 970 per 1000 males in 2001, problematising thereof the postulated link between literacy and women's status. In sum, not only do a quarter of the world's poor live in India, the number of illiterates, school drop-outs, people suffering from communicable diseases, and infant, child and maternal deaths, amount to a staggering proportion of respective world totals. More troublesome is the fact that country has high numbers of hungry people despite the existence of huge buffer stocks of food. And India's record in providing services-sanitation, clean drinking water, electricity, housing, and jobs-is even bleaker. It is clear that political democracy has simply not been accompanied by the institutionalisation of economic and social democracy.

Does it then follow that given a choice between *more* democracy and *more* wellbeing democrats should opt for more wellbeing? The choice is difficult especially when we are confronted with massive poverty, deprivation, and ill-fare in the country. But let me hasten to suggest that democracy is *always* preferable to authoritarianism for one core reason: the possession and exercise of basic rights *enables* citizens to mobilise and press the state to deliver on the promises embedded in the Constitution and in policy pronouncements. Arguably mobilisation leads to enhanced participation, and participation *deepens* democracy simply because it helps realise the prime legitimacy claim of the concept-that of popular sovereignty. In sum, the peculiar virtue of Indian democracy, howsoever formal and minimal our *avatar* of democracy may be, is that it is premised on the recognition of, the grant of, and the codification of basic rights: the right to freedom of expression, of assembly, of association, and more significantly the *root* right to demand other rights. This alone allots to democracy an intrinsic value that outweighs greater wellbeing delivered by non-democratic regimes.

I argue that whereas the codification of Directive Principles of State Policy in part four of the Indian Constitution has *motivated* the enactment of social policy, the *codification* of fundamental rights in part three of the Constitution has inspired and empowered collective action for the implementation of the said Principles. To put it differently, collective action in India has served to connect constitutional entitlements, state policy, and wellbeing via the route of expanding the vocabulary as well as the conceptual repertoire of rights. The argument proceeds in four parts. In the first section I detail the structures of social opportunities provided by the state. In the second section I deal with the structural barriers to wellbeing and also the role of political agents in addressing these barriers. In the third section I discuss some of the contemporary campaigns that press for the effective implementation of the Directive Principles. And in the fourth section I analyse the pre-conditions that are required for achieving wellbeing. I suggest that whereas the compulsions of formal democracy may encourage the enactment of social policies; it is only when civil society mobilises for the strengthening, the expansion, and the effective implementation of these policies, that we can expect a transition from political to social democracy. But civil society interventions have their own limits. What these limits are is discussed in the last section of the essay.

Structures of Social Opportunities

The co-existence of political and civil freedom alongside social and economic unfreedom in India is cause for some regret. For the leaders of the freedom movement had understood as early as the 1920s that the task of attaining political freedom is necessarily hampered unless it is accompanied by social and economic freedom and vice versa. Consequently, it had conceptualised an integrated agenda of political, civil, social, cultural, and economic rights in the 1928 Nehru Constitutional Draft, and in the Karachi Resolution on Fundamental Rights adopted by the Indian National Congress in 1931. This integrated agenda was however split into two units in the Constituent Assembly. Whereas the grant of political, civil, and cultural rights in part three of the Constitution are backed by legal sanction, social and economic rights which are placed in part four under the title of Directive Principles of State Policy are *not* backed by such sanction. For a majority of the members of the Constituent Assembly held that the costs of implementing positive rights were prohibitive.

Consequently, the Directive Principles of State Policy are intended as general guidelines for legislatures and governments. The opening clause of the report of the sub-committee on fundamental rights clearly stated that 'while these principles shall not be cognizable by any court, they are nevertheless fundamental in the governance of the country and their application in the making of laws shall be the duty of the state'.

Some members of the Constituent Assembly were deeply critical of the downgrading of social and economic rights to the status of Directive Principles. K.T Shah alleged that the whole scheme of directives have been reduced to a 'needless fraud'; 'an excellent window dressing without any stock behind that dressing'. However, Dr. Ambedkar the President of the Constituent Assembly assured members that though the Principles were not legally binding 'whoever captures power will not be free to do what he likes with it. In the exercise of it, he will have to respect these Instruments of Instructions, which are called Directive Principles. He cannot ignore them. He may not have to answer for their breach in a court of law. But he will certainly have to answer for them before the electorate at election time.

In pursuance of the general objective of establishing a social order based on social and economic justice, the Directive Principles urge the state to assure the following cluster of social goods to the people of India.

- Firstly, *within the limits of its economic capacity and development* the state shall make effective provision for securing the right to work, a living wage, equal pay for equal work, just and humane conditions of work, adequate means of livelihood and a decent standard of life.
- Secondly, the state is obliged to ensure that health is provided for all, that maternity relief is available to women, which levels of nutrition are raised, and that free and compulsory education is provided to all children till the age of 14.
- The third set of directive principles commit the state to providing public assistance in cases of unemployment, old age, sickness, disablement, and in all cases of undeserved want.
- The fourth set of directive principles oblige the state to ensure that the ownership and control of essential commodities is not concentrated in a few individuals, that the ownership of resources is so distributed as to serve the common good, that workers are enabled to participate

in the management of undertakings, and that the weaker sections, children, and youth are protected against exploitation.

Part 4 of the Constitution thus provides an impressive array of social objectives to guide the formulation of appropriate policies. Further as the legal historian Granville Austin suggests, though Directive Principles are not justiciable, 'they have become the yardstick for the measurement of government's successes and failures in social policy'.

In pursuance of the general objectives of establishing a social order based on social and economic justice the government of India has enacted several policies, which aim at (a) satisfying basic needs and generating social protection and (b) engendering income and employment. Whereas the first set of policies is geared towards providing *all* people with basic goods essential for leading a life of dignity, other schemes are targeted towards raising the purchasing power of the poorer sections.

Social sector programmes fall within the purview of State Governments, and the Central Government supplements these efforts by granting additional resources for specific programmes through centrally sponsored schemes, additional central assistance, and special central assistance. Chart 1 which details expenditure on the social sectors by the Central and the State Governments shows that total spending on this sector has increased but marginally from 1986 to 2004-05. Whereas there has been some increase in spending on education, the budget for health has actually shrunk.

Chart 1 Total Expenditure of Central and State Governments on Social Services

	As percentage of total expenditure		
Years	***1986-87***	***1995-96***	***2004-05***
Social Services	18.9	21.6	19.3
Education	8.6	10.7	9.4
Health	4.5	4.7	4.4
Others	5.7	6.3	5.4

As percentage of expenditure on social services			
Education	45.6	49.4	48.8
Health	24.1	21.6	23.0
Others	30.3	29.0	28.2

Adapted from 2005 Budget, Government of India.

Mapping Social Security

Food Security

Since the Bengal famine of the 1940s, the Government of India has concentrated on establishing food security through (a) achieving self-sufficiency in food grains and (b) building buffer stocks of food grains particularly rice and wheat. The government obtains food grains from direct producers through fixing procurement prices/minimum support prices, by announcing support prices at sowing time, and by agreeing to buy all the food grains offered for sale at this price. Today procurement stands at 20 percent of food grain production. This has resulted in surplus buffer stocks, which by 2002 had risen to 60 million tonnes against the normal standards of 17 million tonnes. Though food stocks declined there on, in January 2004 these still stood at 24.4 million tonnes.

Despite food grain production going up from 175 million tonnes in the 1980s to 206 million tonnes in the 1990s, growth rate in the per capita availability of food grains has actually declined mainly because the poor lack purchasing power. After the food shortages in the 1960s, the Government had instituted a large public distribution system [PDS], which supplies food grains, edible oil, and kerosene at subsidised prices to households. Over the years it was found that the PDS benefited the non-poor more than the poor, and that it was biased towards the urban areas. In 1997 the scheme was converted to a Targeted Public Distribution System. Under the TPDS the government provides Below Poverty Line [BPL] families with 20 kilograms of subsidised food grains per month through a network of 400,000 Fair Price Shops.

The identification of beneficiaries is based on state wise poverty estimates of the Planning Commission. According to the Ministry of Food and Civil Supplies, against a total ceiling of 6.52 crore BPL families in the country as per poverty estimates of the Planning

Commission for 1993-94, State governments have issued more than 8 crore ration cards to BPL families. Correspondingly the food subsidy has jumped from Rs. 2,450 crore in 1990-91 to Rs 25,160 crore in 2003-04. The TPDS is supplemented by other nutrition related schemes. Under the Antodya Anna Yojana, 25 kg of food grains is provided to destitutes at Rs. 2 per k.g. for wheat, and Rs. 3 for rice. This covers 1.5 crores of citizens. The Annapurna Scheme introduced in April 2000 provides free food grains to senior citizens below poverty line.

The country has however not been able to realise food security for poor households. For one, it was found that food grains under the TPDS are diverted to the market. The diversion rate is 64 percent in Bihar and Assam, 100 percent in Nagaland and 69 percent in Punjab. Secondly, most states do not have either adequate infrastructure or funds, which enable them to deliver food grains to BPL families. Thirdly, the offtake by the state governments from the central pool is much lower than the allocations. Fourthly, the poor do not have the resources to buy their quota of food grains. Fifthly the quality of food grains is low; a fact that is exacerbated by poor storage conditions.

Above all weak monitoring, lack of transparency and accountability, and sale of food grains at higher prices than those fixed by the government, have combined to create an unprecedented crisis of food security.

Nutritional Security

Nutritional security is ensured through the provision of midday meals for primary school children. The government of Tamil Nadu, where the scheme had been originally introduced in 1925, adopted the programme in 1957. In 1995 the Ministry of Human Resources conceptualised a fully funded and centrally sponsored scheme of midday meals. The objective of the programme is to supplement nutrition of primary school going children, and thereby to improve school enrolment, retention, and attendance. Each child is provided with 100 grams of raw wheat/rice per school day. 6 states began to provide school children with cooked meals, and a 2001 Supreme Court Order makes it obligatory for each government and government funded school to provide cooked food to the students.

In some states the scheme has been extended to cover students up to Class X. By 2001 105.1 million children were being served midday meals in 576 districts.

Evaluations of the scheme have found that the quality of food served to the children is poor, that proper data on enrolments on the basis of which food grains could be made available is not forthcoming, that transport to transfer food grains to states is not at hand, and that in some states lack of funds prevent meaningful implementation of the scheme. But on balance evaluations hold that most state governments have picked up their quota of food grains under the scheme and that the programme has resulted in increased recruitment of school children as well as ensured attendance.

The Integrated Child Development Services provides food supplements to pre-school children, pregnant women, and lactating mothers in the country. However, the reported coverage is only between 15 to 20 percent of the targeted population. There has been no significant decline in maternal under-nutrition and half of the children below the age of five years continue to be severely malnourished.

Education

Article 45 of the Constitution stipulates that the state shall endeavour to provide within a period of ten years free and compulsory education for children till age 14[3]. The National Policy of Education 1986, which was revised in 1992, provided momentum to the task and has achieved some success. The Census of India defines literacy rates as the proportion of literates to the total population above the age of 7 years. By these standards, at independence literacy stood at merely 18.3 percent for age group 5 years and above. Literacy rose to 43.6 percent in 1981, to 52.21 percent in 1991, to further rise to 65.4 percent in 2001. Of this figure 75.85 percent of males are literate and 54.16 percent of women are literate. In a ten-year period from 1991 to 2000, illiteracy declined for the first time by 32 million in absolute terms. Significantly in rural areas the literacy rate increased from 36 percent in 1981 to 59 percent in 2001. And this was achieved despite the fact that the education budget is clearly insufficient.

The goal of universalizing elementary education is sought to be achieved through setting up of Government or Government aided primary schools. By 1993, 94 percent of the total rural population was served by primary schools; and in the period 1950-1990 the number of schools increased by more than three times. The number of upper primary schools increased 15 times in the same period. The expansion of the school system was accompanied by the provision of midday meals, free uniforms, textbooks, and scholarships in order to increase recruitment and prevent dropouts.

The elementary educational system has been strengthened from time to time by the launch of special campaigns such as 'Operation Blackboard' to upgrade infrastructure, train teachers, and improve the environment. To cover gaps in the educational system, in 2000-01 the Government of India launched the Sarva Shiksha Abihiyan or the movement for education to provide elementary education to children in the age group 6-14, in partnership with state governments, local governments and communities. The school system has been decentralised to enable community participation. This as reports show has led to improved performances, provided community owned education, and bridged gender and social disparities to some extent. The District Elementary Education Plan which was launched in 1994, and which is supported by international agencies, is based on assessments of specific needs of each habitat particularly in the field of Early Child Care and Education.

From 1986 onwards, the Government of India initiated several schemes to bring more than half the children in the age group 6-14 who are outside the school system within the ambit of education, by setting up a parallel stream of non-formal education, through opening up literacy classes to children outside the school system, and through the setting up of World Bank sponsored District Primary Education Programmes. Under the programme, 21,000 new alternative schools have been established, and 10,000 ECCE clusters have been set up. However, these initiatives, which introduced parallel streams of cheap but low quality education for poor children, have been criticised by educationists and activists. For instead of strengthening the existing government and government-aided school system, these schemes provided for contracting often under-qualified youths at low salaries to teach children for a period of nine months. The quality of education has thereby been compromised.

Adults above the age group of 15-35 are provided functional literacy through the National Literacy Mission, which set up in May 1988 is administered in 561 districts through local communities and self-government bodies. The purpose is to achieve full literacy for 75 percent of population by 2005. This, it is expected, will lead to increased productivity, improvement in health care, and betterment of social life. More importantly, 14 states and 4 Union Territories have passed laws making elementary education compulsory. In 2001 the Central government passed the 93rd Constitutional Amendment Bill, subsequently adopted as the 86th Constitutional Amendment Bill, which grants a fundamental right to free and compulsory education.

The right to education however makes little sense unless the school system, which is marked by a high rate of drop-outs, teacher absenteeism, low levels of learning, low participation particularly of the girl child, and critical gaps in the availability of infrastructural facilities and qualitative aspects of education, including teachers training, educational curricula, equipments, and training material, is restructured. It has been estimated that more children drop out of school for these reasons rather than those of poverty. Families would rather incur debt and send their children to expensive private schools.

Given these shortcomings, it is not surprising that despite 53 years of planned development, out of 200 million children in the age group of 6-14 years, 42 million children do not go to school. The National Human Development Report 2001 concluded that 'India's educational development is a mixed bag of remarkable successes and glaring gaps. In the post-independence period, the pace of educational development was unprecedented by any standards. At the same time, perhaps, the policy focus and public intervention in the provision of educational services was not adequately focused or, even misplaced, to the extent that even after 50 years of planned effort in the sector, nearly one-third of the population or close to 300 million people in the age group 7 years and above are illiterate'. These figures vary across regions, whereas literacy rates have improved in Rajasthan, Orissa, and Madhya Pradesh in the 1990s, and whereas Himachal Pradesh is a success story because by the end of the decade of the 1990s 98 percent of children were going to school in the state, literacy rates continue to be modest in Uttar Pradesh and Bihar. The picture on the educational front is simply not encouraging.

Health

In 1946, on the eve of the independence of India, the Bhore Committee had suggested a detailed and comprehensive plan for health security. The report envisaging the establishment of a massive state-managed infrastructure for health stressed that provision of health care is an indispensable function of the government. Health care recommended the report, should be provided to all irrespective of their ability to pay, health services should be placed as close to the people as possible to ensure maximum benefit to communities, and the doctor should be a social physician who combines remedial and preventive measures. If it had been implemented effectively, the Bhore Committee Report would have rendered the private sector in health irrelevant, and the level of health services in the country would have reached to three-fifth of that of Britain during the Second World War.

The most significant suggestion of the Bhore committee was that the focus of health policy should be preventive rather than curative. A preventive health policy would conceptualise the provision of nutrition, safe drinking water, sanitation, hygiene, and education, as well as the institutionalisation of an extensive public health system: immunisation programmes and clinics and community health centres staffed by trained medical personnel and para-health workers, as *essential* preconditions of health. All this requires public investment to the tune of 10 percent of GDP, yet the Government of India invests only 0.9 percent of the GDP on health.

In fact, there is an odd schism between financial outlays and the stated objectives of health policy. The public health system consists of a three-tiered layer of primary health centres, sub-centres, and community centres providing multi-functional outpatient facilities. The number of centres is in direct proportion to the numbers of people being served, with special provisions being made for rural, hill and tribal areas. The Government has also initiated and implemented several disease-control programmes and immunisation schemes, some of which have shown remarkable success. Under the Central Government Health Scheme, health care is provided to government employees, pensioners, and public officials living in big cities. The global debate on health strategy, the signing of the Alma Ata declaration of 'Health for All' by 2000, and the recommendations of various specialised bodies, have resulted in the enunciation of a comprehensive, integrated, approach to health care in the form of the National Health Policy in 1983. The 2002 National Health Policy aims at achieving the basic standards of good health through national public health programmes, extension of infrastructure, medical education, research, enhanced role of stakeholders such as NGOs, enforcement of quality standards in food and drugs, and women's health.

It is not as if India has made no progress in the past several decades in the field of health. There have been no reported cases of small pox since 1985, of guinea worm disease since 1996; and of plague since 1969. Cholera epidemics and related deaths have become more infrequent; in 1950, cholera cases numbered 1,76,307 with 86,997 deaths, by 2001 the total reported cases of cholera were 5000 (Deodhar 2001). The incidence of measles, polio, whooping cough, and tetanus is lower than before. And the proportion of children without immunisation declined from 30 to 14 percent between 1992/93, and 1998/99.

Yet the presence of both communicable and non-communicable diseases casts a heavy miasma over every prospect of wellbeing. Infant mortality rates have still to be brought below 60 per 1000 live births, which was the expressed goal of the 1983 health policy. Maternal mortality rates continue to be 540 per 100,000 live births annually. The main causes of mortality in the age group 0-5 are common diseases, which can be easily avoided, such as lower respiratory tract infection, diarrhoeal diseases, perinatal causes and vaccine preventable diseases. Communicable diseases like viral encephalitis, meningococcal meningitis, rabies kala azhar, dengue fever and tuberculosis have escaped control. Epidemics of food poisoning, infectious hepatitis, typhoid fever, measles, tetanus, and pneumonia regularly appear to bedevil the health scenario. It is estimated that about 15 million people suffer from tuberculosis, and that 2.2 million are added to this figure every year. The emergence of AIDS has begun to affect national and regional epidemiological profiles and priorities, and leprosy cases constitute a major part of the world's cases of leprosy.

Of course the picture is not even across the country; for instance Kerala has made progress on all health indicators, whereas Bihar, Uttar Pradesh, and parts of Madhya Pradesh and Rajasthan show tremendous vulnerability on this front. Moreover, the rural sector much more vulnerable to malnourishment and disease. What is also worrying is the massive social inequity between income groups across all regions of the country in this respect. A study has shown that the richest 20 percent enjoy three times their share of the public subsidy for health compared to the poorest quintile, and that 20 percent of the population which belongs to the poorest section of society has more than double the mortality rates, fertility rates, levels of under-nutrition than of the richest 20 percent of the population.

The malaise of the health scene in India is conceivably due to the interaction of a number of factors. Firstly, much of the government health sector was created through policy pronouncements, which do not legislate the right to health. Secondly, the system is heavily bureaucratised and marked by erosion, corruption, inadequate infrastructure, and non-availability of medicines. Thirdly, whereas the Government of India has concentrated massive resources in specific disease eradication campaigns such as the huge campaign initiated in 1995 to eradicate poliomyelitis through a pulse polio immunisation programme, this has been at the cost of other programmes, which aim at the annihilation of common ailments such as diarrhoea and dysentery. Even though dysentery and diarrhoea along with acute respiratory infections leading to pneumonia happen to be the main killers of children below the age of five, these are not even seen by the Government as diseases. Fourthly, universal programmes of immunisation have failed to establish efficient epidemiological surveillance services for diseases that can be controlled. And fifthly, health policy in India has concentrated more on curative measures rather than on preventive measures.

Above all, from the Fourth Five Year Plan budgetary provisions for health shrank drastically reaching a new low in the first decade of the twenty first century, although the W.H.O has recommended that a minimum of 5 percent of GDP should be allotted to health care. India has one of the lowest health budgets in the world, and in fact, plan allocation for the year 2003-04 has been pegged at 2002-2003 levels that is Rs 1500 crore, leading to reduced allocations for various priority programmes. India, health is a State subject and States are expected to contribute to a major part of the finances allotted to the sector, but the budgetary allocation of State Governments has shown a consistent decline over the years. The general neglect of preventive health care and the increasing push towards the involvement of the private sector in the delivery of health services highlights a dramatic lessening of public commitment to health.

Social Protection

The National Social Assistance Programme launched in 1995 has three components: The National Old Age Pension Scheme, the National Family Benefit Scheme, and the Janani Suraksha Yojana. The schemes are sponsored by the central government in order to ensure minimum standards of social assistance over and above the assistance provided by state governments. The National Old Age Pension Scheme is a tax-financed scheme that provides floor level income assistance of Rs 75 per month to very poor persons over 65 years of age. The NFBS gives Rs 10,000 to BPL families in event of the death of the breadwinner, and JSY is a maternity benefit scheme, which benefits women from BPL families for the first two live births.

The Janshree Bima Yojana, which has been launched through state insurance companies, is a group insurance scheme, which does not require premium contribution by workers. It covers contingencies in cases of natural/accidental deaths and partial or total permanent disability due to accident for people below the poverty line. The Krishi Shramik Samajak Suraksha Yojana 2001, which is a group insurance scheme for agricultural landless labour, provides for pension, insurance and money back schemes. The beneficiaries contribute Rs 1 per day and the government contributes Rs 2 per day to the scheme. In addition public initiatives launched by for instance the Self Employed Womens Association or SEWA provides social security through the setting up of cooperatives.

The Finance Minister has announced a new universal health insurance scheme for the poor, a special group insurance scheme at a low premium, and the setting up of a Rural Health Mission, in the 2005 budget.

The limited coverage of the clearly insufficient social security programme is largely due to resource constraints. For instance, against a target of 8.71 beneficiaries for old age pensions in 1999-2000, only 5 million people were provided assistance from central funds. On the whole the majority of the working people have little or no social protection.

The Employees Provident Fund Scheme is a publicly managed, contributory, and a mandatory scheme to ensure that employed workers save some percent of their wages.

But compliance mechanisms are ineffective and accounting methods are unreliable. In 2004 the Unorganised Sector Workers Social Security Scheme, which was launched on a pilot basis in 50 districts, provides old age pension, personal accident insurance, and medical insurance for workers drawing not more than Rs 6,500 per month. Workers give a single contribution of Rs 50 per month with the government's contribution assessed on a relative basis. The scheme is implemented through the Employees Provident

Fund Organisation

In addition the Government has set up five welfare funds for specific sectors of unorganised workers. Resources are raised outside the employer-employee relationship on a non-contributory basis, and the delivery of welfare services does not have any link to individual contributions. The cess collected from the employers and manufacturers of particular commodities go towards these funds. Some state governments such as West Bengal have introduced state assisted provident funds for unorganised workers. However the coverage under all these programmes is a little more than 10 million out of 370 million workers in the unorganized sector.

Poverty Alleviation

Income Generation Schemes

Since the 1970s the Government of India has enacted several programmes to provide self-employment and supplementary wage employment to BPL families through the extension of bank credit and subsidies. On 1 April 1999 a self-employment programme called the Swaranjayanti Gram Swarozgar Yojana or the Rural Self-Employment Plan merged the earlier mandated Integrated Rural Development Programme [IRDP] and several sub-schemes. The programme, which is credit driven, encourages the development of micro-enterprises through the formation of self-help groups, the extension of credit and subsidies to groups, capacity building, selection of activity clusters, infrastructural development, and access to technology and markets. The Tenth Plan seeks to enhance SGSY by focussing on social mobilisation and group formation in the first phase, thrift and credit augmented by a revolving fund in the second phase, and access to credit from micro-finance institutions in the third phase. The plan stipulates that 50 percent of self-help groups must be formed exclusively by women, and that 50 percent of the benefits should flow to the Scheduled Castes/ Tribes. Some provision has been made for the disabled.

However, the Tenth Plan estimates that the implementation of SGSY between 1999 and 2002 has been hampered because intermediate organisations lack requisite skills to mobilise people into self-help groups, and because they have failed to establish linkages with NGOs, which could have facilitated this process. This resulted in lower releases of funds from the central government as well as lower mobilisation of credit. Consequently only one third of the target of credit allocation could be achieved, and the coverage was considerably lower than the 2.2 million who benefited under IRDP during the Eighth Plan period every year.

But though the IRDP, which was initiated in 1978-79, benefited a large number of recipients, local powerful interests-politicians, contractors, and bureaucrats captured it. Secondly, it was characterised by defective implementation, inefficient targeting, non-availability of bank credit, overcrowding of projects and absence of market linkages. Thirdly, the scheme was subsidy driven and provided credit without follow up action. Fourthly allocations were made poor not on economic but on political grounds: the building of vote banks. All this inhibited income generation to a large extent.

Wage Generation Schemes

In December 2004 the long awaited National Rural Employment Guarantee Bill was introduced in the lower house of Parliament. When it is enacted as law, India will join 30 countries, which grant the constitutional right to work to their citizens. However it is important to note that the Bill does not grant a *generic* right to work because it promises but 100 days of employment per year to only one adult member of a poor rural household. If an eligible applicant is not provided employment within 15 days of receipt of his application, s/he shall be entitled to a daily unemployment allowance, the rate of which shall be specified by the state government. The wage rates will be fixed by the Central Government.

The Bill further provides for the establishment of a Central Employment Guarantee Council at the Central Government level, and State Employment Guarantee Councils in states where the legislation is applicable. The councils will be responsible for the review, the monitoring, and the effective implementation of the scheme. A National Employment Guarantee Fund at the Central and a State Employment Guarantee Fund at the State levels will take care of the funds required for the scheme. In the 2005 budget speech the Finance Minister announced that food-for-work programmes, which have been introduced in 150 districts, will be converted into the National Rural Employment Guarantee Scheme. He also announced a substantial increase in allocations for the programme, from Rs 4020 crores in the current year to Rs 11,000 crores alongside promises of additional funds.

The Bill is significant since rural unemployment has increased over the decade of the 1990s. According to the National Sample Survey data 1999-2000, unemployment rates are as high as 7.2 percent for rural males in the work force and 7 percent for rural women. Since the unemployed constitute the single largest group among the rural poor, there is urgent need that they be assured work. Employment will be offered on asset enhancing works such as public works, afforestation, irrigation facilities, ponds, road connectivity, wasteland development, and regeneration of degraded lands. This is important because though almost 79 percent of agricultural labour owns land, environmental degradation has rendered land holdings unproductive, forcing thereby thousands of poor families to seek work. Assured work on asset creating public works will lead to infrastructural development as well as to greater productivity, because land will be now proofed against drought and floods. This will necessarily result in an improvement of both labour absorbing capacities of small farms and profitability of farming activities. Peasants will consequently move out of state sponsored employment schemes and back to their own land.

The development of infrastructure and enhanced productivity will not only lead to a reduction in rural poverty, but also lessen migration to other parts of the country, both rural and urban. More importantly wages will serve to generate demand for rural goods and services, even as the construction of roads will facilitate the reach of rural markets benefiting thus the rural economy. The development of infrastructure may well boost private investment, and generate secondary employment. Finally, assured employment at minimum wages will ensure that people have the opportunity to participate in other social sector programmes such as the provision of midday meals in schools. And if people are encouraged to participate in the selection of sites for work, in the making of cost estimates, and in the fixing of wages, this will result in an enhancement of popular participation.

The selective initiation of the Bill in 150 districts ensures that the cost of guaranteeing employment will not be more than 2 percent of the GDP. The size of investment will inevitably decrease in time because the need of families to work outside their land will decline over the years. Correspondingly, the programme by assuring Rs 6000 per year to each rural household will result in 75 percent of the rural poor rising above the poverty line.

The introduction of the Bill followed a period of sustained campaign by several civil society groups. Yet social activists are not happy with the Bill for several reasons: it will be introduced only in a few districts, it will replace food-for-work schemes, and it will be confined to only one adult member of BPL households.

Moreover the guarantee of employment will be expanded to other parts of the country only if the experiment proves successful in 150 districts.

The point is that earlier employment schemes-the Jawahar Rojgar Yojana, the National Rural Employment Programme, the Rural Landless Employment Guarantee Scheme, and the Employment Assurance Scheme-which were merged into a single wage payment scheme, the Sampoorna Gramin Rozgar Yojana in 2001-and the 1979 Employment Guarantee Scheme for rural areas and C class municipal councils in Maharashtra have fetc..hed mixed results. On the one hand uncrganised casual labour has unionised to demand stipulated minimum wages and better implementation of projects. Secondly, though the scheme may not have reduced poverty, it has worked well for the poorest of the poor, for only this section of the population opts for often back breaking work on asset creating jobs. Thirdly, some rural infrastructure has been created. Fourthly village self-government bodies, which administer these schemes, have been strengthened. And fifthly the right to work has been put onto the political agenda.

On the other hand these programmes have not generated adequate employment. The reasons for the failure to do so are tediously familiar: indiscriminate universalisation of the programme led to the neglect of poor areas, benefits were cornered by the non-poor, allocations were based on fixed criterion that did not distinguish between needs, and resources were thinly spread over the country. Even in poorer regions employment was provided for only 31 days, works were not labour intensive, and implementation was marked by massive corruption in the form of fictitious muster rolls and bogus employment records. A review of earlier wage employment schemes in the Ninth plan showed a considerable reduction of both allocation and employment generation. Allocations for wage employment declined in the Ninth Plan to only 88 percent of what they were in the Eighth plan. And only 15 percent of the people who sought work in a village panchayat were actually given employment under JRY.

Increasing costs of creating jobs compounded these problems. In 1999, when the JRY was revamped as the Jawahar Gram Samridhi

Yojana, the programme was mainly meant to create rural infrastructure, rendering thereby employment generation to a secondary objective. Above all, village panchayats, which administered the scheme, received inadequate funds. Consequently, the schemes generated lower mandays of employment each successive year. Unemployment continues to stalk the lives of the rural poor. Therefore, unless serious attempts are made to correct existing flaws, the current avatar of the employment guarantee scheme may not prove effective.

Assessing Social Policy

Though the Government of India has enacted a number of policies that target in particular the rural poor, it is precisely this section of the population that remains vulnerable to all kinds of insecurities. Four reasons can be cited for the failure of the Indian state to implement the social goals laid down in part four of the Constitution. Firstly there are huge gaps between policy and implementation, between policy and financial outlays, and between policy and the needs of the people. Secondly, the enactment of social policy has been somewhat incoherent characterised as it is by overlaps between policies, periodic recasting of existing policies in new forms, and in particular the employment of these measures as political tools that address constituencies and forge vote banks more and ameliorate joblessness less.

Thirdly, policies meant for the poor have been indiscriminately generalised, benefited often the non-poor, and been attended by mismanagement, corruption, and tardy implementation. The word 'leakage' must be one of the most inelegant terms in the English language, yet it captures to a nicety the fate of social policy in India. Fourthly, though the provision of social goods falls more or less within the provenance of state governments, the Planning Commission through the Five Year Plans determines strategy, priority, and allocation of resources. However, since the planning process 'was initiated without altering initial structural inequities, the distribution of benefits of economic growth has not been egalitarian'.

An ex-civil servant who is extensively involved in monitoring government sponsored social programmes is more blunt on this front, 'even as the new development state in India has steadily amassed functions, and vastly extended financial powers often in the name of the poor, its capacity to deliver has declined over the years. This is due to rising indiscipline and a growing belief, widely shared among the political and bureaucratic elite, that the state is an arena where public office is to be used for private ends'. The definitive statement on the incapacity of the Indian state to deliver social goods effectively has been made by Dreze and Sen. They conclude that despite some notable successes, India's overall success in promoting social opportunities has been quite limited. The intensities of many basic deprivations have been considerably reduced, but there is nevertheless a long way to go in ensuring anything like acceptable living conditions for all.

This is borne out by the findings of the 2004 ILO report on *Economic Security for a Better World*. The report compliments India for maintaining high growth in the past two decades, but also comments adversely on the country's record of social security. India is ranked 74 out of 90 countries on the economic security index constructed by the ILO. The index is constructed on seven indicators-income, work, representation, job, employment protection, labour market, and skill reproduction. On income security India ranks 94th out of 96 countries, only above Congo and Sierra Leone, both which happen to be fired in civil war. The report concludes that anti-poverty programmes have failed to reach the poor, that the poor are often not aware of the benefits they are eligible for, and that they are less likely to receive benefits than the non-poor. More importantly, the take-up rate of social assistance programmes is very low (ILO 2004). These findings give us cause for some thought-why has economic well being *not* been accompanied by the distribution of benefits especially to the poor?

Constraints on Welfarism

Land Ownership

Axiomatically social policy does not function in a vacuum; it is constrained or enabled by the distribution of resources and the structure of the labour market. Or that ownership of resources/ income dictates access to social opportunities. To put it sharply, in a highly iniquitous society like India social policy can prove effective only if it addresses the structural roots of inequality. For instance the prevalence of deep poverty in the rural areas, where till today 60 percent of the population lives and works, required at the very least a radical restructuring of land relations. However, the conceptualisation and the administration of land reforms in India suffered from serious shortcomings. Though intermediaries were abolished and land was transferred to the tenants vide a series of legislations, not only were land reforms confined to 40 percent of the cultivated area, they suffered both from flawed conceptualisation and sluggish and ineffective implementation. Administered by often recalcitrant bureaucrats, land reforms failed to transfer land to the tiller, failed to correct imbalances in the structure of land relations, failed to provide security to tenants, and failed to secure implementation of land ceiling laws. More significantly, land reforms slowed down because the issue of compensation to erstwhile landowners was bogged down in massive litigation.

By the 1990s land reform was set on the back burner, for the subdivision and fragmentation of land weakened the case for a lowering of the land ceiling. This was despite the fact that inadequate tenancy reforms had resulted in concealed tenancy thereby denying to the tenants security of tenure and rent regulation. Further massive alienation of land from tribal communities that live off the produce of the land reduced many to penury. The decade also heralded the liberalisation of land laws to further corporate farming, in sharp contrast to the post-independence period when considerations of equity and social justice governed land reforms. Therefore, whereas by the end of the Eighth Five Year Plan [1992-1997] 52 lakh acres out of ceiling surplus 75 lakh acres were distributed among 5.5 million beneficiaries, the position remained unchanged at the end of Ninth Five Year Plan [1997-2002]. The net result is that in major parts of the country the poorest of the poor, mainly belonging to the Scheduled Castes, have been unable to access land, productive assets, and skills.

Poverty

From 1950-1970 poverty figures fluctuated between 45 to 60 percent of the population. Poverty began to decline from the 1970s onward partly because of economic growth in primary and tertiary sectors and mainly because of the initiation of the green revolution, which raised productivity. Yet by 2000 three quarters of the rural poor were unable to access the minimal consumption basket that defines the poverty line. What is more disquieting are regional imbalances when it comes to poverty: in Madhya Pradesh and Orissa numbers of the absolutely poor went up 1993-2000 though poverty fell somewhat in other states in the same period. Secondly, states containing larger proportions of the poor are also marked by low human development indicators and slower economic but higher population growth. Thirdly, poverty is much higher among the landless and among the marginal farmers whose small land holdings have been rendered unproductive because of environmental degradation and the vagaries of the monsoon. Above all half of India's 206 million Scheduled Castes/Tribes belong to the category of the absolute poor (NCAER 1996), with no access to employment and minimum wages because they lack educational skills. In sum, the ability of social policy to address deep problems of poverty is limited because it has *not* addressed the issue of redistribution.

Labour Markets

Considering that the contribution of agriculture to GDP has gone down from 50 percent to 25 percent by the beginning of this decade, the labour market in rural areas is marked by near zero elasticity of employment. Even if agricultural productivity rises dramatically in the next ten years it will not be able to absorb much of rural labour. That is why towns and cities witness streams of migrants in search of gainful employment. Here they join thousands of workers who are employed as casual, contract, and sub-contract labour in the informal economy. Around 90 to 93 percent of the working population of about 39.7 crores is in the unorganised sector: 62 percent of unorganised workers are in agriculture, 11 percent in industry and 27 percent in the service sector. Of the 10 percent of the workers employed in the formal sector, 6 percent have jobs in the public sector. But even here the onset of economic reforms has led to a decline in employment opportunities.

Patterns of Unemployment

Even as employment experienced a steady growth of around 2 percent per annum from 1960-1990, even as GDP grew by about

3.5 percent, the labour force grew at the rate of 2.5 percent per annum. Consequently the magnitude of unemployment increased from 6.5 million in 1961 to 16 million in 1990, and the rate of unemployment rose from 3.6 percent to around 5 percent of the labour force in the same period. In the first two years of the decade of the 1990s the rate of employment growth declined to 1.5 percent to further fall to 1.07 percent in the period 1993-2000, with the informal sector absorbing much of the work force.

The growth rate of rural employment however was only 0.5 percent in the same period. Though the growth of GDP accelerated to 6.5 percent by the end of the 1990s from 3.4 percent in 1990-92, the increase failed to generate employment [Papola and Sharma 2004: 19]. This is mainly due to (a) the low capacity of agriculture to absorb the work force and (b) job losses in the public sector. The Tenth Five Year Plan intends to introduce 10 million jobs by the end of 2007. However a study undertaken by the Planning Commission concludes that unemployment will grow from 9.2 percent at the beginning of the Plan to 11 percent of the total work force by the end of the Plan In effect 45 million people are going to be unemployed on the assumption of a 6.5 average GDP growth rate in the rest of the plan period. The economy is doing well but this is not matched by commensurate growth in economic opportunities leading to the phenomena of jobless growth.

Social Policy in a Time of Uncertainty

Societies differ in resources, culture, tradition, wealth, and political power. The same could be said of people. Despite these differences, societies and people share the potential to develop and overcome historical limitations. It is not easy to define this capacity for change in the 1990s, but it includes the expectations, beliefs, and values that cause people to look ahead, to take actions, and to hope that tomorrow will be different, better, and more rewarding than today. This capacity, not easy to measure, is often behind most processes of human change from the migration to urban centres to changes in social mobility, from cultural assimilation to political mobilization, or to the emergence of new forms of community organization. One of the main challenges of the current human development approach is to make this capacity the driving force for social reform.

Social policies are an effective way to face this challenge. Although there is no question about the importance of measures such as antipoverty programs, social integration efforts, political reforms, and employment programs, more than ever before there is an urgent need to design and implement social policies that explicitly address the goals of human development. This means that the conception and operation of social polices must be looked at from a holistic, integrated perspective. This in itself is a major challenge in the prevailing circumstances of crisis of development paradigms, social frustration, economic incertitude, political disorientation, and external conditions, particularly in developing countries. At the same time, however, it seems more important than ever before that these countries have means and opportunities at their disposal to improve the social and human development conditions of their societies.

This perception, perhaps optimistic, emerges, in part, as a result of examining the social reform processes — decentralization, institutional reform, and democratization — under way in countries like Canada and those of the Latin American region. The differences among these countries are indeed many, and common conclusions about these societies, their social reform approaches, and their policy systems cannot be easily drawn from a comparative perspective. In spite of these differences, however, there are also similarities that help to identify lessons and, above all, to identify words of caution about the opportunities and pitfalls that can be faced in social policy making in a world where globalization has become the predominant context of human development.

Although the reality of social reform in Canada and Latin America is too fluid to provide an exhaustive overview of the issues, opportunities, and prospects these countries face, an attempt is made to outline the main points to help set a research agenda on the principal topics related to social reform, the policy making processes, the economic factors influencing social policy making, and the needs for policy evaluation.

Some ideas are also advanced about how a multifaceted research strategy might contribute by providing timely and relevant knowledge to reduce the current uncertainty affecting public policy in these countries.

Some Contextual Factors

The chapters by Filgueira and Lombardi and Morales–Gomez show that some of the countries in Latin America have experienced considerable progress on the economic front. They also show that most countries in the region have gone through painful attempts to reach stabilization and macroeconomic equilibria. The social progress attained through this process, however, has been limited. In most countries of the region, poverty continues to be deeply rooted in persistent social, cultural, political, and economic inequalities. This situation has brought even the viability of productive transformation into question. As a result, there is a new emphasis on the need to implement more effective and efficient social policies. This presents the region with new risks including a wave of future indebtedness resulting from the flow of multilateral funds for social reform programs. In the future, this will be a major issue in relation to the economics of social policy.

This is happening at a time when the countries of Latin America do not seem to have a clear sense of direction in the implementation of their social reforms. A key question in this context is the extent to which actions currently under way in the social sectors will move the region toward a more profound and just change in their social policy system, or if they will simply lead to a relative decrease in poverty to more manageable levels, leaving more or less untouched enduring mechanisms of unequal distribution of income and wealth.

This, however, is not only a dilemma of the less-developed countries of Latin America. Although different, no less worrisome are the dilemmas Canada is facing. Social policy in Canada emerged around the model of a just society where equity and the welfare state model of western European countries were points of reference. Changes promoted by the new economic model, however, based on openness and economic integration have affected the existing social security system.

Under these circumstances, the renegotiation of the federal political model, the "new social contract" and the status of indigenous populations, among others, will have great influence on the reshaping of the Canadian model. To respond to the demands for the reform of a well-crystallized social policy system, Canada needs to take drastic steps to overcome potential social fragmentation and to eliminate existing mechanisms of social exclusion. For Canada, the response to these challenges is of particular importance under the current circumstances where national integration is a major issue and regional integration and globalization are likely to continue affecting its economic and social-welfare policies.

In Latin America, the results of a prolonged economic crisis, the new impacts of globalization, and the conditions of persistent poverty are having a profound effect on the social policy system in the region. Filgueira and Lombardi (this volume) indicate that social policy systems in the region are moving from a universal, public, centralized framework to more focused, private, and decentralized programs. It is not clear, however, how this new social policy model will lead to a more equitable, integrated, and participatory society. Similar changes in other areas, such as in labour market deregulations, have raised questions about the impact of these measures on the structure and role of labour market institutions, associated social security systems, labour organizations, and labour mobility.

Until now, social policies and social programs in the region played the role of economic stabilizers and compensatory redistribution instruments. Today, they are beginning to be recognized as having a different role given the relative stagnation and the difficulties for recovery resulting from structural adjustment policies. It is because of these concerns that the current social reform debate is broadening the focus of social policies from traditional sectoral approaches and poverty alleviation programs toward a more comprehensive and integrated view of social, human, and economic development.

This, however, is not an easy task. Together with the prevailing doubts about the direction social reform should take in the region, there is also a lack of clarity about what social policies really are and what their objectives should be. Among the possible social policy aims are the reduction of poverty, increase of equity, facilitation of economic growth and promotion of competitiveness, promotion of social and cultural integration, and expansion and consolidation of citizenship.

Raczynski (1994) reflects these types of concerns when she identifies the following four question as those in need of urgent response:

- What are the latent and manifest functions of social policies in relation to issues such as social integration, social control, legitimization of the political order, poverty eradication, equity, equal opportunities, democracy, and the strengthening of citizenship?
- Where should social policies be placed in relation to other development policies, including economic and environmental ones?
- What is the impact of social policies in the shaping of the overall social structure?
- What are the opportunities for social change, i.e., social mobility, participation, and more transparent forms of governance, that social policies create?

For the most part, responses to these questions are difficult to find, in part because social policies are no longer a national, domestic issue. In the 1990s, social policies are more a factor in the process of social reform in the context of globalization.

As discussed earlier, globalization can have positive impacts, including the growing integration of international markets for goods, services and finance. In the North, globalization can also lead to new forms of inequality resulting from shifts in the structure and cohesion of key social institutions such as the family. It can also result in an increasing public awareness of the costs of social systems and programs, in a growing sense of social insecurity, in the emergence of an underclass, and in the reduction of the opportunities for younger generations.

Similar situations can be observed in Latin America, particularly in countries with a large middle class. In these countries, the impact of globalization broadens the gap between social classes and affects the state's capacity to allocate fiscal resources to the social policy systems. But what happens in these countries also has a social impact beyond the borders of the countries of Latin America. Low-paid labour and unemployment, for example, have an effect in the polarization of the socioeconomic situation for workers in Canada. In this regard, harmonization and convergence of social policy systems is an issue that requires careful examination. Economic integration, international labour force mobility, capital flows among countries, and areas of economic integration (i.e., the North American Free Trade Agreement, Mercado Comun del Sur) will make it necessary to adapt social policy systems to circumstances that fall outside national boundaries of influence. The situation becomes particularly complex because these external pressures on convergence and harmonization of policies coincide with efforts to reduce social costs while expanding protection. An emerging intellectual and political debate is beginning to question who should pay the costs of social reform in the context of globalization and simultaneous domestic constraints. Should the onus for adapting to globalization and for reaching greater internal efficiency be put on the individual, the family and the community, or should it be on the international system, the business sector, and the state?

Despite these uncertainties, some progress is being made in terms of developing a new framework for social policy making and social policy research that could help to clarify the role of the state and civil society or the responsibilities of individuals in the implementation of the social reform processes in the context of globalization. Because of the complexity of the issues, it is likely that a new framework for social reform will not easily emerge in the near future. The challenge that countries like Canada and those of Latin America face in implementing social reform is to move from a domestic-oriented welfare state approach to social policies to a more comprehensive model. This model would take into account the global economic factors at play while maintaining social justice, equipping citizens with better skills and learning capacities for dealing with economic and technological change, building new forms of political participation, and balancing global demands with domestic priorities.

This challenge makes the need for analysis and evaluation of existing policies and programs and the need for learning experiences in social reform from a comparative perspective even more urgent. To fill this gap, it is necessary to develop a holistic approach in the analysis of social reform.

Social Reform

One of the hardest problems Canada and Latin America face in their attempts to implement social reforms is to provide more effective social services with constrained resources. One of the central concerns, therefore, is to design social policies that are primarily geared toward expanding people's opportunities. How to achieve this goal is perhaps one of the most critical challenges.

Efforts are being made in several directions including social reform processes involving reconceptualization and reorganization of social security systems, the dismantling of key institutions and the creation of others based on a combination of public-and private-sector activities, changes in central and local government responsibilities, and new approaches to consensus building and social participation. These processes, however, are taking place without a specific model. To a large extent, it could be argued that the new model of social reform is taking shape as the process moves along.

In Canada, one of the main concerns in the social reform process is the need to adjust a consolidated welfare state to the new circumstances of globalization and regional integration in such a way that it could respond better to the demands of a changing labour market and family structure. In most Latin American countries, because the welfare state never became fully crystallized, the main challenge to the social reform process is the building up of equity with constrained economic, human and institutional resources, and deeply rooted social inequality.

In such a context, a key issue is not only the eradication of poverty but how to make a new development model viable in social, political, and cultural terms. This is not an easy task. Social reform is taking place while internally oriented economies based on import substitution are shifting to become open economies driven by international competitiveness and privatization efforts. Although in some of these countries adjustment policies have proven to be effective in controlling fiscal deficit and inflation, they need to focus their attention on the new society and on the long-term social processes triggered by these policies and by the changes that have occurred in the development model.

Given these experiences in the region, the examination of social reform, both in Canada and in Latin America, may raise important, common conceptual and policy lessons. Cross-country analyses may help to clarify issues such as the targeting of social programs, social integration, decentralization, strengthening of local administration in search of greater efficiency, and in directing investment in human capital. It should be underlined, however, that this type of analysis also has limitations. Conceptual and policy commonalities across countries do not necessarily mean ready-to-apply responses to realities that remain fundamentally different.

On the one hand, the need to redesign the Canadian social policy system seems to emerge primarily as a response to macroeconomic changes and to changes in the social fibre of society. One of the challenges found in this regard is the harmonization of the changes in society at large and reorganization of the welfare state in a federal–provincial context. The difficulty is to design nationally coherent social policy instruments in a context of political decentralization. On the other hand, in Latin America, there is no well-established tradition of a welfare state. Critical social changes like the demographic transition and the incorporation of women into the labour force, already in effect in Canada, are still in progress in the South. Additionally, in Latin America, social reform is taking place in a context in which almost 40% of the population is poor. Thus, the key issue is drastic redesign of the social policy systems in place rather than adaptation of the Canadian system.

Despite these differences, comparison of the processes and conditions of social reform in Canada and Latin America highlights some important common problems. First, the lack of flexibility of social welfare institutions is often one of the major obstacles for the achievement of greater effectiveness. In Canada, this is of special significance given the fragmentation of social programs. This implies that focusing only on improving delivery systems is not sufficient. A similar situation exists in Latin America, where sectoral programs tend to overlap among themselves and with NGO activities. Social reform will thus need to focus on issues such as the interface between unemployment, training, social security, and antipoverty programs, the latter in the case of Latin

America. To deal with this lack of relative institutional flexibility, it will be necessary to reach a new social consensus and to implement practices of collective bargaining that could permit some degree of control over the impact of the social reform on the economy and the general well-being.

Second, the emphasis on targeting of social programs may have potential negative impacts if, as a result, less importance is given to reorienting universal policies and to self-help programs, including retraining and productive loan programs. A consequence of this in Canada, for example, could be the development of a growing underground or informal economy. In Latin America, in addition to the foregoing, one consequence may be the strengthening of clientelism and the development of a culture of poverty. These consequences may have additional negative effects on tax revenue capacity.

For a number of reasons, there are increasing doubts about giving less importance to universal social policies than to targeted programs. Targeting has limitations as an instrument for poverty alleviation because of its individual rather than family or community focus. There are risks of exacerbating social inequalities by differentiating between social services for the poor and the rest of society, and targeting vulnerable groups may become too costly given that these groups are often politically weak, lack intermediary organizations, and have a culture of economic dependency. Targeted and universal policies should complement each other as they serve different purposes, have different mechanisms, and require distinct organizational frameworks.

Third, in Canada and in Latin America, there are similar economic, political, and institutional limitations at the local and central government levels to conduct social reform processes. In the case of most Latin American countries, however, one of the major constraints is in the availability of qualified human resources. The result is a weak pool of the necessary capacity required to conduct social reform processes and implement new social policies.

Fourth, despite the important differences between the federal and provincial tradition in Canada and the centralism of Latin American countries, which makes policy decentralization a process with very different content in both areas, civil society is acquiring a new importance in relation to the decentralization processes. In addition to local and central capacities, the involvement of civil society is critical to achieve effective political, administrative, and financial decentralization and make local development an effective instrument of social reform. The participation and empowerment of local actors and community organizations are integral to ensuring accountability in the process of decentralization.

Fifth, both in Canada and in Latin American countries the role of national cultures, values, and institutions is critical in the long-term sustainability of social reform processes and in the implementation of effective social policies. They are mutually reinforcing, shaping each other in the processes of reform.

Policymaking Process

Implementing social policy involves many problems. Given the scarcity of resources and institutional bottlenecks, these difficulties require urgent attention. There is a need to examine the approaches and mechanisms to set priorities among different social policies such as antipoverty programs, sectoral policies (education, health, shelter, labour, and social security), labour force training programs, and the strengthening of popular organizations in terms of access to information and decision-making. In this context, research is required to study the extent to which, under constrained economic, human, and institutional resources, the policy making process can become one of the principal mechanisms for equitable allocation of resources.

The availability of funds alone is often a necessary but insufficient condition for good social policy making. In practice, some of the main problems lie in the processes of making policies and in implementing them. For this reason, further analyses are required about the involvement of various social actors in decision-making and the processes that allow or impede their involvement.

There is also a need to understand some of the critical issues regarding the risks in overcoming program fragmentation and reaching increased efficiency. Thus, for example, how to surmount sectoral approaches to reach policy integration, how to manage macro-micro tensions to reach higher levels of policy coordination between central and local government levels, and how to bring together the public and the private sector, including NGOs and grassroots organizations are some of the issues that need careful study. In a democratic context, these issues need to be addressed through appropriate mechanisms for administering conflict and reaching consensus.

Analyses should be carried out on the available means to adopt a holistic approach in articulating more effectively the various stages of the policy making process in social reform. This includes the design, implementation, monitoring, and the evaluation of policy harmonization to address social needs under circumstances of constrained resources.

There is also a need to identify the crucial factors that will improve transparency and accountability. In this regard, study of the new role of local governments is critical as well as the role of information and communication for the participation of new social actors. The local level is where social policies come together and where their interactions and results can be measured, yet, traditional social policy analysis remains national in perspective.

Finally, a better understanding is required of the role of local agents and their instruments in the processes of policy making. In Latin America, this aspect is particularly important given the tendency there to reproduce traditional bureaucratic and clientelistic practices. This implies the need for a better understanding of the role of new actors in social policy making, some being linked to the new processes of change resulting from globalization, integration, and liberalization. In Canada, for example, new political movements, business-sector organizations, community organizations, and professional associations are now playing mediating roles in federal–provincial relations. In Latin America, the situation is similar with the addition of multilateral international agencies that play a very dominant role.

Economics of Social Policy

Program effectiveness and the concern for reducing costs should be stressed as key strategic elements in dealing with social policy reform in an environment of constrained resources. The financing of social policies and programs needs to be examined in the light of issues such as the fiscal deficit, increased tax revenues, reallocation of existing tax revenues, fees for service, and the use of resources from international donors. There is a need to understand the economics of providing different kinds of social services and making that provision effective. This knowledge is indispensable as a basis for evaluation of the relative cost-effectiveness of social measures. Ultimately, the selection of a particular combination of financing measures may depend on a number of political and administrative considerations.

Some key issues that need to be addressed are, first, the political and administrative capacity for expanding tax collection and fiscal resources. What groups, for example, are most likely to be affected and what type of consensus building may be required to implement tax reforms? Second, the shifting of resources between or within programs as a means to reallocate resources among priorities requires assessing the potential negative impacts on programs and groups from which resources are reallocated. Third, the introduction of changes in financial arrangements for the achievement of new social policy objectives requires assessing the potential impact of restructuring financial incentives and the potential role of the private sector in financing social services.

What are the financial pay-offs of reforming and privatizing social programs? Another question that needs further examination is whether privatization can play a role as an expansion of the state, as in the case of private organizations delivering services with fiscal funds. This implies assessing when it is more appropriate to encourage participation of the private sector and if it implies greater effectiveness. Fourth, the promotion of efficiency in the delivery of social services and its impact on their effectiveness requires an understanding of when and under what circumstances and to what extent greater efficiency is conducive to achieving the best policy results.

Analysis of these issues should consider that the handling of incentives is also a powerful social policy instrument. In this regard, Kesselman (1994) mentions some interesting cases of policy implications when pursuing efficiency in the financing of social services.

One case is the incentives that the financing of social programs may exert for efficient behaviour on both sides of the market, the suppliers and users of services, for example through loans to universities and students with income-contingent repayment programs. A second case is the delivery mechanism for public cash transfers to the working poor and employable people on welfare, tied directly to incentives, training, and work effort. These types of mechanisms may avoid reinforcing dependence from welfare programs and a culture of poverty by facilitating access to new work opportunities.

These cases show the need to rethink the financing of social policies from a broader perspective and to adopt a view centred on the user. Provision of social assistance from a supply side has proved to be ineffective because it tends to provoke program dependency. It is necessary to generate a capacity for demand in civil society that makes possible the appropriation of programs by the target populations. Greater emphasis should also be placed on improving the incentive of social programs to facilitate social policies taking a preventive rather than simply an ameliorative or remedial approach. The financing of social policy should contribute to the sustainability of social service delivery by creating more responsibilities for beneficiaries, mutual obligations, and active rather than passive program participation.

Finally, there is also a need to understand the risk of indebtedness in financing social programs. Social investments using national resources or external funds is a topic that has received insufficient attention. There is a need to have better information about who will pay the costs of new debts that will result from implementing new social policies. What can be done to guarantee that new indebtedness will really represent eradication of poverty, strengthening capacity for a more effective social policy implementation, and the attainment of social policy objectives rather than further bureaucracy and eventual corruption?

Social Policy Evaluation

Social policy reform will require close monitoring and evaluation to improve the prospect of meeting the most urgent social needs in Latin America and the central policy goals in Canada. Policy evaluation is a particularly important task where the content and direction of social reform are not yet clearly defined. What should be evaluated, what criteria should be used, and what purposes should be pursued in policy evaluation are some of the key questions. The evaluation of policies is indispensable in ensuring that the civil society plays a role in the follow up of institutional reforms and in identifying new financial arrangements for social service delivery. This, however, is not an easy task.

Similarly complex is the identification of what should be evaluated. A critical area for evaluation is policy integration and implementation at the micro level. Crucial aspects to consider are the institutional capacity for program coordination and the carrying out of social programs, the alternatives for more effective and efficient program delivery, the coordination modalities with local NGOs and the private-for-profit sector, and the alternatives for civil society participation in the policy process. At the macro level, there is a need to evaluate the impact of economic growth on equity and the impact of macroeconomic policies on the effectiveness of social policies.

Regarding the criteria that should be used for policy evaluation, it is often difficult to indicate ex-ante whether these should be related to the policy process, thus focusing on the institutional, legal, political, or financial dimensions of the decision-making framework or to the target populations of policies and programs, or both, giving attention to aspects related to program relevance and effectiveness. The fluidity of current social policy and social reform processes raises the need for continuous evaluation to compensate for the limitations of ex-post facto evaluation. In the current context of globalization, evaluation becomes particularly difficult because the content of social policies tends to change as policies are implemented and as new social actors participate in the process of policy making and implementation. For this reason, evaluation demands support from research to understand the particulars of the impact of social policy on human development in the short, medium, and long term.

Finally, concerning the purposes of social policy evaluation, there is a wide range of possibilities. The most urgent evaluation need from the supply side is the assessment of policy coordination at the central government level and the development of a capacity for policy execution and integration at the local level. From the demand side, an evaluation priority at the micro level is to assess the performance of policies at the individual, family, household, and community level by focusing on the participation and satisfaction levels of users (Cohen, M. personal communication, 1994. Transportation, Water and Urban Development Department, The World Bank, Washington, DC).

Dealing with Uncertainty: Research, Information, Training, and Policy Advice

The current uncertainty in global society affecting the content, structure, and processes of social policy may be addressed by the generation and dissemination of relevant and timely knowledge. To this purpose, the identification of a research agenda is not sufficient. An integrated approach including research, information, training, and policy advice is required. This type of approach is necessary to design and implement effective policies in a new development context characterized by globalization and its effects on communication and information technologies, which have blurred boundaries between academic and applied knowledge, short-and long-term research, and policy analysis and advice. An integrated approach to both research and the generation of policies, may increase the likelihood of a greater impact on the policy making process. An integrated approach to knowledge generation for social policy making requires at least four interacting components: research, information, training, and policy advice.

Research

There are several questions that need to be addressed in relation to the content, outputs, and potential impact of social policy relevant research. Who is the audience and who are the clients of research? Are they other researchers and intellectuals, policymakers and program managers, community leaders, marginal target groups, the general public? What is the vision of society behind the research agenda? Is the final purpose of research, for example, to increase the distributional effects of social policies, to improve transparency and accountability in the policy making processes, and implementing to improve the learning capacities of the actors involved? How does a comprehensive research agenda apply to different countries? Is the purpose of research to obtain general knowledge, or to demonstrate viable new policy alternatives not necessarily replicable in other countries? How can research be democratized and made more participatory? Is this a matter of methods and techniques? What type of information and communication systems and tools should be involved? Are there critical gaps in the dissemination of research results? What is the time span necessary to obtain impact from the research results? Is there a need to rethink research products in terms of short, medium, and long term?

The responses to these questions and the setting of research boundaries will help to identify what "policy space" is available to design and implement social reforms. This is indispensable in efforts to identify the opportunities that research offers to improve the policy making process by introducing a common understanding of social policy issues and a common language among researchers, policymakers, politicians, and other actors of the civil society.

In terms of the type and content of research, there is a need for a multidisciplinary approach that takes into account social, political, cultural, and economic factors to avoid highly descriptive, too specific, sectoral, or broad ideological social policy studies (Pfund, A. personal communication, 1994. Evaluation Office, Inter-American Development Bank, Washington, DC). Traditionally, resources including funding for conducting punctual, sectoral, and very specific research has not been a real limitation. To conduct the type of strategic research that is required today, however, there is a problem in the scarcity of both human and financial resources. It is this type of research that is required to respond to questions about the impact of social policies on development and to provide an overall evaluation of the social policy system.

With this in mind, the content of an agenda should indicate priority areas.

- The first is the interaction between social policy, the social structure, and inequality. This implies giving special attention to the impact on social opportunities of variables, such as demographic changes, changes in family structure, the restructuring of labour markets, and new forms of social vulnerability.

- The second is the role of politics in shaping social policies. This includes the examination of users' perceptions, values, and responsibilities; the processes of public policy priority setting and the processes of decision-making; the linkages between social and economic policies; and the modalities for participation, consensus building, and conflict resolution affecting the design, implementation, and evaluation of social policies.
- The third is the institutional framework of social policies, which encompasses the study of sectoral reform processes (education, health, social security, etc...), the targeting of policies, privatization modalities, policy decentralization, and policy integration.
- The fourth is the role of operational strategies in social policy implementation, which include setting information systems, policy monitoring mechanisms, and policy evaluation systems.

Information

The second component is related to the need for information about the results of social policies as identified and evaluated by research. Information is necessary for adjusting social policies and actions as a means to increase effectiveness, efficiency, and accountability. Information should contribute to identifying for whom social policies are generated and for what purposes. This is fundamental for developing strategies for introducing key themes in the public agenda (Abugattás and Chateau, this volume). Information systems should report on the impact of policy systems and actions and contribute to the effectiveness of social policies in terms of their targets and beneficiaries.

To make social policy information systems accessible and useful to potential users, three issues are critical. First, information systems should be based on the identification and use of strategic social indicators and on the timely gathering of data to improve the capacity for targeting policies. In this regard, information for public awareness and for specific decisions requires special consideration (Durrant, this volume). This type of information is not easy to produce and access in part because of the weak capacity of target populations in identifying their own needs. Two questions that must be addressed are: How can these groups be helped to identify needs and priorities and how can the more dispossessed get access to timely information and contribute to guiding decision-makers in policy areas that affect their lives directly?

A second issue is that in addition to the production, gathering, and retrieval of information, there are other crucial problems that relate to the use and the users of information. Given the difficulties in accessing new software and hardware, attention must be paid to the development of information systems accessible to grassroots and popular organizations. This is a considerable challenge in dealing with the poorest and marginal groups because it means improving the access to equipment, documents, data delivery, and training in the use of resources and "repackaging" of information. "Repackaging" is one of the most strategic entry points to implementing information systems for social policies. It involves pulling together, sorting, analyzing, evaluating, abstracting, and synthesizing relevant information and data. It is perhaps the aspect most relevant to linking researchers and policymakers and to the marketing of information.

A third issue is how to avoid the reproduction of inequities within the information field. How, for example, can the distance between privileged in-groups and out-groups be avoided? In this regard, a number of aspects should be examined in relation to the equitable access to information. A critical topic is who will pay for the information services and systems.

Training

Research results and information are not fully useful unless they serve to generate capacities and learning skills. This leads to the third component, training. This should be a central concern in any research strategy given the scarcity of human resources. In part, the complexity of this component is a result of the variety of possible groups requiring training: researchers, policymakers, social policy managers, grass-root practitioners, and community leaders.

Although the purposes and content of training may vary widely, some general topics deserve mention. Training on social policy issues should generate the capacity to assess the social and political context of social policies; to get acquainted with the local, national, and global trends that condition social policies; to collect and analyze information; to understand the criteria for choosing priorities; and to understand the costs and economic implications of social programs. The training of users of information, especially beneficiaries and actors in the social policy process, should merit special consideration.

Policy Advice

The outputs of research, information, and training will influence social policies if they can be transferred to, adopted, and used at the level of various policy making structures and processes. Policy advice is a mechanism of innovation that embraces activities from the preparation of very specific consultancy reports to the introduction of policy issues into the public agenda. This is not a well known area of work, particularly among academic researchers. It is becoming important, however, under the current scarcity of research funds, in the active role of donors in defining the social policy agenda and in the need for practical and immediate knowledge inputs into the policy making process.

Policy advice requires special attention to improve the current decision-making process by introducing an integrated view of development problems and policy processes. To this end, policy advice requires appropriate support from research and information systems.

Social policy advice usually takes place in a context characterized by conflicting interests. How may objectivity be achieved? What are the opportunities for transferring useful and utilizable knowledge?

How can advice be provided when conditions conducive to the exacerbation of social inequity and conflict persist? Appropriate social policy advice requires that special attention be given to issues such as social inequalities, social participation, social conflicts, the perceptions of the actors involved, ethics, and the needs of the more affected groups. This makes social policy advice a complex task requiring expertise that goes beyond disciplinary training.

From the perspective of the policy making process, policy advice is a means to introduce into the research, information, and training agendas the need to improve the decision-making process. Policy advice closes the circle in the production of knowledge. There is accumulated research experience in the anglo–saxon research tradition about models and processes for policy advice. More research, however, is needed in Latin America to identified explanatory models of the decision-making process. There is a need for further research in this area to discover how knowledge can more effectively reduce uncertainty and enhance opportunities for effective social policy implementation and evaluation.

3

Administrative Responsibility and Complexity of Function

The Role of the Social Worker Sub-Group (RSW) has based its recommendations to the Review Group on evidence gathered, commissioned research, evidence presented to the Review Group and on its own experience. Its substantive conclusions about the role of the social worker in the 21st Century are set out at the end of its recommendations.

The RSW has come to the firm view that social work is and should remain a generalist profession with a strong common value, skills and knowledge base.

It sees the social worker in the 21st century as a confident and competent professional working with and along side people who use social work services, their advocates and other professionals to help them achieve the best possible outcomes in their lives.

It considers that the organisations have a responsibility to ensure that social workers are properly equipped and supported to undertake their roles and functions. This includes promoting a positive public message of support for social workers as well as creating a working environment which encourages and enables social workers to reflect critically on their practice.

Social workers must uphold public trust and confidence in social work services. Their primary responsibility is to protect and provide the welfare and well being of children, vulnerable adults and communities. For these reasons the Role of the Social Worker sub-group makes the following Recommendations:

1. Social work is and should remain a generalist profession, with a strong common value, skills and knowledge base.
2. Certain functions should be reserved to social workers and should be set out in Regulations. This is to ensure the protection of the public.
3. All organisations employing social workers and social workers professional organisations should adhere to and promote the Codes of Practice for Social Service Workers and Employers of Social Service Workers.
4. A national framework for post registration, training and learning of social workers should be established by the Council, be resourced by the Scottish Executive and organisations held to account for their provision of appropriate arrangements.
5. The Review Group should define the role, responsibility and status of the Chief Social Work Officer and require organisations to locate the post appropriately to safeguard the public.
6. The level of complexity and responsibility carried by social workers should be reflected in the career structures and remuneration available to them.
7. Employing organisations must have arrangements in place to ensure the workload of social workers is commensurate with the tasks required of them. This will include ensuring sufficient time is made available to allow the development of helping relationships which is an essential part of social work practice.
8. Social workers must have access to professional consultation, support and advice from appropriate, experienced social workers. This consultation and management should focus on assisting social workers to reflect critically on their practice, use their powers effectively and make complex decisions.
9. All organisations employing social workers must have in place formal arrangements which define the status of line management and professional consultation and clearly set out their parameters.

10. All organisations employing social workers must implement development and appraisal processes that give due recognition to service requirements and individual development needs.
11. All organisations employing social workers must ensure effective work force planning and development at local level to meet emerging need, maintain a competent and effective work force and contribute to work force planning at a national level.
12. Executive must have in place an effective mechanism to create a coherent overview of policy development relevant to social work and to monitor and evaluate this properly.
13. Executive must take account of work force issues and resource allocation at local level when introducing national initiatives.
14. Employers must provide social workers with access to appropriate, skilled professional and administrative support, within an organisation fit for purpose.
15. Employers and social workers must work together to develop a culture of learning, valued and promoted throughout agencies and organisations which reinforces the importance of being aware of current research and putting this into practice.
16. Social workers should intervene earlier with complex cases to avert crises but simple early interventions and preventive work should be the role primarily of universal services and/or social work services/social care.
17. Easily accessible and available social work services should not require complex assessment processes. All organisations require a shared understanding and agreed protocols which define the roles and responsibilities of different professionals at different stages of intervention and articulate how to access more specialist services, across agency boundaries, as people move through the stages and tiers.
18. Executive should invest in research to provide evidence on which social worker knowledge and practice would be

developed. Leadership at all levels is necessary, at the front line and politically – both locally and nationally. The Scottish executive should support and ensure this.

Underpinning Principles

The social worker in the 21st century is a confident and competent professional committed to working with and along side people who use social work services, their advocates and other professionals to help them achieve the best possible outcomes in their lives. The primary responsibility of the social worker will remain the protection and promotion of the welfare and well being of children, vulnerable adults and communities.

Social workers operate within the Codes of Practice for Social Services Workers and Employers and subscribe to the value base most recently set out in the International Federation of Social work Code of Ethics as "...based on respect for the inherent worth and dignity of all people, and the rights that follow from this. Social workers should uphold and defend each person's physical, psychological, emotional and spiritual integrity and well-being. They will work holistically taking account of the individual, their family and their community. They will build supportive relationships with people in order to help them effect change in their lives and work collabouratively with other professionals. They are committed to continuously developing their own professional skills, knowledge and expertise.

Social workers are skilled in coordinating complex networks of integrated service delivery particularly in those situations of uncertainty where relationships are complex and where there is a high degree of risk to the person using social work services and to the wider community. Social work will continue to be a demanding profession.

Social workers must possess the maturity and strength of character to confront challenging and complex situations; the emotional intelligence to establish relationships with people in these situations and the intellectual curiosity to acquire and use research evidence to achieve better outcomes for people who use services. Their employing organisations must recognise the importance of the social worker's role and ensure they are properly equipped and supported to operate effectively. Social workers constantly manage the twin roles of care and control in discharging their duties in a varied and complex environment.

It is important service users and the general public understand the complexity of balancing the two roles. This means there must be a robust evidence base for the decision making process, for example through using consistent approaches to risk assessment. The ability to identify acceptable levels of risk and put in place appropriate risk management mechanisms is a highly skilled task. This involves respecting individuals rights while balancing these with public safety. There must also be collaboration, transparency and openness with clients particularly in relation to using statutory powers.

Social workers must uphold public trust and confidence in social services. They must be aware of society's values and operate in accordance with legal obligations. They must be able to balance need in the risk in the face of constant uncertainty and competing demands. Communities will always include people who are vulnerable and who pose challenges for themselves and others. Social workers intervene in situations where not to do so could lead to a continuation or escalation of harm. They may work with people who have no wish to use social work services as well as people whose needs and demands challenge stretc..hed resources. Social Workers have a role to play in promoting social justice and in identifying and addressing obstacles to social inclusion.

In seeking to achieve the best possible outcomes for people who use social work services, social workers will use the knowledge and skills and understanding which are set out in the Standards in Social Work Education in order to:

- Prepare for and work with, individuals, families, careers, groups and communities to assess their needs and circumstances;
- Plan, carry out, review and evaluate social work practice with individuals, families, careers, groups and communities and other professionals;
- Assess and manage risk to individuals, families, careers, groups, communities, self and colleagues;

- Demonstrate professional competence in social work practice; and
- Manage and be accountable, with supervision and support, for their own social work practice within their organisation; and support individuals to represent and manage their needs, views and circumstances.

They must also contribute to the development of effective policy, practice and research within social work services and in the context of partnership working.

Social workers already work in statutory, voluntary and private settings and as independent practitioners. While this will continue to be the case, the evolving nature of service delivery will inevitably have an impact on where social workers are located. Given the nature of the complexities, interactions and risks involved in the lives of people using social services social workers do not and must not work in isolation from their colleagues in health, education, housing, employment and justice services as well as with voluntary and private sector providers Increasingly services are being integrated around the individual needs of people who use services in order to produce better outcomes for children and adults. Integrated service delivery requires a high level of sharing of skills, knowledge and roles, involving a wide variety of professionals in working with, assessing, recommending and reviewing action plans for vulnerable children and adults. This in turn requires professionals to have a clear and well developed understanding of their own distinctive contribution and those of others.

Seeing people's situations in the round includes recognising the effects on them of having to engage with a variety of agencies, and assessing where action or change by other agencies may open up opportunities, remove barriers to achieving the outcomes they seek. Social work skills are often deployed to good effect in collaborative work with other professionals, either in on-going multi-disciplinary teams or in ad hoc joint work around the needs of an individual or family. The distinctive social work contribution combines a developing body of knowledge and skills, a set of core values and priorities, and a range of personal qualities and includes working through the medium of a qualitative personal relationship.

The commencement of Protection of the Title "social worker" has in turn led to the definition of a 'social worker' as someone who meets the registration requirements of the Scottish Social Services Council and has a live and current registration as a social worker with the Council. Following the introduction of protection of title, these will be the only people entitled to call themselves social workers.

The professional practice of social workers should always be underpinned by the following principles:

- The primary responsibility of the social worker is the protection and promotion of the welfare and well being of children, vulnerable adults and communities.
- social workers should use their professional knowledge and expertise to make judgements and decisions for which they are professionally accountable.
- social workers must have access to professional consultation through line management arrangements which provides support and advice from appropriate, experienced social workers. This consultation should focus on assisting practitioners to reflect on their practice, use their powers effectively and make complex decisions for which they are personally and professionally accountable.
- The level of complexity and responsibility carried by social workers should be reflected in the career structures and remuneration available to them, and the continuing professional development they undertake.
- Leadership within local government for social workers undertaking protected functions should be exercised by the Chief Social Work Officer.

Social Workers' Roles and Functions

Developing Effective Relationships

Adopting a holistic approach and forging therapeutic relationships are not unique to social work. What makes the role of the social worker distinct is that it combines both. The social worker seeks to understand the person's entire situation (the holistic approach) and to work with this. Developing an effective helping relationship with people who use services is central to the role of the social worker in order to ensure better outcomes. Social workers need sufficient time to combine knowledge of skills and values and demonstrate the effective listening, respect and sensitive engagement which this involves. The ability to form and maintain such relationships can be eroded by a workload which exceeds resources, by over management of risks and by increasing expectations from people who use services of the social worker's capacity to meet their needs.

The development of a staged and tiered approach to social work intervention should ensure that the time and skills of social workers are invested appropriately in supporting those with the most complex needs, i.e. where there are multiple risk factors and vulnerability.

Social workers may not be the only professionals engaged in care management but will be the most appropriate professionals in complex care management where adults are in need of protection, are in danger of exploitation or significant harm and are at risk of causing significant harm to themselves or others. This role is being further clarified and developed, in light of care management guidance issued by Scottish Executive in August 2004. Such care management arrangements must be predicated on a continuing therapeutic relationship.

Social workers have a key role in working alongside people to help them take more control of their lives where this is possible and appropriate. Social workers should always aim to promote independence for users, even if this is a long-term goal. However, it will always be the case that for some people, creating a long term supportive relationship with social work services may be an appropriate response to managing risk and promoting the well-being of vulnerable children or adults. Some people will need high levels of support throughout their lives in order to achieve their full potential.

Social workers may work with people who have no wish to engage with social services but who are required to do so in the interests of the protection of their own or other's safety. In these circumstances, the development of a therapeutic relationship or working alliance with the involuntary service user is an essential element in bringing about the achievement of positive change in their lives.

Recommendations

Employing organisations must have arrangements in place to ensure the workload of social workers is commensurate with the tasks required of them. This will include ensuring sufficient time is made available to allow the development of helping relationships which is an essential part of social work practice.

Generalist or Specialist

Social work services work alongside a range of universally provided services. There are many points of entry to these universal services. Part of the social worker's task is to assist people maximise the opportunities available to them from universal services e.g. education and health and to advocate for them with these services.

Not every person looking for assistance from social services will need the level of intensity or duration of contact central to developing a therapeutic relationship with a social worker. For some, engagement with social services is purely a means of accessing a necessary service or resource. For this group of people, any necessary support may be more appropriately delegated to another social services worker.

Social work is and should remain a generalist profession, with a strong common values, skills and knowledge base. Individuals' social problems are often multi faceted and vulnerable people should expect to find continuity of service from their allocated social worker and be confident that worker will in turn be able to draw on the specialist knowledge and expertise of colleagues.

Generalist professionals need the back up of specialist expertise and knowledge. A good generalist service depends on good supporting specialist services. However, we also recognise that social workers need to build up their knowledge, skills and expertise in specific areas (for instance, substance misuse, autism, bereavement counselling) as they operate in increasingly specialist environments. Their knowledge and expertise must be available to people who use services as well as to colleagues elsewhere in social work services and within other professions.

In order to do this:

- Teams and organisations need a comprehensive knowledge base about the skills and expertise of the work force, both to provide ready access for advice and consultancy and to identify and fill any gaps.
- Individual professionals need to know the limit of their own competence. Professional consultation should provide a vehicle to support this and encourage practitioners to seek expertise when and where they need it.
- We must clearly define accountabilities in this process and the parameters within which this happens.
- We should recognise that there may increasingly be sharing of expertise across sectors, both in terms of sharing good practice and in providing access to particularly scarce specialist expertise.
- Organisations should ensure access to specialist expertise when and where that is required. This may be in giving advice to a practitioner or in taking over responsibility for users with particular needs.
- We should promote the development of generalists with specialist interests – similar to the model increasingly developing in general medical practice.
- If we are to maintain social work as a generalist profession, whilst ensuring that each social worker has the necessary competence to fulfil their current role effectively, then we will need to undertake the following actions:
- Provide the necessary training opportunities to allow social workers to develop excellent knowledge and skills.
- Develop a contemporary and relevant educational framework that allows people to develop the competence to undertake their current role and to add additional competencies required for new roles.
- Build development appraisal processes that ensure matching between service requirements and individual development needs.
- Promote the Social Services Council Code of Practice for Employers and Social Service workers.

- Organisations need to encourage workers to expand and develop their knowledge and skills.
- Ensure effective work force planning at local level to meet emerging need, maintain a competent and effective work force and contribute to work force planning at a national level.

Recommendations

Social workers must have access to professional consultation, support and advice from appropriate, experienced social workers. This consultation and management should focus on assisting social workers to reflect critically on their practice, use their powers effectively and make complex decisions.

All organisations employing social workers must have in place formal arrangements which define the status of line management and professional consultation and clearly set out their parameters.

All organisations employing social workers must implement development and appraisal processes that give due recognition to service requirements and individual development needs.

- All organisations employing social workers must ensure effective work force planning and development at local level to meet emerging need, maintain a competent and effective work force and contribute to work force planning at a national level.
- Council Executive must have in place an effective mechanism to create a coherent overview of policy development relevant to social work and to monitor and evaluate this properly.
- Council's Executive must take account of work force issues and resource allocation at local level when introducing national initiatives.

Access to Services

We will always deliver services within finite resources. Social workers are legitimately involved in making decisions about how these are deployed. However, we recognise that social workers and users can see this "gate-keeping" function as a barrier to building effective therapeutic relationships. In order to make this function more effective, a number of actions are proposed:

- Develop more effective collaborative approaches to decision making with service users and careers which are built on openness and transparency and develop individual and community capacity.
- Ensure that the provision of services is fair and equitable through effective communication between front line staff and finance and strategy leads, including influencing where resources are inadequate and recommending where resources could more effectively meet need.
- Devolve budget responsibilities nearer to the front line, with a proportionate approach, recognising that costly scarce resources may need agreement by senior managers. To support this, organisations should ensure that all staff have a good understanding of the big picture in financial terms and corporate spending priorities.

All of this requires effective communication, financial controls and sound governance which the review group will need to address in considering systems and processes.

Role Boundaries in Integration

We anticipate that social workers will work in integrated settings and teams reflecting the skill mix needed to produce the best possible outcomes for service users. There are examples of integrated work between partner agencies at strategic and operational level across the country. They include Community Mental Health Teams, Rapid Response Teams (to achieve early discharge from hospital) Integrated Community Schools. Good integration however also needs to take place across social work services e.g. expertise in services in addiction and mental health supporting children and families work or criminal justice social work and vice versa. Key features of successful integrated team working involve an understanding of different role, a willingness and capacity to work across role boundaries and a shared understanding of the desired outcomes. This approach is fully taken into account in the draft paper describing the reserved functions of the social worker. This paper also identifies the circumstances in which the social worker will be the designated 'Lead Officer' responsible for the management and co-ordination of services in cases requiring complex arrangements among different workers or agencies.

Integration of services means integration around the needs of the service user, i.e., that the service user experiences a service in which their individual needs are met in a coherent way with clarity around lines of accountability. Integrated teams may be "real" i.e. they are a group of people working together to meet the needs of a particular group of users, or "virtual" i.e. a group of professionals who are brought together around one or more particular service users needs. The make up of teams may be variable and will change over time according to the task. Effective team work will not happen simply by putting people together. Creating new teams may simply result in new boundaries elsewhere. It also requires the investment of time and effort in supporting the development of teams with proper accountability and management. In order to be effective in integrated team's social workers must be competent, confident practitioners able to articulate their roles and responsibilities and locate these within a theoretical framework based on up-to-date research about effective practice. Team members and agencies must define their common goals and clarify the contributions of individual team members.

Recommendations

Employers must provide social workers with access to appropriate, skilled professional and administrative support, within an organisation fit for purpose.

Employers and social workers must work together to develop a culture of learning, valued and promoted throughout agencies and organisations which reinforces the importance of being aware of current research and putting this into practice.

Prevention and Early Intervention

Although often used in tandem, these are separate concepts which are relevant to all aspects of well-being and health, at individual and community level, for all ages and service users. There are many ways of defining these concepts, but in effect, 'prevention' refers to activities designed to stop a problem arising and early intervention is activity aimed at halting the development of a problem which is already evident.

There are economic as well as professional arguments in favour of these approaches. They are closely linked to developing community capacity as well as individual capacity. The skills and knowledge possessed by social workers can add to local intelligence of services and resources needed to strengthen and develop communities. They can influence universal service providers in developing preventative strategies and services. Their particular skills and knowledge when used in relation to assessment of individual service users can determine where prevention and/or early intervention will be most effective in preventing escalation of problems and risk.

Using this approach, the point of intervention will be on a continuum from prevention to crisis management, to long term, complex, care management. This tiered and staged approach to intervention is described on the next page as a pyramid, with the tip being those areas where a social worker should always be involved. This includes managing crises, complex cases and those cases where statutory powers may be invoked. The base is the responsibility primarily of universal services, but where social workers may have a role in contributing intelligence and advising universal services.

Accountability and Risk Management

When a case is allocated to a social worker he/she is directly responsible through their line management arrangements for the management and delivery of care to the user. In addition, as lead professionals they may receive information and assistance from colleagues and other professionals in meeting their responsibilities. They will retain professional accountability for their own contribution and for the overall coordination and management of cases allocated to them.

There is a need to ensure that social work professional practice is based upon evidence of effectiveness, promotes professional autonomy within a legislative and organisational framework with access to professional consultation. This means that individual social workers will exercise and act on professional judgement. Organisations need to be able to support the practice of social workers within a clear framework of accountability, ensuring that the organisation is able to deliver its statutory duties, whilst giving practitioners sufficient flexibility to practice innovatively.

This requires clear, well developed and user friendly practice guidelines, policies and procedures as well as a sound professional understanding of accountability at all levels within the organisation. There must also be a proactive approach to professional consultation and management which promotes reflective practice explores and where appropriate, challenges decision making and identifies development needs. Newly qualified social workers require an approach which allows them to grow professionally and promotes confidence and independence whilst allowing their practice to be closely supervised during the development phase.

Social workers are responsible for the assessment and management of complex and inter-connecting risks rather than simply risk avoidance. This requires social workers to work with individuals to help them assess the risks they face and may present to others and to promote the independence of service users while helping to protect them as far as possible from danger or harm. At the same time they must respect their rights while seeking to ensure that their behaviour does not harm themselves or other people. Social workers need to be able to develop and maintain their skills in this field throughout their careers, and in all settings. They should also have a range of methods to assess and manage risk, based on evidence that can be used to support professional judgement and where necessary, to explain it.

While managing risk is a key skill of social workers, other professionals are required to accept shared responsibility also. They need to improve their skills in addressing the needs of individuals who challenge their services.

Conclusion

Social workers do a job which is spiritually, ethically and physically daunting, a job which is a permanent test of character and intelligence, a job which requires rare determination and commitment". *Jonathan Dimbleby.*

At its heart, social work is about real people living real lives. Lives that are uniquely different; each bringing its own complexity and adversity, hope and frustration. Some people will never need a social worker but others will rely on social workers to help them deal with the challenges, threats and disadvantages they face throughout their lives. Some will seek the help of a social worker, others will have no option but to accept their involvement because their actions pose a threat to themselves or others.

The social worker's task is to work alongside people to help them build resilience, maintain hope and optimism and develop their strengths and abilities. It is also to confront and challenge behaviour and manage situations of danger and uncertainty. Social workers must meet people on their own terms, in their own environment whilst retaining the professional detachment needed to help service users to understand, come to terms with or change their behaviour.

India today faces its own challenges and opportunities-changing demography and employment patterns, continuing inequality and growing expectations of public services. It is in this complex and ever changing environment that social workers must function. Their contribution to making an India a healthy and thriving society is vast, but can only be realised if we recognise and strengthen the role of the social worker in the context of a modern India. The intention of this paper is to set out a new vision for social work, based on existing values and to strengthen social workers' capacity to practice efficiently and effectively and ultimately bring about better outcomes for people who use their services.

Guidelines for Social Work Supervision

In 2006, Social Workers Registration Board conducted a large-scale survey on the practice of supervision among all social workers in Hong Kong. After that, a discussion paper was sent to every registered social worker (RSW) for consultation. In the consultation process, various social work organizations (e.g. Hong Kong Council of Social Services, Hong Kong Social Workers Association, Hong Kong Social Workers General Union, training institutes, staff associations, and agency heads) and were also consulted. One of the recommendations proposed after the consultation is to formulate a set of guidelines for the practice of supervision in Hong Kong.

In 2007, a task force on supervision guidelines under the Working Group on Professional Development was formed to look into the issue. A review of the practice of supervision in 14 human service organizations was conducted. The guidelines adopted by overseas social workers organizations were also examined. It was found that the supervision guidelines used by the Australian Association of Social Workers (AASW) is the most comprehensive one in developed countries. Based on the AASW supervision guidelines and the context of the social work field in Hong Kong, the task force drafted this document for the purpose of collecting the views of social workers in Hong Kong.

The aim of this document is to develop a set of recommended standards for discussion in the social work field. It has clarified the responsibility of the agency, the worker, and the supervisor in relation to professional supervision.

Supervision is one of the core elements in the development and maintenance of high standards of social work practice. Supervision is important to the quality of human service delivery and professional development of front line social work practitioners. The primary objective of professional supervision is to enhance, ensure, and enable humanistic, competent, and independent social work practice. Ultimately, supervision should benefit service users.

The term "supervision" has a specific meaning in the social work field. It goes beyond the concept of line management which mainly monitors the job performance of the employees and efficiency of service programs.

The concept of supervision is broader than consultation. Supervision encompasses hierarchical administrative responsibility, which is part and parcel of social work practice as it is practised in an organizational context of a social service agency.

Supervision is most effective when it is valued by the agency, the supervisor, and the supervisee, when all these parties give supervision a high priority, and where there is recognition of the importance of supervision to the quality of service and the needs of the supervisee as a professional practitioner. Social work supervision consists of administrative, educational, and supportive functions. All these three functions are inter-related and should be fulfilled, but the ration could be based on the service context and needs of the staff.

Administrative Function

This is a management function which includes the setting of service objectives and priorities, clarification of roles, planning and assignment of works; review and evaluation of work, and accountability of and responsibility for the supervisee's work.

Educational Function

This involves socialization of professional values, provision of knowledge, and training of practice skills, which are the worker's necessary tools for effective professional practice. It also includes the development of self-awareness and sensitivity of the social worker. Educational supervision should be emphasized as a core component in the professional development of the worker.

Supportive Function

It enables the supervisee deal with job-related issues, and with developing attitudes and feelings conducive to effective job performance. It sustains staff morale and gives the supervisee a sense of professional self worth, and a feeling of belonging to the agency and the profession.

Organizational Standards

Supervision should meet the needs of the supervisee, the supervisor, and the agency; in order to provide effective services to the client(s) within the context of the human service agency.

Rationale

Supervision should serve administrative, educational, and supportive functions unless it is specified with reasonable considerations.

Operationalization

It is preferably to have written supervision agreement in the human service agency which includes long-term professional development objectives and should be mutually negotiated and periodically reviewed by both the supervisor and supervisee. A reporting form of the supervisory practice or practice-related records, appropriate to the service setting(s) of the agency, should also be developed. While the criteria for assessing supervision will differ from agency to agency, the following simple guidelines are provided for reference:

a. Are both the supervisor and the supervisee(s) well prepared for the supervision sessions?
b. Is the supervisee's workload monitored by the supervisor regularly?
c. Is the supervisee's practice-related records reviewed by the supervisor regularly?
d. Is the process of professional intervention discussed in the supervision sessions?
e. Is there professional advice on service delivery giving by the supervisor?
f. Are the client outcomes reviewed and discussed?
g. Is there discussion on evaluation of service effectiveness and efficiency as accountability to the service agency and the community?
h. Are the ethical and legal issues implied in direct practice considered?
i. Is there discussion of the working relationships with other colleagues within the agency?
j. Are there opportunities for the supervisee to give feedback to the supervisor and the supervision?
k. Are issues related to the supervisee's roles, professional identity, and staff morale discussed?
l. Are the supervisee's long-term professional development needs addressed in supervision sessions?
m. Is there a supportive learning atmosphere for both the supervisor and the supervisee(s)?

The job duties of a social work supervisor related to supervisory responsibility in terms of time allocation, accountability, and lines of authority should be formally recognized by the agency. The duty list should also be periodically reviewed and assessed in regard to the feasibility of carrying out the specified duties.

Rationale

Adequate resources, accountability, and authority should be provided to support the practice of effective supervision.

Operationalization

The time fraction required for the supervision of each supervisee should be calculated (including time for preparation and evaluation) and the other responsibilities of the supervisor should be adjusted accordingly.

A minimum level of individual supervision should be one uninterrupted hour every two months, exceptional cases could only be allowed with substantial reasons.

The proposed supervision time is subject to the following conditions of the supervision interview:

a. for professional growth
b. scheduled and prepared, and with aim
c. one-to-one
d. periodic and progressive
e. regular and systematic (Reasons should be recorded if not conducted.)

The agency should provide opportunities for the further development of the supervisor's knowledge and skills in relation to supervision.

Rationale

The quality of supervision is dependent on the supervisory capacity and practice expertise of the supervisor.

Operationalization

The agency should enable the supervisor to attend courses, seminars, and conferences etc... relating to supervision and this should be included in the budget for staff development.

Agencies should develop an appropriate mechanism to assess and negotiate situations in which the supervisor-supervisee relationship is in difficulty.

Rationale

Supervision can be implemented effectively in an atmosphere of trustful and positive working relationship.

Operationalizaiton

Procedures for dealing with a potential conflict which cannot be directly resolved between the supervisor and supervisee should be developed and this should be specified in the supervision agreement. Conflicts could be resolved by different means. For example, (a) peer mediation; if this fails, (b) the superior of the supervisor should try to mediate and review the possible structural sources of the conflict which are being expressed in the supervisor-supervisee relationship; (c) ultimately, of course, it may be necessary for the top management of the agency to arbitrate in relation to this conflict.

Supervisor Standards

It is recommended that the supervisor should possess at least five years of practice experience preferably in a relevant field of practice (but not necessarily in the particular sub-field).

(Note: The term 'field' used here refers to a broad client population and service system, such as "youth". Specialized 'sub-field' is the specific areas which constitute the broad 'field' such as 'outreaching services'. It should be recognized that where a supervisor does not meet these standards they will have to get professional support in carrying out their supervisory duties.) It is encouraged that the supervisor has successfully completed a course in social work supervision.

It is encouraged that the supervisor has undergone further training in a field of practice or method of intervention relevant to the service, for example, specific training in a field or method on the job.

Rationale

Supervisors should have a higher level of practice experience than their supervises and have had some training in supervision. It is unlikely that a person would be able to acquire and integrate the complexity of social work theory and practice without basic working experience.

Minimum Supervision Standards at Different Levels of Experience

Recent graduates (less than three years of full time experience) should receive face-to-face supervision at least one uninterrupted hour individual face-to-face supervision every month. The form of the supervision may vary according to the characteristics of the agency and practice situation. Group supervision is also encouraged to provide as a supplement. Attendance at staff meetings, team meetings, in-service training, workshops, and seminars, while constituting valuable sources of professional development, are not acceptable substitutes for supervision.

Rationale

Recent graduates have a particular strong need for supervision in order to consolidate the knowledge and skills attained in their social work education; successfully manage the stress related to assuming the responsibilities of a social work position; and be adequately prepared for becoming a supervisor themselves.

Operationalization

Supervision programs for recent graduates need to be tailored to the specific practice context which can be described as supervised practice. Social workers with three or more years' full time experience should have the equivalent of one uninterrupted hour of supervision in every two months. If peer supervision (by a colleague of the same rank) is chosen, responsibility for accountability and review should remain the duty of the occupant of a senior position.

a. Experienced social workers also need and have a right to expect an opportunity to formally use social work colleagues as a "sounding board" for consultation and reflection upon their own practice.

b. On occasions it may be appropriate for an experienced social worker to use the expertise of consultants of other professions/disciplines to further their own professional development goals.

c. If peer supervision is to be effective it is necessary that members be sufficiently experienced to know their own limitations as well as be able to share their strengths.

4

Social Policy and its Responsibility

Social policy primarily refers to guidelines and interventions for the changing, maintenance or creation of living conditions that are conducive to human welfare. Thus, social policy is that part of public policy that has to do with social issues. The Malcolm Wiener Centre for Social Policy at Harvard University describes it as *"public policy and practice in the areas of health care, human services, criminal justice, inequality, education, and labour"* Social policy often deals with issues which Rittle & Webber (1973) called wicked problems.

Social Policy is also distinct as an academic field which focuses on the systematic evaluation of societies' responses to social need. London School of Economics professor Richard Titmuss is considered to have established Social Policy (or Social Administration) as an academic subject and many universities offer the subject for undergraduate and postgraduate study.

History of Social Policy

Early proponents of scientific social planning, such as the sociologist Auguste Comte, and social researchers, such as Charles Booth, contributed to the emergence of social policy. Surveys of poverty that exposed the brutal conditions that existed, such as in the urban slum conurbations of Victorian Britain, pressured changes such as the reform of the Poor Law and welfare reforms by the British Liberal Party. Other significant examples of social policy are the social security policies introduced by the New Deal in the United States between 1933 and 1935 and health reforms in the UK following the Beveridge Report of 1942.

Types of Social Policy

Social policy aims to improve human welfare and to meet human needs for education, health, housing and social security. Social policies will be approached in vastly different ways depending on the ideological leanings of the governing power. Important areas of social policy are:

- The welfare state
- Social security
- Unemployment insurance
- Pensions
- Healthcare
- Family Policy
- Social housing
- Social care
- Social exclusion
- Education policy
- Crime and Criminal justice
- Labour regulation.

The term 'social policy' can also refer to policies which govern human behaviour. 'Social policy' may refer to the following issues:

- abortion and the regulation of its practice
- the legal status of euthanasia
- the legal status of homosexuality
- the rules surrounding issues of marriage, divorce, and adoption
- poverty, welfare, and homelessness and how it is to deal with these issues
- the legal status of recreational drugs
- the legal status of prostitution.

The Population Crisis

Few in India can deny that India is facing an intense crisis of resources. There is intense competition for the nation's limited natural resources that is leading to quarrels between states, between communities and even families. Our land and water resources are being exploited to the hilt. The exploitation of our mineral resources is threatening our forests, nature reserves, and general ecology. Seventy percent of our energy resources need to be imported putting constant pressure on us to export more or face a currency devaluation. Over use of resources is contributing to natural disasters ocurring more frequently and with greater devastation. For many Indians, life is a big struggle just to put together the bare essentials for survival, and shortages of resources works most against the poor and under privilged. Even as sections of India's middle-class struggle with scarcities-it is the poor and vulnerable sections of society who suffer most.

As famine rages in many parts of India, reports from Gujarat and Rajasthan indicate that Dalit villagers are the last to get access to water. Reports also indicate that much of the burden of collecting water is placed on women who often walk for miles a day to fill a pot or two of water.

It is true that better management of resources could reduce this problem-that states like Gujarat and Rajasthan have neglected traditional water-harvesting methods that could be vital to augment scarce water resources. Others have argued that if the Narmada project were to be completed in some acceptable form, that could alleviate such problems in the future. But even with appropriate development schemes and optimum utilization of scarce resources, it would be hard to argue, that on a per capita basis, India's natural resources are not becoming severely strained.

So far, these resources have been shared in a very unequal way. Some Indians have the luxury of taking long showers twice or thrice a day- even their pets are bathed daily, and their cars scrubbed from top to bottom. Other Indians are lucky if they get to bathe once a week. And many Indians are lucky just to have access to clean drinking water. If in the future, India were to become a more egalitarian nation, and attempt to share it's water-resources in a fairer and more just way, it is evident that with projected population growth rates, it is unlikely that every Indian citizen will have access to a reasonable ammount of water every day. The same would be true of other precious resources like land, energy and scarce minerals.

Twenty years ago, it may have been possible to argue that in a socialist system, the country would find the resources to provide every Indian citizen a comfortable life. Today, it is becoming more and more difficult to make such assertions with any degree of confidence. While there is no doubt that increased research and more ingenuous and creative management of our resources could be quite effective, we must accept that compared to most nations we are becoming exceedingly resource poor.

To a large extent this is a result of the post-colonial division of the world. During colonial rule, Europe was much more densely populated than India, and it's population was growing faster.

But Europeans had the option of migrating to the so-called "new world". Very quickly, Europe's excess population was absorbed by the US, Canada, South America, Australia, New Zealand, and South Africa. Some of the world's resource-richest places on the planet were settled by European migrants, who then quickly closed their borders to non-European migrants by enforcing racially biased quotas and other immigration restrictions.

By the time colonized nations like India had won independence, and begun to improve their national health system (leading to rapid population growth), the borders in the "new world" were closed to them. As India's life expectancy has doubled from 31 to about 62 in 50 years, and it's infant mortality rate fallen dramatically, it's population has grown to almost a billion. But except for a small trickle-most Indians cannot expect to migrate to "greener pastures". They must endure life on one of the most densely populated resource-limited lands on the planet.

Even as "globalization of the media" has created amongst many Indians the desire for a more comfortable and even extravagant life-style, our growing population makes it almost impossible for anything more than a tiny elite to actually live that way. This is creating tremendous stress in terms of rising middle class and even working class expectations and what is actually possible for India's limited geography to deliver. With the population still growing rapidly amongst the poor peasants, (particularly in the Hindi belt)-the consequences for the future are serious, if not catastrophic.

Socio-Economic Consequences of a Burgeoning Population

Even more serious than the physical consequences of expected scarcities are the potential social consequences. As is already quite evident worldwide, industrial growth can, and is taking place with virtually no increase in the demand for labour. Improved agricultural implements and expanded availiability of tractors and mechanical threshers and harvesters, has meant that there has also been little growth in the demand for agricultural labour. Since most of the population growth in India is taking place amongst those who will have the least skills when entering the job market-India is likely to be inundated with either completely illiterate or poorly schooled youth and children in a stagnant or pehaps even shrinking job market. The social consequences could be simply devastating-and to some extent hints of this impending crisis are already visible in the slums of our metros.

More and more children from the slums are being pushed into the job market as their parents find it impossible to feed their families. Village youth and young adults from poor and desperate villages migrate to the cities to compete with the existing pool of unskilled workers for a very limited supply of service-sector jobs. Wages are pushed down and in the long run could head to near-starvation levels even as per-capita city budgets for social spending are cut. Even when allocations for social spending are made, little of the money sanctioned is actually spent on the poor. As their numbers explode, the bargaining power of these desperately poor slum dwellers diminishes to the point where they cannot exercise any control on corrupt officials cheating them out of the few schemes the government runs in their name.

This has been particularly true during the Orissa cyclone, and now during the famine that has afflicted much of the country. There have been almost daily reports of the needy being paid a fraction of the wages due to them under the food-for-work programs. Corrupt officials are milking the poor out of every last rupee they possibly can. When people are desperate, they work for even less than what it takes to survive. And they have no energy to fight it out.

But an army of poor and unemployed cannot be expected to tolerate their miseries for ever. In the absence of strong social organizations that represent the interests of the poor and help build a more humane and just society-their seething discontent could manifest itself in many unexpected and unpleasant ways. With the present disarray in India's left movement and the inability of the unions to organize the unorganized-it is not unlikely that India's urban slums could become centres of social anarchy. While some may take to petty or violent crime, others may let out their frustrations in sudden and volcanic explosions of social discontent. It may be quite difficult to predict as to which direction this frustration will take.

Cheap Labour-Asset or Liability?

So far, large sections of India's elite, while viewing the poor and their "tendency to over-reproduce" with disgust and contempt, have done little to push for a serious population policy. In large part this has been because they have benefited from this unending supply of cheap labour. But this unending supply of cheap and largely unskilled labour has serious unrecorded economic consequences. It severely constricts demand-growth and limits Indian industry to producing low quality, low-valued added goods. In the global market, this eventually puts Indian industry at a great competitive disadvantage rather than advantage.

Modern-day production fetc..hes larger profits when labour productivity is multiplied manifold. With some exceptions (like the Gulf oil industry), even in the extractive industries like mining, India's cheap labour cannot always compete against advanced mechanized procedures. Industries that rely excessively on human labour are generally becoming unrenumerative, and generate low rates of profit.

Higher rates of profit are to be found in those industries where the labour force must be well-educated and highly well-trained. Those Indians who wish to sell India's cheap labour in the world market will find that the scope for selling commodities produced by cheap labour is ultimately quite limited. That will not turn India into the "Asian tiger" that they wish. On the contrary.

It is important to abserve that years of high-growth in the ASEAN nations were also accompanied by rapidly falling birth rates, rapidly increasing literacy rates, and what is most significant-also rising wages. Virtually every ASEAN member has a literacy rate of over 85%, with much lower infant mortality rates and higher life-expectancy than India. Their work-force on the average is better trained, better paid, and more skilled than India's. Without investing in the social sector it is futile to dream about India becoming like an ASEAN "tiger". It is their highly skilled work-force-especially in nations like Korea and Taiwan that has helped these nations build advanced products that can compete with the best in the world.

India's industrialists ought to know that a poorly-trained and demoralized work-force cannot be compensated for by simply importing tools and machinery. Even to use modern machinery effectively and to keep it in working order requires certain skills that do not come automatically.

Another dimension to the cheap work-force scenario is that the demand for labour-saving inputs and devices grows very slowly. This means that both in the industry and in the home, the switch to higher quality machines, and tools does not take place or takes place very slowly. If it is cheaper to hire labour than buy a labour-saving device-who will make the switch?

But since human endeavour can rarely match the precision and accuracy of well-designed computer-controlled electronic machines-the quality of Indian goods remains uncompetitive in the world market, even as the internal market for capital goods and appliances stalls.

A cheap labour market also implies a restricted market for consumption. When workers are well-paid they are able to buy more goods produced by industry. This leads to increased demand fuelling new investment and new opportunities for industries to expand. But if wages are so low that people can just about eat and spend on nothing else-even the market for consumer goods stagnates or shrinks. This means that industry has to constantly contend with demand-recessions.

If Indian industry is to ever grow at double-digit rates, the entire Indian mindset will have to change from tolerating a growing but cheap and unskilled work force into building the social infrastructure that will rapidly control population growth and spend the money on improving the all-round quality of India's work force.

While it is imperative that India quickly address it's growing population, a problem that threatens to grow dangerously out of hand-it must do so without the prejudices and lackadaisical attitudes of the past. The problem should be taken up not just by the social welfare ministry but by all government and non-governmental agencies, as well as by progressive organizations and unions.

However, rather than come out with undemocratic and discriminatory schemes like freezing the representation of the Hindi-belt states in parliament, schemes ought to be designed with compassion and sympathy for the poor. Issues such as gender inequality, social pressures concerning marriage and sexuality, social pressures for having more children, especially male children ought to be confronted. Pressures from religious orthodoxy ought to be challenged. Above all, the well-being of small families ought to be guranteed.

So far, India's family planning programs have seen only limited success because the programs have not tackled the issue in a holistic way. There have been few concrete incentives for the poor to keep their families small. There has been little attention paid to enforcing a liveable minimum wage, so that children are not pushed into work early. There has been little attention paid to guaranteeing jobs or decent schooling for those amongst the poor who do adopt family planning methods and restrict their birth rates. There has also been little attention to the need for old age pensions, for affordable health-care and disability insurance so that the poor feel secure enough not to want to have more children as an "insurance" for the future.

Of course, in practice, with the growth of capitalism-the values of the traditional family system have rapidly broken down. As a result, there is little solidarity amongst family members. Few family members chip in when a health emergency strikes or when a family member is seriously injured or disabled. The elderly are often abandoned by their children when they migrate far away from their ancestral villages. All the old reasons for having more children are disappearing. It is consequently imperative that concerned social agencies educate India's illiterate or poorly schooled about the dangers and negative consequences of having large families.

India's population policy needs to be based on concrete measures that not only help solve our population problem but also helps the poor to improve their lives in tangible and meaningful ways. In this regard, our film industry and television industry also need to play a socially responsible role in creating the value-systems that not only rewards small families but also makes society collectively responsible for looking after the poor when they do adopt socially responsible measures. Blaming or ridiculing the poor and denying them their democratic rights will not be helpful in this regard. Neither will an escapist or careless attitude.

Based on the past record of most state and national governments to delay constructive intervention until the nation becomes overawed by a full-blown crisis, there is a danger that a time may come when as the problem becomes more intense and perceived to be more and more intolerable, there may be a chorus of calls for more intrusive and coercive measures.

Rather than wait for the crisis to grow out of hand, progressive organizations need to be especially pro-active. It is particularly important that India's progressive community see to it that the population issue is seriously and adequately addressed-and addressed in an ethical and socially constructive way.

For too long, some in the Indian left have dismissed the problem of India's population growth as a problem for the "bourgeoisie" and not a "class" problem. They have not always tried to see the connection between child labour and large families, or the connection between large families and diminished bargaining power for the working class as a whole.

It is high time that unions, progressive social organizations and working-class oriented parties and all other concerned organizations and citizens understand this problem in all it's depth and assist India's poor peasantry and young and growing urban proletariat to intervene in the population debate in a constructive and socially redeeming and socially conscious way.

World Social Forum India-Policy Guidelines

Proposed Preamble

The consultation of Indian organisations and individuals that took place in the city of Bhopal in India, on April 19-20 2002, and that constituted the World Social Forum-India It was decided that WSF's Charter for India needs to be evolved with certain additions required for India. It accordingly entrusted the task to the WSF India Working Committee.

Starting with the original Preamble to the WSF Charter of Principles, as prepared by the Brazil Organising Committee, the following constitutes the revised text as prepared by the WSF India Working Committee.

1. The World Social Forum is an open meeting place for reflective thinking, democratic debate of ideas, formulation of proposals, free exchange of experiences and inter linking for effective action, by groups and movements of civil society that are opposed to neo-liberalism and to domination of the world by capital and any form of imperialism, and are committed to building a world order centred on the human person.
2. The World Social Forum at Porto Alegre – held from January 25th – 30th, 2001, was an event localized in time and place. With the Porto Alegre Proclamation that "another world is possible", it becomes a permanent process of seeking and building alternatives, which cannot be reduced to the events supporting it.
3. The World Social Forum is a world process. All the meetings that are held as part of this process have an international dimension.
4. The alternatives proposed at the World Social Forum stand in opposition to a process of capitalist globalisation commanded by the large multinational corporations and by the governments and international institutions at the service of those corporations' interests. They are designed to ensure that globalisation in solidarity will prevail as a new stage in world history. This will respect universal human rights, and those of all citizens – men and women–

of all nations and the environment and will rest on democratic international systems and institutions at the service of social justice, equality and the sovereignty of peoples.

5. The World Social Forum brings together and interlinks only organisations and movements of civil society from all the countries in the world, but intends neither to be a body representing world civil society nor to exclude from the debates it promotes those in positions of political responsibility, mandated by their peoples, who decide to enter into the commitments resulting from those debates.
6. The meetings of the World Social Forum do not deliberate on behalf of the World Social Forum as a body. No one, therefore, will be authorized, on behalf of any of the editions of the Forum, to express positions claiming to be those of all its participants. The participants in the Forum shall not be called on to take decisions as a body, whether by vote or acclamation, on declarations or proposals for action that would commit all, or the majority, of them and that propose to be taken as establishing positions of the Forum as a body.
7. Nonetheless, organisations or groups of organisations that participate in the Forum's meetings must be assured the right, during such meetings, to deliberate on declarations or actions they may decide on, whether singly or in coordination with other participants. The World Social Forum undertakes to circulate such decisions widely by the means at its disposal, without directing, creating hierarchies, censuring or restricting them, but as deliberations of the organisations or groups of organisations that made the decisions.
8. The World Social Forum is a plural, diversified, non-confessional, non-governmental and non-party context that, in a decentralized fashion, interrelates organisations and movements engaged in concrete action at levels from the local to the international — to built another world. It thus does not constitute a locus of power to be disputed by the participants in its meetings, nor does it intend to

constitute the only option for interrelation and action by the organisations and movements that participate in it.

9. The World Social Forum asserts democracy as the avenue to resolving society's problems politically. As a meeting place, it is open to pluralism and to the diversity of activities and ways of engaging of the organisations and movements that decide to participate in it, as well as the diversity of genders, races, ethnicities and cultures.
10. The World Social Forum is opposed to all authoritarian and reductionist views of history and to the use of violence as a means of social control by the State. It upholds respect for Human Rights, for peaceful relations, in equality and solidarity, among people, races, genders and peoples, and condemns all forms of domination and all subjection of one person by another.
11. The meetings of the World Social Forum are always open to all those who wish to take part in them, except organisations that seek to take people's lives as a method of political action and those organisations that exclude groups/communities based on ethnic, racial, religious or caste considerations from the democratic world.
12. The WSF process in India must necessarily make space for all struggling sections of society to come together and articulate their struggles and visions, individually and collectively, against the neo-liberal economic agenda of the world and national elite, which is breaking down the very fabric of the lives of ordinary people all over the world and marginalizing the majority of the world people, keeping profits as the main criteria of development rather than society and destroying the freedoms and rights of all women, men, and children to live in peace, security, and dignity. It must make space for workers, peasants, indigenous peoples, dalits, women, hawkers, minorities, immigrants, students, academicians, artisans, artists and other members of the creative world, professionals, the media, and for local businessmen and industrialists, as well as for parliamentarians, sympathetic bureaucrats and other concerned sections from within and outside the

state. Most importantly, it must make space for all the 'sections' of society that remain less visible, marginalised, unrecognised, and oppressed.

13. In India today, all civil and political organisations/groups that are organising around people's issues — economic, political, social, and cultural — are being profoundly challenged by the religious and political intolerance that is raging in the country, and increasingly across the world. There is the threat of growing communal fascism and fundamentalism. The WSF India will strive to encourage a process that allows all of those who are combating communal fascism and fundamentalism to come together, to hear and understand each other, to explore areas of common interest, and also our differences, and to learn from the experiences and struggles of people here and in other countries.

14. The WSF India process involves not only events but also different activities across the country. These processes, in the spirit of the WSF, would be open, inclusive and flexible and designed to build capabilities of local groups and movements. The process should also be designed to seek and draw out peoples' perceptions regarding the impact of neo-liberal economic policies and imperialism on their daily lives. The language of dissent and resistance towards these will have to be informed by local idioms and forms.

15. WSF India will strive as far as possible for self reliance based on local resources generation in its activities. However, recognising that global solidarity, against the global neo-liberal agenda may involve international events. For such events and activities, resources may need to be mobilised from external resources.

16. As a forum for debate, the World Social Forum is a movement of ideas that prompts reflection, and the maximum possible transparent circulation of the results of that reflection, on the mechanisms and instruments of domination by capital, on means and actions to resist and overcome that domination, and on the alternatives that can be proposed to solve the problems of exclusion and

inequality that the process of capitalist globalisation currently prevalent is creating or aggravating, internationally and within countries.

17. As a framework for the exchange of experiences, the World Social Forum encourages understanding and mutual recognition among its participant organisations and movements, and places special value on all that society is building to centre economic activity and political action on meeting the needs of people and respecting nature.
18. As a context for interrelations, the World Social Forum seeks to strengthen and create new national and international links among organisations and movements of civil society, that – in both public and private life – will increase the capacity for social resistance to the process of dehumanisation the world is undergoing and reinforce the humanizing measures being taken by the action of these movements and organisations.
19. The World Social Forum is a process that encourages its participant organisations and movements to situate their actions as issues of world citizenship, and to introduce onto the global agenda the change-inducing practices that they are experimenting in building a new world.

Social Policy for Street Children

The street children issue can best be addressed through preventive programs and policies that will strike at its social and economic causes. Special protection measures are also needed to increase development opportunities for young persons currently suffering the hardships of street life.

As mentioned earlier, goodwill alone cannot guarantee a positive, lasting impact on the lives of children. Focusing only on assistance is just as ineffective and can even make the problem worse, by increasing the child's dependence on charity and destroying its incentive to leave the street. The right kind of program is one that will help young participants strengthen their connections with family, school, and the community. Lobbying and advocacy can make the voices of street children heard, by producing changes in policies and laws that affect their life. The impact and sustainability of NGO programs can be increased by networking and cooperating with municipalities and local services in developing initiatives geared to a broad range of vulnerable groups.

To date, few programs for street children have been adequately evaluated. Those that are able to show and quantify their results are usually operated by the largest and the best-endowed NGOs. But a significant part of the work in this field is carried out by small, low-funded organizations, whose results are undocumented and unavailable to the public at large. As this report makes clear, funding can assist street children programs in various ways, depending on each donor's mandate and ultimate goals.

The following list outlines areas in greatest need of support at present.

- *Program services, including salaries or incentives for expert staff.* The Bulgaria experience shows that the quality of programs increases in proportion to the extent that funding is continuous over a defined period of time. Better quality in turn enables NGOs to raise public support and become sustainable.
- *Training of program staff.* Funding allows programs to continuously upgrade their level of professionalism. This is particularly important for small young NGOs.
- *Monitoring and evaluation.* Small NGOs need to be able to train staff in this area of expertise and to conduct regular monitoring activities. Donors could not only contribute financial support but also provide guidelines or conduct external evaluations.
- *Institutional cooperation.* Donors should facilitate and support the establishment of municipal, multiagency development programs with street children as one of their components.
- *Lobbying, advocacy, and networking.* Funding these activities is a way to help NGOs overcome their isolation and give a stronger voice to street children themselves. Finally, not all donors have the mandate and experience to directly support street children activities. Some of them can however play an important role in promoting policies and

legislation that encourage the positive development of all children in need of special protection and that help governments remove some of the social and economic causes of child vulnerability.

Instruments of Social Policy and Mechanisms of Welfare Delivery in India

Independent India's commitment to democratic politics meant that its polity had to grapple with the harsh reality of India's poverty: the sheer number of the poor (who were also now voters), the intensity of poverty and destitution and a deeply stratified and hierarchical society. Addressing the needs of vulnerable and marginalised groups in society has preoccupied the energies of intellectuals and policy makers and a focus of political rhetoric in India to a degree that is uncommon among developing countries. Yet, India's record on this count has been decidedly modest notwithstanding the gargantuan scale of the problem in that country.

India's social heterogeneity and the limited nature of accountability in areas of public service delivery creates political incentives to provide narrow private and club goods than pure public goods and promote discretionary policy instruments rather than broad programmatic efforts. This tendency is further amplified by India's clientelist politics. The puzzle is perhaps less why these countless targeted interventions have performed poorly, but rather why the state – and India's intellectual class – persists in reposing faith in these instruments.

Typology of Social Policy Instruments

The efforts by the state have encompassed a wide range of domains and instruments. Traditional Keynesian wage and price policies have limited utility in a country like India where more than 90 percent of the labour force is outside the formal sector institutionalized wage bargaining in the organized sector. Monetary policy has been relative conservative largely because of the risk aversion towards inflation since a very large number of voters are poor, and inflation inevitably acts like a regressive tax. However, the Indian state has been a fervent user of controls – on prices of products and services, trade, industrial licensing, location and bankruptcy, foreign exchange, etc.....-which more than often resulted in massive rationing and the development of parallel "black" markets. While many of these have been abolished after 1991, controls continue to flourish at the state and local level.

However, in this paper we do not address macro instruments that are a major part of social policies in industrialized countries and focus instead on targeted social policy instruments. The various mechanisms for welfare delivery in India are classified as per the following broad categories:

Set-Asides

Two broad streams have characterized set-asides. The first, where the focus is on redistribution of end products, like jobs and housing, and the second, which relates to intermediate inputs like education, and specially targeted schemes such as credit directed to particular social groups with the intention to equip them to participate more effectively in a market economy.

The key instrument used – to a much broader extent than almost any other country – is affirmative action, which are set-asides (or "reservations" as they are commonly referred to in India) in education, jobs and political representation for historically marginalised sections of society. The Constitution had provided these guarantees for India's indigenous peoples (referred to as Scheduled Tribes or STs) and the social group at the bottom of India's caste hierarchy. Over time other social groups began clamouring for similar status, arguing that their "backward status" required special dispensation by the state.

In turn this has fuelled the rise of identity politics in India. The result has been considerable success in giving political representation to a wide range of social groups. However, this has come at a high price. The success in providing "symbolic goods" and group benefits has intensified identity politics and militated against broad programmatic efforts. As a result outcomes – in terms of improvements in socioeconomic conditions – have been weak, with the political leadership reaping most of the benefits. Indeed, in many areas of education and employment, the set-asides are not fully utilised because, as we note later, of the failure to provide basic public services.

Income Augmenting

Another major thrust of social policy schemes has been to provide food security with the additional intent of increasing agricultural output. In this case however, the focus is on guaranteeing a minimum support price (MSP) for particular agricultural products, especially grains (wheat and rice), purchasing, storing and transporting the foodgrains by a government intermediary and then releasing a part of it at subsidized rates to families below the poverty line (BPL) through the public distribution system (PDS). The subsidy accrues to grain producers (confined mainly to the North Western states of Punjab, Haryana and Western UP, and the Southern state of Andhra Pradesh where the procurement takes place and where consequently the support is more effective) and the parastatal agency in charge of the logistics of grain procurement, storage and distribution. A part eventually reaches BPL households through the PDS though its targeting performance has been commented upon adversely even in many government reports. The food subsidy is the most expensive of the government schemes, costing the government about Rs. 250 billion (approximately $6 billion) in 2003-04 (more than half of all explicit subsidies of the central government). The other large item in this set, targeted to the same group, is the fertilizer subsidy, which tries to moderate the price of fertilizers to the farmer.

It does so, however, by subsidising the producer, in an ill-designed cost-plus scheme that has for many years now, allowed inefficiency in the industry to persist. The design is now in the process of being altered, but it remains a producer based subsidy.'

A second set of policies has focused on augmenting incomes of the rural poor through a variety of job creation programs. The largest and most vulnerable group in India is rural landless labour.

Lacking assets, it has little bargaining power and is particularly vulnerable to the vagaries of agricultural output. Over the years large resources – administrative, financial and intellectual –have been deployed on employment programs through public works. While these vary in the nature of payment, type of work, number of days of work, etc..... it must be emphasized that the really poor in India do not have the option of remaining unemployed and therefore these public works schemes can benefit only to the extent the wages paid to these workers on the public works projects are higher than what they could earn elsewhere and the knock-on effects of increasing wages in the non-public works labour market as a result of the general increase in demand for labour.

A third set of policies has focused on augmenting incomes through asset redistribution. Although land reform has been on the agenda since independence, there has been only limited land redistribution in part because such efforts were sabotaged by extant rural elites, but also because India simply did not have the sorts of massive landholdings as in Latin America, Pakistan or Philippines. In general legislation aimed at land ceilings and land consolidation has had little impact on poverty while legislation targeting tenancy reform and abolition of intermediaries has had a more positive impact by improving tenants' claims on the returns from land.

The limited scope (and political intransigence) of land reforms has led the Indian state to try other measures to augment incomes through asset redistribution. To this end a flagship antipoverty program was created in the 1970s, called the Integrated Rural Development Program (IRDP). This program has been recreated in different forms since then, including schemes to make entrepreneurs of the poor through schemes such as TRYSEM (Training of Rural Youth for Self-Employment), which provide training and a toolkit, and most recently as a self-employment scheme (the Swarnajayanti Grameen Swarozgar Yojana (SGSY), or Golden Jubilee Rural Self Employment Scheme). The basic idea in these programs is to transfer a productive asset to the target population.

However, they have chronically underestimated the barriers facing the poor in participating in the market place, managing an enterprise, or the costs of insuring the very asset (e.g. milk cattle) supposed to provide a livelihood. As we will note later, the Indian state's attempts to provide targeted benefits to the poor has been severely hampered by its inability to provide generic skills through mass education and literacy. Consequently the initial beneficiary was soon separated from his/her asset defeating the very purpose of the scheme.

Another form of asset transfer has been to provide access to credit at subsidized rates to the poor given the well recognized market failures in this area. These micro-finance programs have been marked by low recovery rates (less than a third, with defaults often at the behest of politicians), resulting in severe credit rationing. Recently efforts have been made to improve outcomes by directing credit to self-help groups (SHGs), comprising women. There has been a remarkable growth of bank credit to SHGs, particularly since the late 1990s. By 2003, the number of SHGs receiving some credit from banks was close to 800,000 compared to just 33,000 in 1999 covering about 12 million women and their households. Some of these have been very innovative in terms of their chosen occupation which has extended even to the delivery of public services. However, while large in absolute numbers the program's coverage is still modest in terms of the proportion of poor households served.

Safety Nets for Old-age

India lacks a comprehensive population-wide old age income security system. The two important mandatory pension mechanisms are the civil servants' defined benefit pension and the 'organized sector' system run by the Employees Provident Fund Organization (EPFO), an arm of the Ministry of Labour. The key weakness in India's pension system is its very limited coverage which extends to just 11 percent of the labour force (which automatically diminishes the extent of risk pooling that takes place). The vast majority of the population lies in the 'unorganized sector' and is outside the formal pension system. For this group support from their children continues to be the principal means of old age insurance. In addition, many states have now introduced oldage pension schemes, but the benefits under these are limited, typically about USD 5 per month.

Direct Provision of Basic Needs

One might presume that a government that is so energetic in trying to implement targeted poverty programs would have got the basics right first. In India's case this would be grossly erroneous presumption. India continues to do poorly on the public provision of basic services even those such as education which are constitutionally obligated. India's private health expenditure (78%) is one of the highest in the world, reflecting the abysmal provision of public health services. Child mortality and malnutrition are worse than Bangladesh and India's literacy rates are one of the worst in Asia as is the extremely limited coverage of sanitation services.

India's poor record in providing basic public goods – minimal levels of education, health, nutrition, water and sanitation – while spending vast public resources on targeting the poor, indicates that the problem is not one of limited resources, but political priorities and incentives.

Why has Social Policy in India Performed Poorly?

A democracy with a large number of poor voters, who vigorously participate in elections, where hitherto marginalised social groups have made significant inroads in capturing political power, might be expected to have powerful incentives to address issues of poverty and social development. Indeed, there is little doubt that India has made some progress in reducing poverty with the fraction of population that is defined as poor having fallen by about half since the late 1960s. But much of this decline has come from old fashioned growth rather than the welter of anti-poverty programs.

Creative Use of Subsidies to the Poor to Improve Urban Services

Kukatpally town in the state of Andhra Pradesh has an area of 72 sq. km and a population of 200,000 (1991 census). The township area was plagued by poor sold waste management and consequent accumulation of garbage resulting in community dissatisfaction, complaints, and protests by citizen groups. In 1998, the urban local body (ULB) in Kukatpally initiated discussions with poor women who had experience in sanitation and solid waste management.

Those who evinced interest were called for meetings and given details about the scheme, including the financial support they were likely to receive from commercial banks and the nature of assistance and guidance from the municipality. As a result, twelve women formed a group that was registered under the Cooperative Societies Act and began with a pilot area of 12.24 sq. km.

The project involved a financial outlay of Rs. 324,000, mainly to purchase a vehicle (such as a tractor) for transporting solid waste. Under the DWCUA scheme, Rs. 125,000 was provided as a grant. The remaining financing came from loans (Rs. 184,000, obtained from financial institutions) and the women's group contributed Rs. 16,000, i.e., 5% of the project cost. The group was paid a monthly tractor hire charge of Rs. 9,000 by the ULB for lifting the garbage.

Out of the hire charges, the ULB would deduct Rs. 8000 towards the repayment of bank loan and directly remit it to the bank. The tractor belonged to the group when the loan was completely repaid. As a DWCUA group could consist of only 12 members, additional persons were employed by the women's group with the ULB paying for the persons so employed.

The Kukatpally initiative of using DWCUA groups for urban sanitation, the first of its kind in the state became a trailblazer and was soon adopted by 61 urban local bodies (ULBs) in Andhra Pradesh with about 165 women groups providing sanitation service. In part this was also because the government decided to entrust environmental sanitation work to the women self-help groups in all the urban local bodies in a phased manner. These 165 women's groups have made a total investment of Rs. 53.6 million, of which the Government sanctioned Rs. 20.6 million as grant and Rs. 30.3 million was borrowed from financial institutions. The remaining Rs. 2.7 million was mobilised by the groups themselves. The scheme is both replicable and sustainable. Both the ULBs and the communities stand to gain. The gains for low income women's self help groups are self-evident, while for the ULBs, usually unable to maintain and improve environmental sanitation, the scheme provides a workable low cost alternative.

It is estimated that growth has been responsible for about 80% of the decline in the poverty headcount ratio (which measures the number of people below a defined poverty line) and 60 percent in the decline of the poverty gap measure (which measures the intensity of poverty).

Thus redistribution has been responsible for 20 and 40 percent of the decline in the two poverty measures. Not surprisingly, redistribution matters most for the ultra-poor. Given the large number of rural poor in India, an important predictor of poverty decline is agricultural growth. In the last decade, however, this sector has grown much more slowly, and hence the impact of India's impressive growth rate on poverty decline has been less than in the past.

There are several reasons why programs specifically directed at poor and marginalised populations in India have done poorly. We group them broadly into two heads:

(a) Structural and

(b) Political. The nomenclature is more classificatory than descriptive.

The structural reasons stem in large part from the fiscal crises of state (i.e. provincial) governments. This has led to an increasing dependence on centrally sponsored schemes (CSS).

The programs are designed and substantially funded by the central government, but since the issue areas are in the state list of the Constitution, implementation is at the hands of states. In the two decades since the early 1980s, the share of the CSS in the Plan budget of the Central Ministries increased from 30 to 70 percent. This expansion has taken place at the expense of investments in infrastructure, energy and industry sectors.

The key problematic consequence of this is purely administrative, but no less important because of that. While each centrally sponsored scheme has the resources of a particular central ministry to call upon to aid in its design, stipulate conditionalities for disbursement, etc..., the picture at the delivery level is very different. All centrally sponsored schemes must pass through the eye of the needle that is the district administration – and now increasingly the Panchayati Raj institutions (which are the 3rd tier of government i.e. local government). Few states have the administrative capacity to access grants from 200 plus schemes, spend money as per each of its conditions, maintain separate accounts and submit individual reports. This administrative capacity is even more limited in those states where the need is the most. The multiplicity of centrally sponsored schemes makes it difficult for the local level administrative machinery to even monitor, let alone execute, the schemes. Even though many schemes have common objectives, targeting the same population, each develops a Hydra-like new administrative structure – fragmenting already weak and limited resources to begin with. If local level administrative capacity for implementation is weak, equally there is little incentive for the concerned central ministry to monitor these schemes. Even financial monitoring is weak, with funds released without questioning the utilization of previous assistance. As for impact or sustainability, the issue is hardly ever raised. The few evaluation reports prepared are themselves seldom monitored for quality and even otherwise seldom read. Fear of adverse publicity leads to any reports of shortcomings to be suppressed.

A top-down approach and uniformity across states means that there is little local ownership, with the result that even if states are aware that the scheme is performing poorly, they become indifferent to its implementation. States do not attach importance to spending on CSSs, and thus are in no hurry to sanction expenditure. And mounting fiscal problems at the state level leads them to divert GOI funds for paying salaries.

Not surprisingly, the Comptroller and Auditor General (CAG) found a common pattern of shortcomings in the execution of all Centrally Sponsored Schemes:

Inability of the Union ministries to control the execution of the schemes with a view to ensuring the attainment of the stated objectives in the most cost effective manner and within the given time-frame, as a result of which, the programmes continued to be executed in uncontrolled and open-ended manner without quantitative and qualitative evaluation of delivery.

The controlling Union ministries confined their role to the provision of budget and release of the funds to the state governments rather mechanically without reference to the effective utilisation of the funds released earlier in accordance with the guidelines and capacity of the respective state governments to actually spend the balance from the previous years and releases during the current year.

The ministries were unable to ensure correctness of the data and facts reported by the state governments. Overstatement of the figures of physical and financial performance by the state governments was rampant. No system of accountability for incorrect reporting and verification of reported performance were in vogue.

The Ministry was more concerned with expenditure rather than the attainment of the objectives. Large parts of funds were released in the last month of the financial year, which could not be expected to be spent by the respective state governments during that financial year.

The state government's attitude to the execution of the programs was generally indifferent. They laid emphasis on release of assistance by the ministry rather than ensuring the quality of expenditure and attainment of the objectives. Misuse of the funds provided for vulnerable sectors and sections of the society was rampant. The state governments' attitude towards such misuse was one of unconcern. The controlling Union ministries had no clue to such misuse. Thus, in many cases, the figures of expenditure booked in accounts assumed precedence over the bona fide and propriety of the expenditure.

Nobody could be held responsible for shortfall in performance, poor delivery of output, wanton abuse of the authority to misuse the funds provided for succor to the victims of calamity, economic upliftment of the poor Schedules Tribes, eradication of Malaria, *sheltering from the suffering of repeated droughts, etc.*

A critical understanding of the links between politicians, political parties and citizens is needed to appreciate the political reasons for the varying outcomes in the delivery of social services. In India (as in many other democracies), the linkage between citizens and politicians is based less on broad indicators and provision of collective goods such as economic growth and stability or national health care and more on the private or club goods available to individual citizens. This patronage based party voter linkages based on direct material inducements targeted to individuals and particular social groups are at the core of clientelist relations. The resulting clientelist accountability represents a transaction linking the direct exchange of a citizen's vote in return for direct payments or continuing access to employment goods and services. Clientelist citizen politician relations are distinctive in that benefits are targeted only to individuals or groups in exchange for electoral support. Thus the goods provided are either those that have excludability characteristics i.e. private goods (if rivalrous), such as housing or credit) or club good (if nonrivalrous) such as affirmative action benefits to specific social groups.

A Number of Interlinked Factors have Ensured the Vitality of Clientelist Politics in India

Increasing political competition together with a growth of identity politics (in turn the result of ethnocultural heterogeneity and a history of set-asides), and a first-past-the-post political system, has simply scaled up clientelist networks from local politics with personalistic face-toface relations to the national level of hierarchical political machines. The continued high degree of discretion in the enforcement of rules, whether land encroachment or loan repayment, further adds to the phenomena.

Under such conditions appealing to a narrow group of voters can be sufficient to win elections. High levels of poverty fuel clientelist linkages in that poor voters can be more easily bought over by the provision of immediately provisional goods (small amounts of cash, liquor, clothes) because of the higher discount rates of poor voters. In India's case, another intervening variable has been a shift in the structure of political parties with regional political parties gaining share at the expense of national political parties. For the latter holding power at the centre matters more, while the former, by definition, are state based. The division of constitutional responsibilities means that the regional and state based parties have little role in the provision of national collective goods, further increasing their incentives to provide private and club goods through the social policies that are within their constitutional mandate.

The prevalence of clientelist politics also helps understand the weakness from the *demand side*. A puzzle about Indian politics and social provisioning is why the poor have not articulated their demands more forcefully for better social services since they do express their voice when it comes to issues that bear on the "politics of dignity". In part this may be due to the inhibiting effects of social heterogeneity on building broad class-based coalitions. The selective provisioning of goods and services and enforcement of rules that are the hallmark of clientelist politics also reduce the incentives for collective action and mute voice.

A related puzzle stems from the acquiescence of state level politicians in the progressive centralisation of the financing of social programmes, given the general reluctance of central politicians to let go of the power of the purse. National electoral constituencies in India are large (with an average of almost a million voters) and in this case voter identification with political parties is relatively more salient than with individual legislator's. However, state electoral constituencies are much smaller and here voter identification with individual legislators is more powerful. In terms of popular political support or a mass electoral base, therefore, state legislators have an advantage. National legislators try to counterbalance by retaining control over financial allocations for social schemes. The rise of regional parties makes this dichotomy a little less sharp. To add to this, many states with strong regional parties like Tamil Nadu and Andhra Pradesh would prefer to see less transparent devolution and more centrally sponsored schemes since these favour states that have good absorption capacity in terms of execution capability and preparation of state level schemes for central funding.

Central schemes are also easier to manipulate, e.g., regional choice in the procurement operations of the Food Corporation of India is an administrative decision. Given that increased devolution will probably be more equalising and less performance based than is the case now, the transformation of central schemes into state devolutions may paradoxically leave better performing states with fewer resources than they currently have. Hence they have little incentives to press for a change in the status quo.

Corporate Social Responsibility in India

Corporate Social Responsibility (CSR) has been on the agenda in India for a considerable period. Most big Indian corporations are engaged in some CSR activities. As is the case in many countries, the private sector is generally more active in this area than the governmental/public sector. Several major CSR initiatives have been launched in India since the mid-1990s. Among these is the first voluntary code of corporate governance, *"Desirable Corporate Governance: A Code"*, established in April 1998. This was an initiative by the Confederation of Indian Industry (CII), India's largest industry and business association.

A *National Foundation for Corporate Governance* (NFCG) has been established by the Ministry of Corporate Affairs. This is a partnership with the Confederation of Indian Industry (CII), the Institute of Company Secretaries of India (ICSI) and the Institute of Chartered Accountants of India (ICAI). The purpose of the *National Foundation for Corporate Governance* is to promote better corporate governance practices and raise the standard of corporate governance in India towards achieving stability and growth.

Legislation authority in India is shared between the Central Government and the State Governments. Some laws, such as those regulating minimum wages, differ from state to state. Likewise, the implementation and supervision mechanisms may vary between states.

Child Labour and Right of Organization

India is member of the International Labour Organization, and has ratified 40 of the ILO conventions. However, India has not ratified four of the ILO core conventions:

- o 087 Freedom of Association and Protection of the Right to Organize (1948)
- o 098 Right to Organize and Collective Bargaining (1949)
- o 138 Minimum Age Convention (1973)
- o 182 Elimination of the Worst Forms of Child Labour (1999).

India's domestic law on child labour, *Child Labour (Prohibition and Regulation) Act* (1986), ban employment of children in some dangerous occupations, such as factories and mines, and regulate the working conditions in others. According to this law, anyone above the age of 14 will be regarded as an adult and will not protected by the child labour regulations.

According to UNICEF, insufficient attention has been given in India to eliminate the worst forms of child labour. The 1986 child labour law does not cover children in all sectors. India has the world's highest number of child labourers under years.

Labour Laws

India has altogether ratified 333 labour laws. The ways these laws are supervised and implemented, vary. Sub-contracts are common in India. One challenge is that 90% of the Indian labour is in the informal sector, which is not protected by the labour regulations.

Most Indian states have enforced an act for minimum wages for labourers in scheduled employment, as stipulated in the *Minimum Wage Act* from 1948. However, the minimum wage is often not paid. According to ILO, labour under minimum wage is considered a form of forced labour. According to ILO estimates, there are more than one million forced labourers in India, particularly in the southern part. Many of these are children.

India was in 1976 the first country in the South Asian region to enact legislation against bonded labour. Contract labour in India is another complex area. The contract workers do not get the same protection and benefits as permanent workers. Many work as contract labour for longer periods of time. Although the ILO Conventions related to forced Labour have been ratified, certain forms of bonded labour still persists, especially in the informal sector.

India has enacted legislation that prohibits discrimination due to gender, religion, ethnicity or caste. Again, the record of implementation is varied. ILO has observed some violations in India's implementation of the Discrimination (Employment and Occupation) Convention, (No 111, from 1958). This convention obligates the state parties to hinder discrimination due to e.g. caste or gender, such as different salary scales and labour conditions.

The Environment

The main law on environment and production is *The Environment (Protection) Act* (1986). This law gives the central government the authority to protect and improve environmental quality, as well as control and reduce pollution from all sources. The responsibility for environmental governance is shared between the corporations and the government. Many Indian institutions have come up with voluntary guidelines on environmental friendly practice. Among these is a partnership on voluntary pollution control, developed by the Indian Ministry of Environment and Forests together with the industrial sector. Other initiatives include the Energy Efficient Initiative by the Indian Chamber of Commerce, the Indian Ecomark and the Clean Technology initiative by the Confederation of Indian Industry and others.

With regard to the implementation of environmental laws, a challenge has been lack of knowledge on how to fulfil the laws in practice. There are also weaknesses in the implementation and control mechanisms, The budget and infrastructure for control has not been sufficient, although greatly improved over the last years.

Right to Information and Corruption

In the Transparency International Corruption Perceptions Index in 2008 in was ranked as number 85 out of 180 countries. The biggest problems were found in regards to politics and governance. According to a Global Compact report, there are low levels of government capacity for law enforcement and implementation in India, causing relatively high levels of corruption. *In 2005, Right to information (RTI) act* was established, This law gives the general public right to government information, and is meant to promote transparency and responsibility in the work of all governmental institutions.

The introduction of RTI has led to changes in the transparency regarding establishment and implementation of strategies, programmes and laws. It is also opening for access to information in areas where the authorities have left out important aspects, and give the public a possibly to require important information. RTI is additionally an important tool in regards to environmental management.

5

The Position of Women

Introductory Quotes

Various calls for women's freedom, liberation and equal rights have been heard all over the world, and many slogans have been coined for the marches. In some societies women have indeed lived under oppression, cruelty and injustice, and have been denied basic rights of humanity. Nor is it denied that some Muslims have deviated from the Islamic principles and teachings. Islamic law, on the other hand, has collected women's rights in a comprehensive and balanced system of human rights and obligations. Close examination of the slogans propagated by the international women's liberation movements show that they revolve around three elements: women's liberation, equal rights with men and women's rights. We will examine them in the light of Islamic law and teachings, regardless of the practices of some of the ignorant and deviant Muslims.

Firstly, the word "liberation" indicates that there are shackles, bonds and restrictions in place, and secondly, that women are enslaved and must be liberated. This is ambiguous and misleading since absolute liberty is impossible, regardless of whether they are men or women. Mankind is naturally restricted by the limitations of innate limited abilities, and necessities of social organization. Both men and women must live in a social environment under certain laws, rules and regulations that govern and organize the various affairs of life. Does that mean that man is not free and independent in his actions, or that he is clear from the responsibility of his deeds? Can anyone be free of natural limits and legal restrictions? If they are slaves, then the question becomes, to whom? Any so called freedom and liberty has natural and legal limits, which, if exceeded, will lead to destructive activities that all recognize as indecent, uncivilized and criminal.

Islamic law decreed that both men and women seek freedom and liberation from idolatry, tyranny, exploitation and injustice. The divinely revealed principles and laws teach and advocate strict monotheism, justice and noble morality. Within this framework men and women have inter-dependent and complementary roles. Islamic law granted women the right to deal in many affairs within the society directly, rather than dealing via a guardian. Women in Islam are officially responsible and in charge of running all their affairs whether economical, social or otherwise, as in many societies. For her protection and maintenance, her father, brother, uncle and husband-the stronger sex-are obligated and legally bound to guard her honour and maintain her sustenance and proper living circumstances according to their abilities, throughout the stages of her life. Is this demeaning her position, or elevating it? Islam has forbidden men and women equally from being indecent publicly, and this translates differently for the two sexes for natural reasons. All must protect virtue in private, and guard themselves in public.

Islamic law protects women from intimidation and molestation, and this demands that no one of either gender commit acts that are sexually provocative or enticing to the other. For this reason Islamic law requires modest clothing for her protection when going out of the home, and prohibits open ended free intermingling, and any type of physical touching of the other sex. Islam illustrates the concept of freedom and liberty in such a way that individual behaviour must not be harmful to the individual or destructive to the society at large, as graphically illustrated in the words of the Messenger of Allah when he said in an authentic tradition:

"The example of a person who observes the laws of Allah and the person who violates them are examples of two groups of people who gathered on a ship and decided to divide their places. One group received the upper deck as their lot, while the other group received the lower part of the ship. Whenever the people in the lower part needed water they had to pass through the people on the upper deck. The people in the lower part thought to themselves: If we drill a hole in our portion of the ship, we can have access to the water without disturbing the party on the upper deck.' If the group on the upper deck allows them execute their plan, all the people will be destroyed, and if they forbid them from doing so, they all will be safe" A well-known German thinker and philosopher, Schopenhauer said:

"Grant woman total and absolute freedom and liberty for One Year Only, and check with me after that to see the results of such freedom. Do not forget that you (all), along with me, will inherit virtues, chastity and good morals. If I die you are free to say either: "He was wrong!" or "He hit the heart of the truth!"

An American female reporter, Helesian Stansbery, who is syndicated in over 250 newspapers, worked in the area of journalism and broadcasting for over 20 years, and visited numerous Muslim countries had this to say at the end of one of her visits to a Muslim country:

"The Arab-Islamic society is wholesome and healthy. This society must continue to protect its traditions that restrict both its males and females to a certain and reasonable degree. This society definitely differs from the European and American societies. The Arab-Islamic society has its own traditions that impose certain restrictions and limitations on women and give special respect and status to parents... First and foremost, the most strict restrictions and limitations are on absolute sexual freedom that truly threatens both the society and the family in Europe and the United States of America. Therefore, the restrictions that are imposed by the Arab-Islamic society are valid and beneficial as well. I strongly recommend that you adhere to your traditions and code of ethics. Forbid coeducation. Restrict female freedom, or rather, return back to the full *'purdah'* (veiling) practices. Truly this is better for you than the sexual freedom of Europe and the United States of America. Forbid coeducation because we have suffered from it in the USA.

The American society has become sophisticated, full of all forms and terms of sexual freedom. The victims of sexual freedom and coeducation are filling the prisons, sidewalks, bars, taverns and whorehouses. The (false) freedom that we have granted to our young females and daughters has turned them to drugs, crime and white slavery. Coeducation, sexual freedom and all other types of "freedom" in the European and American societies have threatened the family and shaken moral values and ethics."

The question that poses itself to women's liberation advocates is: What is the truly the best, most beneficial and most protective system for the preservation of the honour, dignity and protection of women?

The worth of a civilization can be judged from the position that it gives to women. Of the several factors that justify the greatness of India's ancient culture, one of the greatest is the honoured place ascribed to women. Manu, the great law-giver, said long ago, 'where women are honoured there reside the gods'. According to ancient Hindu scriptures no religious rite can be performed with perfection by a man without the participation of his wife. Wife's participation is essential to any religious rite. Married men along with their wives are allowed to perform sacred rites on the occasion of various important festivals. Wives are thus befittingly called 'Ardhangani' (betterhalf). They are given not only important but equal position with men.

But in the later period the position of women went on deteriorating due to Muslim influence. During the Muslim period of history they were deprived of their rights of equality with men. They were compelled to keep themselves within the four walls of their houses with a long veil on their faces. This was definitely due to Islamic influence. Even today in some Islamic countries women are not allowed to go out freely. The conservative regimes of Iran and Pakistan, for example, have withdrawn the liberties given to women folk by the previous liberal governments. Even in India the Muslim women are far more backward than their Hindu, Christian and Sikh counterparts. The sight of Muslim women walking with long 'Burkas' (veils) on their person is not very rare. The women are, as a matter of fact, regarded as captive and saleable commodities in Muslim families. One man is allowed to have so many wives with the easiest provision of divorce. The husband can divorce a wife just by saying 'I divorce you' under the provision of Muslim laws. This is what the emperors did hundred years back and the men are doing it even now in almost all Islamic countries. Even in this last phase of the twentieth century rich and prosperous men of Islamic countries keep scores of wives in their harems. It was natural outcome of the Muslim subjugation of India that woman was relegated to a plaything of man, an ornament to decorate the drawing room. Serving, knitting, painting and music were her pastimes and cooking and cleaning her business.

In the wake of Raja Ram Mohan Roy's movement against women's subjugation to men and British influence on Indian culture and civilization the position of women had once again undergone a change. However, it was only under the enlightened leadership of Mahatma Gandhi that they re-asserted their equality with men. In response to the call of Gandhi they discarded their veil and came out of the four walls of their houses to fight the battle of freedom shoulder to shoulder with their brothers. The result is that the Indian Constitution today has given to women the equal status with men. There is no discrimination between men and women. All professions are open to both of them with merit as the only criterion of selection.

As a result of their newly gained freedom Indian woman have distinguished themselves in various spheres of life as politicians, orators, lawyers, doctors, administrators and diplomats. They are not only entrusted with work of responsibility but also they perform their duties very honestly and sincerely. There is hardly any sphere of life in which Indian women have not taken part and shown their worth. Women exercise their right to vote, contest for Parliament and Assembly, seek appointment in public office and compete in other spheres of life with men. This shows that women in India enjoy today more liberty and equality than before. They have acquired more liberty to participate in the affairs of the country. They have been given equality with men in shaping their future and sharing responsibilities for themselves, their family and their country.

It is a fact that women are intelligent, hard-working and efficient in work. They put heart and soul together in whatever they undertake. As typists and clerks they are now competing successfully with men. There are many women working in the Central Secretariat. They are striving very hard to reach highest efficiency and perfection in the administrative work. Their integrity of character is probably better than men. Generally it was found that women are less susceptible to corruption in form of bribery and favouritism. They are not only sweet tongued but also honest, efficient and punctual in their jobs as receptionists, air-hostesses and booking clerks at railway reservation counters. As a matter of fact they are gradually monopolising the jobs of receptionists and air-hostesses.

Another job in which Indian women are doing so well is that of teachers. In country like India where millions are groping in the darkness of illiteracy and ignorance efficient teaching to the children is most urgently needed. By virtue of their love and affection for the children the women have proved the best teachers in the primary and kindergarten schools. They can better understand the psychology of a child than the male teachers. Small children in the kindergarten schools get motherly affection from the lady teachers. It is probably significant that the Montessori system of education is being conducted mostly by the women in this country.

Women have been serving India admirably as doctors and nurses. Lady doctors have been found to perform efficient surgery by virtue of their soft and accurate fingers. They have monopolised as nurses in the hospitals and nursing homes. Very few men have been able to compete with them in this sphere because the women have natural tendency to serve and clean. It is thus natural tendency found in women which motivated Florence Nightingale to make nursing popular among the women of the upper classes in England and in Europe. She showed the way to women kind how nobly they can serve humanity in the hours of sufferings and agonies.

Women's contributions in politics and social services have also been quite significant. We cannot fail to mention the name of Indira Gandhi who shone so brilliantly and radiantly in the firmament of India's politics. She ruled this country for more than a decade and took India victorious out of Pakistan-war which resulted in the historic creation of a new country, Bangladesh. In the field of social service Indian women have also done some excellent jobs. They have not only served the cause of the suffering humanity but have also brought highest laurels for the country.

The name of Mother Teressa cannot but be mentioned. She brought the Nobel Prize for India by her selfless services to the poor, destitute and suffering people of our country in particular and the needy and handicapped people of the world in general. Today, we need the services of the educated women who can tour throughout the country and help in removing human sufferings. The Government is alarmed at the rapid growth of population in the rural areas in particular. Women volunteers can more easily take up the task of canvassing the advantages of family planning among the rural womenfolk. They can, more easily than men, carry on propaganda against hazards of unhygienic conditions under which the villagers live. In urban areas they can efficiently take up the task of visiting and teaching the orphans and the helpless widows in the orphanages and the widow welfare centres. They can train them in sewing, knitting, embroidery and nursing in which women by nature excel. They can also train them in the art of music and dancing.

But all this should not lead us to conclude that the women should look down upon domestic life. The main sphere of action for them who have not taken up jobs outside should be essentially a happy home which is their real kingdom and where their sweet manners and mature advices as wife, mother, sister and daughter make tremendous effects on the male members of the family. The progress of a nation depends upon the care and skill with which mothers rear up their children. The first and foremost duty of Indian women should, therefore, be to bring forth noble generations of patriots, warriors, scholars and statesmen. Since child's education starts even in the womb and the impressions are formed in the mind of a child while in mothers arms women have to play a role of vital importance. They have to feel and realise at every step of their life that they are builders of the fate of our nation since children grow mainly in mothers arms. They should also discourage their husbands and sons from indulging in bribery and other corrupt practices. This they can do only when they learn the art of simple living by discarding their natural desires for ornaments and a living of pomp and show. In many cases families have been running in deficit due to the extravagance of the housewives in maintaining a high standard of living. The result is that the earning male members of the family are forced to fill up the gap in the budget by corrupt practices. Corruption has been so far the greatest impediment in way to India's progress. Minus corruption India would have been one of the most developed nations of the world.

There is no denying the fact that women in India have made a considerable progress in the last fifty years but yet they have to struggle against many handicaps and social evils in the male dominated society.

The Hindu Code Bill has given the daughter and the son equal share of the property. The Marriage Act no longer regards woman as the property of man. Marriage is now considered to be a personal affair and if a partner feels dissatisfied she or he has the right of divorce. But passing of law is one thing and its absorption in the collective thinking of society is quite a different matter. In order to prove themselves equal to the dignity and status given to them in the Indian Constitution they have to shake off the shackles of slavery and superstitions. They should help the government and the society in eradicating the evils of dowry, illiteracy and ignorance among the eves.

The dowry problem has assumed a dangerous form in this country. The parents of the girls have to pay thousands and lacs to the bridegrooms and their greedy fathers and mothers. If promised articles are not given by the parents of brides, the cruel and greedy members of the bridegrooms' family take recourse to afflicting tortures on the married women. Some women are murdered in such cases.

The dowry deaths are really heinous and barbarous crimes committed by the cruel and inhumane persons. The young girls should be bold enough in not marrying the boys who demand dowry through their parents. The boys should also refuse to marry if their parents demand dowry.

But unfortunately the number of such bold and conscientious boys is very few. Even the doctors, engineers, teachers and the administrative officers do not hesitate in allowing themselves to be sold to the wealthy fathers of shy and timid girls. Such persons have really brought disgrace to their cadres in particular and society in general. The government should enact stringent laws to afflict rigorous punishment on dowry seekers, women's murderers and rapers.

Ancient India

Scholars believe that in ancient India, the women enjoyed equal status with men in all fields of life. However, some others hold contrasting views. Works by ancient Indian grammarians such as Patanjali and Katyayana suggest that women were educated in the early Vedic period Rigvedic verses suggest that the women married at a mature age and were probably free to select their husband. Scriptures such as Rig Veda and Upanishads mention several women sages and seers, notably Gargi and Maitreyi.

Some kingdoms in the ancient India had traditions such as *nagarvadhu* ("bride of the city"). Women competed to win the coveted title of the *nagarvadhu*. Amrapali is the most famous example of a nagarvadhu.

According to studies, women enjoyed equal status and rights during the early Vedic period. However, later (approximately 500 B.C.), the status of women began to decline with the Smritis (esp. Manusmriti) and with the Islamic invasion of Babur and the Mughal empire and later Christianity curtailing women's freedom and rights.

Although reformatory movements such as Jainism allowed women to be admitted to the religious order, by and large, the women in India faced confinement and restrictions. The practice of child marriages is believed to have started from around sixth century.

Medieval Period

The Indian woman's position in the society further deteriorated during the medieval period when Sati, child marriages and a ban on widow remarriages became part of social life in India. The Muslim conquest in the Indian subcontinent brought the purdah practice in the Indian society. Among the Rajputs of Rajasthan, the Jauhar was practised. In some parts of India, the Devadasis or the temple women were sexually exploited. Polygamy was widely practised esp. among Hindu Kshatriya rulers. In many Muslim families, women were restricted to Zenana areas.

In spite of these conditions, some women execeled in the fields of politics, literature, education and religion. Razia Sultana became the only woman monarch to have ever ruled Delhi. The

Gond queen Durgavati ruled for fifteen years, before she lost her life in a battle with Mughal emperor Akbar's general Asaf Khan in 1564. Chand Bibi defended Ahmednagar against the mighty Mughal forces of Akbar in 1590s. Jehangir's wife Nur Jehan effectively wielded imperial power and was recognized as the real force behind the Mughal throne. The Mughal princesses Jahanara and Zebunnissa were well-known poets, and also influenced the ruling administration Shivaji's mother, Jijabai was deputed as queen regent, because of her ability as a warrior and an administrator. In South India, many women administered villages, towns, divisions and heralded social and religious institutions.

The Bhakti movements tried to restore women's status and questioned some of the forms of oppression. Mirabai, a female saint-poet, was one of the most important Bhakti movement figures. Some other female saint-poets from this period include Akka Mahadevi, Rami Janabai and Lal Ded. Bhakti sects within Hinduism such as the Mahanubhav, Varkari and many others were principle movements within the Hindu fold to openly advocate social justice and equality between men and women.

Shortly after the Bhakti movement, Guru Nanak, the first Guru of Sikhs also preached the message of equality between men and women. He advocated that women be allowed to lead religious assemblies; to perform and lead congregational hymn singing called Kirtan or Bhajan; become members of religious management committees; to lead armies on the battlefield; have equality in marriage, and equality in Amrit (Baptism). Other Sikh Gurus also preached against the discrimination against women.

Historical Practices

Traditions such as sati, jauhar, and devadasi have been banned and are largely defunct in modern India. However, some cases of these practices are still found in remote parts of India. The purdah is still practiced by many Indian women, and child marriage remains prevalent despite it being an illegal practice, especially under current Indian laws.

Sati : Sati is an old, largely defunct custom, in which the widow was immolated alive on her husband's funeral pyre. Although the act was supposed to be a voluntary on the widow's part, it is believed to have been sometimes forced on the widow. It was abolished by the British in 1829. There have been around forty reported cases of sati since independence. In 1987, the Roop Kanwar case of Rajasthan led to The Commission of Sati (Prevention) Act.

Jauhar : Jauhar refers to the practice of the voluntary immolation of all the wives and daughters of defeated warriors, in order to avoid capture and consequent molestation by the enemy. The practice was followed by the wives of defeated Rajput rulers, who are known to place a high premium on honour.

Purdah : Purdah is the practice of requiring women to cover their bodies so as to cover their skin and conceal their form. It imposes restrictions on the mobility of women, it curtails their right to interact freely and it is a symbol of the subordination of women. It does not reflect the religious teachings of either Hinduism or Islam, contrary to common belief, although misconception has occurred due to the ignorance and prejudices of religious leaders of both faiths.

Devadasis : Devadasi is a religious practice in some parts of southern India, in which women are "married" to a deity or temple. The ritual was well established by the 10th century A.D. In the later period, the illegitimate sexual exploitation of the devadasi's became a norm in some parts of India.

British Rule

European scholars observed in the 19th century Hindu women are "naturally chaste" and "more virtuous" than other women. During the British Raj, many reformers such as Ram Mohan Roy, Ishwar Chandra Vidyasagar, Jyotirao Phule etc... fought for the upliftment of women. While this list might suggest that there was no positive British contribution during the Raj era, that is not entirely so, since missionaries' wives like Martha Maultnee Mead and her daughter Eliza Caldwell Mault are rightly remembered for pioneering the education and training of girls in south India-a practise that initially met with local resistance, as it flew in the face of tradition. Raja Rammohan Roy's efforts led to the abolition of the Sati practice under Governor-General William Cavendish-Bentinck in 1829. Ishwar Chandra Vidyasagar's crusade for the improvement in condition of widows led to the Widow Remarriage Act of 1856. Many women reformers such as Pandita Ramabai also helped the cause of women upliftment.

Kittur Chennamma, the queen of the princely state Kittur in Karnataka, led an armed rebellion against the British in response to the Doctrine of lapse. Abbakka Rani the queen of coastal Karnataka led the defence against invading European armies notably the Portugese in 16th century. Rani Lakshmi Bai, the Queen of Jhansi, led the Indian Rebellion of 1857 against the British. She is now widely considered as a nationalist hero. Begum Hazrat Mahal, the co-ruler of Awadh, was another ruler who led the revolt of 1857. She refused the deals with the British and later retreated to Nepal. The Begums of Bhopal were also few of the notable female rulers during this period. They did not observe purdah and were trained in martial arts. Chandramukhi Basu, Kadambini Ganguly and Anandi Gopal Joshi were few of the earliest Indian women to obtain educational degrees.

In 1917, the first women's delegation met the Secretary of State to demand women's political rights, supported by the Indian National Congress. The All India Women's Education Conference was held in Pune in 1927. In 1929, the Child Marriage Restraint Act was passed, stipulating fourteen as the minimum age of marriage for a girl through the efforts of Mahomed Ali Jinnah. Though Mahatma Gandhi himself married at the age of thirteen, he later urged people to boycott child marriages and called upon the young men to marry the child widows.

Women played an important part in India's independence struggle. Some of the famous freedom fighters include Bhikaji Cama, Dr. Annie Besant, Pritilata Waddedar, Vijayalakshmi Pandit, Rajkumari Amrit Kaur, Anjali Ammal, Aruna Asaf Ali, Sucheta Kriplani and Kasturba Gandhi. Other notable names include Muthulakshmi Reddy, Durgabai Deshmukh etc... The Rani of Jhansi Regiment of Subhash Chandra Bose's Indian National Army consisted entirely of women including Captain Lakshmi Sahgal. Sarojini Naidu, a poet and a freedom fighter, was the first Indian woman to become the President of the Indian National Congress and the first woman to become the governor of a state in India.

Independent India

Women in India now participate in all activities such as education, politics, media, art and culture, service sectors, science and technology, etc...

The Constitution of India guarantees to all Indian women equality, no discrimination by the State (Article 15(1)), equality of opportunity (Article 16), equal pay for equal work. In addition, it allows special provisions to be made by the State in favour of women and children, renounces practices derogatory to the dignity of women, and also allows for provisions to be made by the State for securing just and humane conditions of work and for maternity relief..

The feminist activism in India picked up momentum during later 1970s. One of the first national level issues that brought the women's groups together was the Mathura rape case. The acquittal of policemen accused of raping a young girl Mathura in a police station, led to a wide-scale protests in 1979–1980. The protests were widely covered in the national media, and forced the Government to amend the Evidence Act, the Criminal Procedure Code and the Indian Penal Code and introduce the category of custodial rape. Female activists united over issues such as female infanticide, gender bias, women health, and female literacy.

Since alcoholism is often associated with violence against women in India, many women groups launched anti-liquor campaigns in Andhra Pradesh, Himachal Pradesh, Haryana, Orissa, Madhya Pradesh and other states. Many Indian Muslim women have questioned the fundamental leaders' interpretation of women's rights under the Shariat law and have criticized the triple talaq system.

In 1990s, grants from foreign donor agencies enabled the formation of new women-oriented NGOs. Self-help groups and NGOs such as Self Employed Women's Association (SEWA) have played a major role in women's rights in India. Many women have emerged as leaders of local movements. For example, Medha Patkar of the Narmada Bachao Andolan.

The Government of India declared 2001 as the Year of Women's Empowerment (*Swashakti*). The National Policy For The

Empowerment Of Women came was passed in 2001. In 2006, the case of a Muslim rape victim called Imrana was highlighted in the media. Imrana was raped by her father-in-law. The pronouncement of some Muslim clerics that Imrana should marry her father-in-law led to widespread protests and finally Imrana's father-in-law was given a prison term of 10 years, The verdict was welcomed by many women's groups and the All India Muslim Personal Law Board.

Culture

Sari (a single piece of a long cloth wound around the body) and salwar kameez are worn by women all over India. *Bindi* is part of the women's make-up. Traditionally, the red bindi (or sindhur) was worn only by the married Hindu women, but now it has become a part of women's fashion.

Education and Economic Development

According to 1992-93 figures, only 9.2% of the households in India were female-headed. However, approximately 35% of the households below the poverty line were found to be female-headed.

Education

Though it is gradually rising, the female literacy rate in India is lower than the male literacy rate. Compared to boys, far fewer girls are enrolled in the schools, and many of them drop out. According to the National Sample Survey Data of 1997, only the states of Kerala and Mizoram have approached universal female literacy rates. According to majority of the scholars, the major factor behind the improved social and economic status of women in Kerala is literacy.

Under Non-Formal Education programme, about 40% of the Centres in states and 10% of the Centres in UTs are exclusively reserved for females. As of 2000, about 0.3 million NFE Centres were catering to about 7.42 million children, out of which about 0.12 million were exclusively for girls. In urban India, girls are nearly at par with the boys in terms of education. However, in rural India girls continue to be less educated than the boys.

According to a 1998 report by U.S. Department of Commerce, the chief barrier to female education in India are inadequate school facilities (such as sanitary facilities), shortage of female teachers and gender bias in curriculum (majority of the female characters being depicted as weak and helpless).

Work Force Participation

Contrary to the common perception, a large percent of women in India work. The National data collection agencies accept the fact that there is a serious under-estimation of women's contribution as workers. However, there are far fewer women in the paid work force than there are men. In urban India Women have impressive number in the work force. As an example at software industry 30% of the work force is female. They are at par with their male counter parts in terms of wages, position at the work place.

In rural India, agriculture and allied industrial sectors employ as much as 89.5% of the total female labour. In overall farm production, women's average contribution is estimated at 55% to 66% of the total labour. According to a 1991 World Bank report, women accounted for 94% of total employment in dairy production in India. Women constitute 51% of the total employed in forest-based small-scale enterprises.

One of the most famous female business success stories is the Shri Mahila Griha Udyog Lijjat Papad. In 2006, Kiran Mazumdar-Shaw, who started Biocon-one of India's first biotech companies, was rated India's richest woman. Lalita Gupte and Kalpana Morparia (both were the only businesswomen in India who made the list of the Forbes World's Most Powerful Women), run India's second-largest bank, ICICI Bank.

Land and Property Rights

In most Indian families, women do not own any property in their own names, and do not get a share of parental property. Due to weak enforcement of laws protecting them, women continue to have little access to land and property. In fact, some of the laws discriminate against women, when it comes to land and property rights.

The Hindu personal laws of mid-1956s (applied to Hindus, Buddhists, Sikhs and Jains) gave women rights to inheritance. However, the sons had an independent share in the ancestral property, while the daughters' shares were based on the share received by their father. Hence, a father could effectively disinherit a daughter by renouncing his share of the ancestral property, but the son will continue to have a share in his own right. Additionally, married daughters, even those facing marital harassment, had no residential rights in the ancestral home. After amendment of Hindu laws in 2005, now women in have been provided the same status as that of men.

In 1986, the Supreme Court of India ruled that Shah Bano, an old divorced Muslim woman was eligible for maintenance money. However, the decision was vociferously opposed by fundamentalist Muslim leaders, who alleged that the court was interfering in their personal law. The Union Government subsequently passed the Muslim Women's (Protection of Rights Upon Divorce) Act.

Similarly, the Christian women have struggled over years for equal rights of divorce and succession. In 1994, all the churches, jointly with women's organisations, drew up a draft law called the Christian Marriage and Matrimonial Causes Bill. However, the government has still not amended the relevant laws.

Crimes Against Women

Police records show high incidence of crimes against women in India. The National Crime Records Bureau reported in 1998 that the growth rate of crimes against women would be higher than the population growth rate by 2010. Earlier, many cases were not registered with the police due to the social stigma attached to rape and molestation cases. Official statistics show that there has been a dramatic increase in the number of reported crimes against women.

Sexual Harassment

Half of the total number of crimes against women reported in 1990 related to molestation and harassment at the work place. Eve teasing is a euphemism used for sexual harassment or molestation of women by men. Many activists blame the rising incidents of sexual harassment against women on the influence of "Western culture". In 1987, The Indecent Representation of Women (Prohibition) Act was passed to prohibit indecent representation of women through advertisements or in publications, writings, paintings, figures or in any other manner.

In 1997, in a landmark judgement, the Supreme Court of India took a strong stand against sexual harassment of women in the workplace. The Court also laid down detailed guidelines for prevention and redressal of grievances. The National Commission for Women subsequently elaborated these guidelines into a Code of Conduct for employers.

Dowry

In 1961, the Government of India passed the Dowry Prohibition Act, making the dowry demands in wedding arrangements illegal. However, many cases of dowry-related domestic violence, suicides and murders have been reported. In the 1980s, numerous such cases were reported.

In 1985, the Dowry Prohibition (maintenance of lists of presents to the bride and bridegroom) rules were framed. According to these rules, a signed list of presents given at the time of the marriage to the bride and the bridegroom should be maintained. The list should contain a brief description of each present, its approximate value, the name of whoever has given the present and his/her relationship to the person. However, such rules are hardly enforced.

A 1997 report claimed that at least 5,000 women die each year because of dowry deaths, and at least a dozen die each day in 'kitchen fires' thought to be intentional. The term for this is "bride burning" and is criticized within India itself. Amongst the urban educated, such dowry abuse has reduced considerably.

Child Marriage

Child marriage has been traditionally prevalent in India and continues to this day. Historically, young girls would live with their parents till they reached puberty. In the past, the child widows were condemned to a life of great agony, shaving heads, living in isolation, and shunned by the society. Although child marriage was outlawed in 1860, it is still a common practice.

According to UNICEF's "State of the World's Children-2009" report, 47% of India's women aged 20–24 were married before the legal age of 18, with 56% in rural areas. The report also showed that 40% of the world's child marriages occur in India.

Female Infanticides and Sex Selective Abortions

India has a highly masculine sex ratio, the chief reason being that many women die before reaching adulthood. Tribal societies in India have a less masculine sex ratio than all other caste groups. This, in spite of the fact that tribal communities have far lower levels of income, literacy and health facilities. It is therefore suggested by many experts, that the highly masculine sex ratio in India can be attributed to female infanticides and sex-selective abortions.

All medical tests that can be used to determine the sex of the child have been banned in India, due to incidents of these tests being used to get rid of unwanted female children before birth. Female infanticide (killing of girl infants) is still prevalent in some rural areas. The abuse of the dowry tradition has been one of the main reasons for sex-selective abortions and female infanticides in India.

As of March 2001, the female population stands at 495.4 million out of total 1,028 million Indian population. Thus, in the present population of 1.03 billion, there ought to be 528 million women. Instead, estimates show only 496 million women in the population today. This implies that there are some 32 million "missing" women in India. Some are never born, and the rest die because they do not have the opportunity to survive. Sex-ratio (number of female per 1,000 male) is an important indicator of women's status in the society. In 1901 there were 972 females per 1,000 males, while by 1971; the ratio has come down to 930 females per 1,000 males. In 1981 there has been only a nominal increase in the female sex ratio within 934 females to 1,000 males. There were only 926 females per 1000 males in India according to 1991 census.

The 2001 census indicate that the trend has been slightly arrested with the sex ratio at 933 females per 1000 males, with Kerala at 1058 females. The sex ratio of the 0-6 age group has declined sharply from 945 in 1991 to 927 in 2001. According to UNFPA State of world population 2005, Punjab (793), Haryana (820), Delhi (865), Gujarat (878) and Himachal Pradesh (897) have worst child sex ratio. Scheduled Tribes have fairly respectable CSR of 973 but that falls for Scheduled Castes it falls at 938. For non SC/St. population it stands at 917. Rural India has 934 per 1000 and for urban India it stands at 908. In most states least literate districts have superior CSR compared to their most literate counterparts.

One reason for the adverse juvenile sex ratio is the increasing reluctance to have female children. For women the literacy rate stands at 54.16 percent. Still, 245 million Indian women cannot read or write, comprising the world's largest number of unlettered women. National averages in literacy conceal wide disparities. For instance, while 95 percent of women in Mizoram are literate, only 34 percent of women in Bihar can read and write. The average Indian female has only 1.2 years of schooling, while the Indian male spends 3.5 years in school. More than 50 percent girls drop out by the time they are in middle school. Similarly, life expectancy has increased for both the sexes; it has increased to 64.9 years for women and 63 years for men according to UN Statistic Division (2000). The Working women population has risen from 13% in 1987 to 25% in 2001.

However the UNFPA State of World Population 2005 states that about 70% of graduate Indian women are unemployed. Women constitute 90 percent of the total marginal workers of the country. Rural women engaged in agriculture form 78 percent of all women in regular work. They are a third of all workers on the land. The traditional gender division of labour ensures that these women get on average 30 percent lower wages than men. The total employment of women in organized sector is only 4 percent. Although industrial production increased in the 1980s; jobs in factories and establishments — or non-household jobs — stagnated at eight percent of the work force. Increasingly, companies tend to rely on out sourcing, using cheap labour. It is well known that women and children work in huge numbers in bidi-rolling, agarbatti-rolling, bangle making, weaving, brassware, leather, crafts and other industries. Yet, only 3 percent of these women are recorded as labourers. They are forced to work for pitiable wages and are denied all social security benefits. A study by SEWA of 14 trades found that 85 percent of women earned only 50 percent of the official poverty level income.

Indian women enjoy a low status in their households because family decisions relating to finances, kinship relations, selection of life partner are made by the male members and women are rarely consulted. Although there has been an expansion in health facilities maternal mortality rate continue to be high at 407 per 1, 00,000 live births (1998). WHO estimates show that out of the 529,000 maternal deaths globally each year,136,000 (25.7%) are contributed by India. A factor that contributes to India's high maternal mortality rate is the reluctance to seek medical care for pregnancy-it is viewed as a temporary condition that will disappear. The estimates nationwide are that only 40-50 percent of women receive any antenatal care. Evidence from the states of Bihar, Rajasthan, Orissa, Uttar Pradesh, Maharashtra and Gujarat find registration for maternal and child health services to be as low as 5-22 percent in rural areas and 21-51 percent in urban areas. Even a woman who has had difficulties with previous pregnancies is usually treated with home remedies only for three reasons: the decision that pregnant women seek help rests with the mother-in-law and husband; financial considerations; and fear that the treatment may be more harmful than the malady.

Domestic Violence

The incidents of domestic violence are higher among the lower Socio-Economic Classes (SECs). The Protection of Women from Domestic Violence Act, 2005 came into force on October 26, 2006.

Trafficking

The Immoral Traffic (Prevention) Act was passed in 1956. However many cases of trafficking of young girls and women have been reported. These women are either forced into prostitution, domestic work or child labour.

Other Concerns

Health : The average female life expectancy today in India is low compared to many countries, but it has shown gradual improvement over the years. In many families, especially rural ones, the girls and women face nutritional discrimination within the family, and are anaemic and malnourished.

The maternal mortality in India is the second highest in the world. Only 42% of births in the country are supervised by health professionals. Most women deliver with help from women in the family who often lack the skills and resources to save the mother's life if it is in danger. According to UNDP Human Development Report (1997), 88% of pregnant women (age 15-49) were found to be suffering from anemia.

Family planning : The average woman in rural areas of India has little or no control over her re-productivity. Women, particularly women in rural areas, do not have access to safe and self-controlled methods of contraception. The public health system emphasises permanent methods like sterilisation, or long-term methods like IUDs that do not need follow-up. Sterilization accounts for more than 75% of total contraception, with female sterilisation accounting for almost 95% of all sterilisations.

Notable Indian Women

Arts and Entertainment

Singers and vocalists such as M.S. Subbulakshmi, Gangubai Hangal, Lata Mangeshkar and Asha Bhosle are widely revered in India. Many actresses such as Aishwarya Rai. Anjolie Ela Menon is a famous painter.

Sports

Although the general sports scenario in India is not very good, some Indian women have made notable achievements in the field. Some of the famous female sportspersons in Indian include P. T. Usha, J. J. Shobha (athletics), Kunjarani Devi (weightlifting), Diana Edulji (cricket), Saina Nehwal (badminton), Koneru Hampi (chess) and Sania Mirza (tennis). Karnam Malleswari (weightlifter), is the only Indian woman to have won an Olympic medal (Bronze medal in 2000).

Politics

Through the Panchayat Raj institutions, over a million women have actively entered political life in India. As per the 73rd and 74th Constitutional Amendment Acts, all local elected bodies reserve one-third of their seats for women. Although the percentages of women in various levels of political activity has risen considerably, women are still under-represented in governance and decision making positions.

Some of the notable women leaders in India include Indira Gandhi, Sushma Swaraj, Vasundhara Raje Scindia, Sheila Dikshit,

Jayalalitha, Uma Bharati, Mayawati, Mamata Banerjee Sindhu Joyand Sonia Gandhi. On July 25, 2007 the country's ever first woman president Pratibha Patil was sworn in.

Literature

Sudha Murthy, Sarojini Naidu, Chandabai, Subhadra Kumari Chauhan, Mahadevi Varma, Shivani, Anita Desai, Arundhati Roy, Shashi Deshpande, Shobha De, Kiran Desai, Jhumpa Lahiri, etc... are some of the notable female Indian authors.

Religion

Mata Amritanandamayi, Mother Meera, Mate Mahadevi.

Other Fields

Shahnaz Husain is one of the popular Indian beauticians and entrepreneur. Mirudhubashini Govindarajan is a women's healthcare specialist.

Status of Indian Women and the Role of Legislation

In Indian society the status of women has changed from time to time; position of women in society is the index to the standard of social organization.We can divide the past [history] in to three phases to analyse the status of women. They are: ancient India, Medival India and Modern Indian period.

In ancient India women enjoyed equal status with man in all fields of life, she received the same education like man, many Hindu religious books like Vedas, Upanishads, Ramayana, Mahabharata have mentioned the names of several women who were great scholars, poets, philosophers of the time. The wife was 'Ardhangini' which means she is half of her husband. An unmarried man was considered to be incomplete man. All religious ceremonies were performed by the husband along with the wife. This shows the importance given to the women in ancient period.

But in the Medival period, the status of women went down considerably. She was considered to be inferior to man. Any historians have called this age as the 'dark age'. Her position became very miserable. Decline in the status of women in Indian society begins with the muslims rule in India: customs of pardha, sati, child marriage & restrictions on widow marriage are prevalence of joint family system have been the factors responsible for the injustice done towards women. The position of women in modern India has changed considerably. Her position in modern Indian society is equal to that of men, socially, economically, educationally, politically & legally. Her sufferings from Sati, Child marriage, Institution of Temple prostitution are no longer existing.

Now, she has the right to receive education, inherit & own property, participate in public life & political life of the nation. She has become economically independent. She can seek employment anywhere and remains not a domestic slave. So, she is certainly enjoying the equal status with man in all respect.

For this change in the status of women several factors like women's education, reform movements by many social reformers, women participation in politics and many social legislation are held responsible.

Role of Legislation

Today Indian womanhood is marching towards liberty and equality. For this march towards liberty and equality, various social legislation passed from time to time are mainly responsible. This legislation aimed at eradication of social evils. Following are the significant enactment, which helped in bringing about the change:

The Hindu Widow Re-marriage Act of 1856: In the traditions Hindu society there was a ban on widow remarriage. Ban on widow remarriage was one of the most important evils from which women in the traditional Hindu society suffered a lot. This Act allowed widows to remarry and section 5 of this Act ensured her to enjoy all the rights which a married woman did.

The Child Marriage Restraint Act of 1929: The practice of child marriage was another social evil from which woman in traditional Hindu society suffered a lot. Age at marriage for girls was 9 or 10 and after passing this Act the minimum marriageable age of women was fixed to 15 years. Later it was increased to 18 years.

The Hindu Womens Right to Property Act Of 1937: In traditional society women had no property right. In the eyes of law she was miner or ward. This Act recognized a widow of a deceased person as his surviving personality with the same right as his in the joint property. Thus through this Act women in the Hindu society received the property right to a limited extent.

The Hindu Marriage Act of 1955: This Act has recognized the equal rights of man and woman in the matters of marriage and divorce. Under the provision of this Act either the man or woman can present a petition in a court of law for divorce, wife has got an equal right to divorce her husband as he can do.

The Hindu Succession Act of 1956: This Act recognized an equal right for women in the matter of inheritance of property. She can inherit the property of father along with her brothers. She can also sell or mortgage the inherited property or use it for herself. For the first time absolute ownership was conferred to a woman by this Act.

The Suppression of Immoral Traffic in Women and Girls Act of 1956-57: This Act aims to deal with the problem of prostitution and to promote the welfare of fallen women. Main objectives of this Act are to reduce the scope of prostitution and to reform the prostitution under this Act. Every state is expected to set up protective homes and to appoint women police and women social workers. In protective homes these fallen women will be given training in tailoring, toy and basket making and other crafts so that they may earn for their maintenance in a proper way.

The Dowry Prohibition Act of 1961: The main objective of this Act is to abolish giving and taking dowry at the time of marriage. The term dowry refers to a valuable property or thing which is determined by the parties to a marriage for a marriage. The practice of dowry had produced very bad effects. Dowry has become a social evil. Even though this Act prohibits dowry system, the dowry cases have not been reduced. Still this Act makes some effort in bringing social change.

Above mentioned are the important legislations which brought upward trend in the status of women in India. Today what women are enjoying their status is because of legislations. She is protected in every way of life. Thanks to legislations, women in India are gaining better status, recognition and respect.

6

War and Social Policy

How Does War Effect and Change People

On the battlefield soldiers are seen fighting bravely for their countries. The machine guns blast and the cannons boom, lives are lost and battles won. Finally, when the dust settles and the battle seems to be over, for some, it is just the beginning. The war which is fought in the minds of people affected by it lasts a lifetime, and its effects stretc..h far beyond just the battlefield which it is fought.

For example, in the story "Ambush", by Tim O'Brien, the author is writing the story as a sign of his guilt for a man he killed in war. He is ashamed of his actions, and will forever live in guilt. No matter how hard he tries to forget it, it will always be there; lingering in the back of his mind. Near the end of the story he states, "Even now I haven't finished sorting it out." (Ambush, 1224), and, "In the ordinary hours of life I try not to dwell on it, but now and then, when I'm reading a newspaper or just sitting alone in a room, I'll look up and see the young man coming out of the morning fog." (Ambush, 1224). This event will always remain in O'Brien's mind, and affect him for the rest of his life.

Nearly all combatants who have fought in a war are said to come back changed. They become very quiet, and reserved. "Why Soldiers Don't Talk", written by John Steinbeck, explains in detail some psychological effects of war, and why people become this way. Steinbeck says that many individuals who fight in war return in these quiet states of mind because they usually are very ashamed of what they did, or they simply just do not remember it all. The memories that battles and wars leave behind will never be forgotten by the people who lived through, or fought in the war, but will many times also not be told.

People must also remember that these memories and feelings do not only stay with the fighters of the war who experienced it first hand, but many families are greatly affected also.

Home Front During World War II

The home front is the name given to the activities of the civilians when their nation is at war. Since World War II could be described as total war, homeland production became even more invaluable to both the Allied and Axis powers. Life on the home front during World War II was a significant part of the war effort for all participants and had a major impact on the outcome of the war. During the war, Government became involved with their respective home fronts to educate them on how to protect themselves, their country, and aid the war effort. Nations routinely used propaganda to influence the civilian population. Frequently, women were needed to work during this period because the men were at war.

Jews in Warsaw Ghetto: 1943

On September 1, 1939, Germany invaded Poland, conquering it in three weeks, as the Soviets invaded the eastern areas. During the German occupation, there were two distinct civilian uprisings in Warsaw, one in 1943, the other in 1944. The first took place in an entity, less than two square miles in area, which the Germans carved out of the city and called "Ghetto Warschau." Into the thus created Ghetto, around which they built high walls, the Germans crowded 550,000 Polish Jews, many from the Polish provinces. At first, people were able to go in and out of the Ghetto, but soon the Ghetto's border became an "iron curtain." Unless on official business, Jews could not leave it, and non-Jews, including Germans, could not enter.

Entry points were guarded by German soldiers. Because of extreme conditions and hunger, mortality in the Ghetto was high. Additionally, in 1942, the Germans moved 400,000 to Treblinka where they were gassed on arrival. When, on April 19, 1943, the Ghetto Uprising commenced, the population of the Ghetto had dwindled to 60,000 individuals. In the following three weeks, virtually all died as the Germans fought to put down the uprising and systematically destroyed the buildings in the Ghetto.

Warsaw Uprising of 1944

The uprising by Poles began on August 1, 1944 when the Polish underground, the "Home Army," aware that the Soviet Army had reached the eastern bank of the Vistula, sought to liberate Warsaw much as the French resistance had liberated Paris a few weeks earlier. Stalin had his own group of Communist leaders for the new Poland and did not want the Home Army or its Catholic leaders (based in London) to control Warsaw. So he halted the Soviet offensive and gave the Germans free rein to suppress it. During the ensuing 63 days, 250,000 Poles of the Home Army surrendered to the Germans. After the Germans forced all the surviving population to leave the city, Hitler ordered that any buildings left standing be dynamited and 98% of buildings in Warsaw were destroyed.

France

The UK's total mobilization during this period proved to be successful in helping topple the Axis Powers, but carried a steep cost postwar. Public opinion strongly supported the war, and the level of sacrifice was high. The war was a "people's war" that enlarged democratic aspirations and produced promises of a postwar welfare state.

Munitions

In mid-1940, the R.A.F. was called on to fight the Battle of Britain but it had suffered serious losses. It lost 458 aircraft—more than current production—in France and was hard pressed. The government decided to concentrate on only five types of aircraft in order to optimize output. They were Wellingtons, Whitley V's, Blenheims, Hurricanes, and Spitfires. They received extraordinary priority. Covering the supply of materials and equipment and even made it possible to divert from other types the necessary parts, equipments, materials and manufacturing resources. Labour was moved from other aircraft work to factories engaged on the specified types. Cost was not an object. The delivery of new fighters rose from 256 in April to 467 in September—more than enough to cover the losses—and Fighter Command emerged triumphantly from the Battle of Britain in October with more aircraft than it had possessed at the beginning.

Rationing

Food, clothing, petrol, leather and other such items were rationed. However, items such as sweets and fruits were not rationed, as they would spoil. Access to luxuries was severely restricted, though there was also a significant black market. Families also grew victory gardens, and small home vegetable gardens, to supply themselves with food. Many things were conserved to turn into weapons later, such as fat for nitroglycerin production. People in the countryside was less affected by rationing as they had greater access to locally sourced unrationed products than people in metropolitan areas and were more able to grow their own.

Evacuation

From very early in the war, it was thought that the major industrial cities of Britain, especially London in the south east, would come under Nazi German Luftwaffe air attack, which did happen with The Blitz. Some children were sent to Canada, the USA and Australia and millions of children and some mothers were evacuated from London and other major cities when the war began under government plans for Evacuations of civilians in Britain during World War II, but they often filtered back. When the Blitz bombing began in September 1940, they evacuated again. The discovery of the poor health and hygiene of evacuees was a shock to many Britons, and helped prepare the way for the Beveridge Report. Children were evacuated if their parents agreed but in some cases they did not have a choice. The children were only allowed to take a few things with them, including a gas mask, books, money, clothes, ration book and some small toys.

Canada

Canada joined the war efforts on September 10, 1939. This was a week after Britain joined because of the Statute of Westminster, which meant Canada had to vote before entering a war. With the war going on in Europe and Asia, Canada didn't have any major problems in building supplies for the war other than switching factories to make war equipment. Many factories were set up which helped increase the employment rate. More or less out of range of Axis attacks, Canada became one of the largest trainers of pilots for the Allies. Many Canadian men joined the war efforts, so with the men overseas and industries pushing to increase production, women took up positions to aid in the war effort.

Women

At this time of war many supplies were needed and there was a low supply of goods. Women took the initiative to recycle and salvage in order to come up with needed supplies. They gathered recycled goods, handed out information on the best methods to use that one may get the most out of recycled goods and organized many other events to decrease the amount of waste. Volunteer organizations led by women also, prepared packages for the military overseas or for prisoners of war in Axis countries.

With World War II came the dire need for employees in the workplace, without women to step in the economy would have collapsed. By autumn 1944 the number of women working full-time in Canada's paid labour force was twice what it had been in 1939, and that figure of between 1,000,000 and 1,200,000 did not include part-time workers or women working on farms." Women had to take on this intensive labour and while they did this they still had to find time to make jams, clothes and other such acts of volunteering to aid the men overseas.

India

With the massive demands of manpower for the British Indian Army fighting in European, African and Burmese theaters of war, there was a shortage of able bodied men for agriculture. The British were also afraid the Bengali plains might fall into Japanese hands, so cultivation of border areas was prevented, all rice stocks were moved back towards Kolkata, and there was forced procurement of rice for the war effort in Europe. This led to severe food shortages, made worse by mal administration, culminating in the Bengal famine of 1943 in which 3 million Indian civilians are said to have perished.

With the British recruiting Indian soldiers in large numbers as well as the Japanese recruiting Indian expatriates into the Indian National Army (INA), a state of civil war existed on the east Indian border with Indians killing Indians. This, in turn, led to civilians who supported either the British or the INA rioting against each other.

Soviet Union

During rapid German advances in the early months of the war, nearly reaching the cities of Moscow and Leningrad, the bulk of Soviet industry which could not be evacuated was either destroyed or lost due to German occupation. Agricultural production was interrupted, with grain harvests left standing in the fields that would later cause hunger reminiscent of the early 1930s. In one of the greatest feats of war logistics, industries were evacuated on an enormous scale, with 1523 factories dismantled and shipped eastwards along four principal routes to the Caucasus, Central Asian, Ural and Siberian regions. In general, the tools, dies and production technology were moved, along with the blueprints and their management, engineering staffs and skilled labour.

The whole of the Soviet Union become dedicated to the war effort. Conditions were severe. In Leningrad, under German siege, over a million people died of starvation and disease. Many factory workers were teenagers, women and old people. Despite harsh conditions, the war led to a spike in Soviet nationalism and unity. Soviet propaganda toned down socialist rhetoric of the past as the people now rallied by a belief of protecting their motherland against the evils of German invaders. Ethnic minorities thought to be collaborators were forced into exile. Religion, which was previously shunned, became a part of Communist Party propaganda campaign in the Soviet society.

United States

Taxes and Controls

Federal tax policy was highly contentious during the war, with Roosevelt battling a conservative Congress. Everyone agreed on the need for high taxes to pay for the war. Roosevelt tried to impose a 100% (incorrect fact) tax on incomes over $25,000 (which failed to pass), while Congress enlarged the base downward. By 1944 nearly every employed person was paying federal income taxes (compared to 10% in 1940).

Many controls were put on the economy. The most important were price controls, imposed on most products and monitored by the Office of Price Administration. Wages were also controlled. In addition, the military imposed priorities that largely shaped industrial production.

Labour

The unemployment problem ended in the United States with the beginning of World War II, when stepped up wartime production created millions of new jobs and the draft pulled young men out.

Women also joined the work force to replace men who had joined the forces, though in fewer numbers. Roosevelt stated that the efforts of civilians at home to support the war through personal sacrifice was as critical to winning the war as the efforts of the soldiers themselves. "Rosie the Riveter" became the symbol of women labouring in manufacturing. The war effort brought about significant changes in the role of women in society as a whole. At the end of the war, many of the munitions factories closed. Other women were replaced by returning veterans. However most women who wanted to continue working did so.

In the figure below the development of the United States labour force by sex during the war years.

Year	*Total labour force (*1000)*	*of which Male (*1000)*	*of which Female (*1000)*	*Female share of total (%)*
1940	56,100	41,940	14,160	25.2
1941	57,720	43,070	14,650	25.4
1942	60,330	44,200	16,120	26.7
1943	64,780	45,950	18,830	29.1
1944	66,320	46,930	19,390	29.2
1945	66,210	46,910	19,304	29.2
1946	60,520	43,690	16,840	27.8

Labour shortages were felt in agriculture, even though most farmers were given an occupational exemption and few were drafted. Large numbers volunteered or moved to cities for factory jobs. At the same time many agricultural commodities were more needed for the military and for the civilian populations of Allies.

In some areas schools were temporarily closed at harvest time to enable students to work. Several hundred thousand enemy prisoners of war were used as farm labourers.

Labour Unions

The war mobilization changed the relationship of the Congress of Industrial Organizations (CIO) with both employers and the national government; much less is known about the rival American Federation of Labour (AFL) during the war.

Nearly all the unions that belonged to the CIO were fully supportive of both the war effort and of the Roosevelt administration. However the Mine Workers, who had taken an isolationist stand in the years leading up to the war and had opposed Roosevelt's reelection in 1940, left the CIO in 1942. The CIO, in particular the United Auto Workers (UAW), supported a wartime no-strike pledge that aimed to eliminate not only major strikes for new contracts, but also the innumerable small strikes called by shop stewards and local union leadership to protest particular grievances.

The CIO did not, on the other hand, strike over wages during the war. In return for labour's no-strike pledge, the government offered arbitration to determine the wages and other terms of new contracts. Those procedures produced modest wage increases during the first few years of the war but not enough to keep up with inflation, particularly when combined with the slowness of the arbitration machinery.

Even though the complaints from union members about the no-strike pledge became louder and more bitter, the CIO did not abandon it. The Mine Workers, by contrast, who did not belong to either the AFL or the CIO for much of the war, engaged in a successful twelve-day strike in 1943.

But the CIO unions on the whole grew stronger during the war. The government put pressure on employers to recognize unions to avoid the sort of turbulent struggles over union recognition of the 1930s, while unions were generally able to obtain maintenance of membership clauses, a form of union security, through arbitration and negotiation. Workers also won benefits, such as vacation pay, that had been available only to a few in the past while wage gaps between higher skilled and less skilled workers narrowed.

The experience of bargaining on a national basis, while restraining local unions from striking, also tended to accelerate the trend toward bureaucracy within the larger CIO unions. Some, such as the Steelworkers, had always been centralized organizations in which authority for major decisions resided at the top. The UAW, by contrast, had always been a more grassroots organization, but it also started to try to rein in its maverick local leadership during these years.

The CIO also had to confront deep racial divides in its own membership, particularly in the UAW plants in Detroit where white workers sometimes struck to protest the promotion of black workers to production jobs, but also in shipyards in Alabama, mass transit in Philadelphia, and steel plants in Baltimore. The CIO leadership, particularly those in further left unions such as the Packing house Workers, the UAW, the NMU and the Transport Workers, undertook serious efforts to suppress hate strikes, to educate their membership and to support the Roosevelt Administration's tentative efforts to remedy racial discrimination in war industries through the Fair Employment Practices Commission. Those unions contrasted their relatively bold attack on the problem with the timidity and racism of the AFL.

The CIO unions were progressive in dealing with gender discrimination in wartime industry, which now employed many more women workers in non-traditional jobs. Unions that had represented large numbers of women workers before the war, such as the UE and the Food and Tobacco Workers, had fairly good records of fighting discrimination against women. Most union leaders saw women as temporary wartime replacements for the men in the armed forces. It was important that the wages of these women be kept high so that the veterans would get high wages.

Civilian Support for War Effort

The Civil Air Patrol was established, which enrolled civilian spotters in air reconnaissance, search-and-rescue, and transport. Its Coast Guard counterpart, the Coast Guard Auxiliary, used civilian boats and crews in similar roles. Towers were built in coastal and border towns, and spotters were trained to recognize enemy aircraft. Blackouts were practiced in every city, even those far from the coast. All lighting had to be extinguished to avoid helping the enemy in targeting at night. The main purpose was to remind people that there was a war on and to provide activities that would engage the civil spirit of millions of people not otherwise involved in the war effort. In large part, this effort was successful, sometimes almost to a fault, such as the Plains states where many dedicated aircraft spotters took up their posts night after night watching the skies in an area of the country that no enemy aircraft of that time could possibly hope to reach.

The United Service Organizations (USO) was founded in 1941 in response to a request from President Franklin D. Roosevelt to provide morale and recreation services to uniformed military personnel. This request led six civilian agencies—the Salvation Army, Young Men's Christian Association, Young Women's Christian Association, National Catholic Community Service, National Travellers Aid Association and the National Jewish Welfare Board—to unite in support of the troops. The United Service Organizations, or USO, was incorporated in New York on February 4, 1941.

Legions of women previously employed only in the home, or in traditionally female work, took jobs in factories that directly supported the war effort, or filled jobs vacated by men who had entered military service.

Draft

In 1940 Congress passed the first peace-time draft legislation, which was led by Grenville Clark. It was renewed (by one vote) in summer 1941. It involved questions as to who should control the draft, the size of the army, and the need for deferments. The system worked through local draft boards comprising community leaders who were given quotas and then decided how to fill them. There was very little draft resistance.

The nation went from a surplus manpower pool with high unemployment and relief in 1940 to a severe manpower shortage by 1943. Industry realized that the Army urgently desired production of essential war materials and foodstuffs more than soldiers. (Large numbers of soldiers were not used until the invasion of Europe in summer 1944.) In 1940-43 the Army often transferred soldiers to civilian status in the Enlisted Reserve Corps in order to increase production. Those transferred would return to work in essential industry, although they could be called back to active duty if the Army needed them. Others were discharged if their civilian work was deemed absolutely essential. There were instances of mass releases of men to increase production in various industries.

In the figure below an overview of the development of the United States labour force, the armed forces and unemployment during the war years.

Year	*Total labour force (*1000)*	*Armed forces (*1000)*	*Unemployed (*1000)*	*Unemployment rate (%)*
1939	55,588	370	9,480	17.2
1940	56,180	540	8,120	14.6
1941	57,530	1,620	5,560	9.9
1942	60,380	3,970	2,660	4.7
1943	64,560	9,020	1,070	1.9
1944	66,040	11,410	670	1.2
1945	65,290	11,430	1,040	1.9
1946	60,970	3,450	2,270	3.9

One contentious issue involved the drafting of fathers, which was avoided as much as possible. The drafting of 18-year olds was desired by the military but vetoed by public opinion. Supposedly, Blacks and Asians were drafted at the same rate as Whites. The experience of World War I regarding men needed by industry was particularly unsatisfactory—too many skilled mechanics and engineers became privates (there is a possibly apocryphal story of a *banker* assigned as a *baker* due to a clerical error, noted by historian Lee Kennett in his book "G.I."). Farmers demanded and were generally given occupational deferments (many volunteered anyway, but those who stayed at home lost postwar veteran's benefits.)

Later in the war, in light of the tremendous amount of manpower that would be necessary for the invasion of France, many earlier deferment categories became draft eligible.

Population Movements

There was large-scale migration to industrial Centres, especially on the West Coast. Millions of wives followed their husbands to military camps. Many new military training bases were established or enlarged, especially in the South. Large numbers of African Americans left the cotton fields and headed for the cities. Housing was increasingly difficult to find in industrial Centres; commuting by car was limited by gasoline rationing. People car pooled or took public transportation, which was seriously overcrowded. Trains were heavily booked, so people limited vacation and long-distance travel.

Rationing

At the beginning of World War II, a rationing system was begun in the United States. Tires were the first item to be rationed in January 1942 because supplies of natural rubber were interrupted. Soon afterward, passenger automobiles, typewriters, sugar, gasoline, bicycles, footwear, fuel oil, coffee, stoves, shoes, meat, lard, shortening and oils, cheese, butter, margarine, processed foods (canned, bottled and frozen), dried fruits, canned milk, firewood and coal, jams, jellies and fruit butter, were rationed by November 1943.

To get a classification and a book of rationing stamps, one had to appear before a local rationing board. Each person in a household received a ration book, including babies and small children. When purchasing fuel, a driver had to present a gas card along with a ration book and cash. Ration stamps were valid only for a set period to forestall hoarding.

Employment

Women took on many paid jobs in temporary new munitions factories and in old factories that had been converted from civilian products like automobiles. This was the "Rosie the Riveter" phenomenon.

They also filled many traditionally female jobs that were created by the war boom—as waitresses, for example. And they broke into jobs that had almost always been held by men--such as bank teller or shoe salesperson. Nearly one million women worked as so called "government girls," taking jobs in the federal government, mainly in Washington, DC, that had previously been held by men or were newly created to deal with the war effort.

During World War II, women began to gain more respect and men realized that women actually could work outside of the home. They fought for equal pay and made a huge impact on the United States work force. They began to take over "male" jobs and gained confidence in themselves.

In general when they replaced men they came with fewer skills. Industry retooled its machine jobs so that unskilled workers could handle them. (This opened many jobs for men who had been unemployed in the 1930s). Some unions tried to maintain the same pay scale as men had because they expected men to resume their jobs after the war. At the Oak Ridge plant separating U-235 for the Manhattan Project, it was noted that the girl "hill-billy" operators employed by Tennessee Eastman outperformed the scientists first used on the calutrons.

Volunteer Activities

Women staffed millions of jobs in community service roles, such as USO and Red Cross while the men were at war.

Women Airforce Service Pilots

The Women Airforce Service Pilots, also known as WASP, and the predecessor groups the Women's Flying Training Detachment (WFTD) and the Women's Auxiliary Ferrying Squadron (WAFS) (official from September 10, 1942) were each a pioneering organization of civilian female pilots employed to fly military aircraft under the direction of the United States Army Air Forces during gender-sensitive days of World War II that eventually would number in the thousands of female pilots, each freeing up a male pilot for combat service and duties. The WFTD and WAFS were combined on August 5, 1943 to create the para-military WASP organization.

Baby Boom

Marriage and motherhood came back as prosperity empowered couples who had postponed marriage. The birth rate started shooting up in 1941, paused in 1944-45 as 12 million men were in uniform, then continued to soar until reaching a peak in the late

1950s. This was the "Baby Boom." In a New Deal-like move, the federal government set up the "EMIC" program that provided free prenatal and natal care for the wives of servicemen below the rank of sergeant.

Housing shortages, especially in the munitions Centres, forced millions of couples to live with parents or in makeshift facilities. Little housing had been built in the Depression years, so the shortages grew steadily worse until about 1948, when a massive housing boom finally caught up with demand. (After 1944 much of the new housing was supported by the GI bill.)

Federal law made it difficult to divorce absent servicemen, so the number of divorces peaked when they returned in 1946. In long-range terms, divorce rates changed little.

Housewives

Juggling their roles as mothers due to the Baby Boom and the jobs they filled while the men were at war, women strained to complete all tasks set before them. The war caused cutbacks in automobile and bus service, and migration from farms and towns to munitions Centres. Those housewives who worked found the dual role difficult to handle.

The worst psychological pressure came when sons, husbands, brothers and fiances were drafted and sent to faraway training camps, preparing for a war in which nobody knew how many would be killed. Millions of wives tried to relocate near their husbands' training camps.

Role of Minorities

FEPC

The FEPC was a federal executive order requiring companies with government contracts not to discriminate on the basis of race or religion. It assisted African Americans in obtaining jobs in industry. Under pressure from A. Philip Randolph's growing March on Washington Movement, on June 25, 1941, President Roosevelt created the Fair Employment Practices Committee (FEPC) by signing Executive Order 8802. It said "there shall be no discrimination in the employment of workers in defence industries or government because of race, creed, colour, or national origin".

In 1943 Roosevelt greatly strengthened FEPC with a new executive order, #9346. It required that all government contracts have a non-discrimination clause. FEPC was the most significant breakthrough ever for Blacks and women on the job front. During the war the federal government operated airfield, shipyards, supply Centres, ammunition plants and other facilities that employed millions. FEPC rules applied and guaranteed equality of employment rights. Of course, these facilities shut down when the war ended. In the private sector the FEPC was generally successful in enforcing non-discrimination in the North, it did not attempt to challenge segregation in the South, and in the border region its intervention led to hate strikes by angry white workers.

African American: Double V Campaign

The African American community in the United States resolved on a Double V Campaign: Victory over fascism abroad, and victory over discrimination at home. Large numbers migrated from poor Southern farms to munitions Centres. Racial tensions were high in overcrowded cities like Chicago; Detroit and Harlem experienced race riots in 1943. The derogative name jig was coined during this time. The *Pittsburgh Courier* created the Double V Campaign after readers began commenting on their second class status during wartime.

Internment of Japanese Americans

In 1942 the War Department demanded that all enemy nationals be removed from war zones on the West Coast. The question became how to evacuate the estimated 120,000 people of Japanese citizenship living in California. Roosevelt looked at the secret evidence available to him: the Japanese in the Philippines had collaborates with the Japanese invasion troops; most of the adult Japanese in California had been strong supporters of Japan in the war against China. There was evidence of espionage compiled by code-breakers that decrypted messages to Japan from agents in North America and Hawaii before and after the attack on Pearl Harbor. These MAGIC cables were kept secret from all but those with the highest clearance, such as Roosevelt. On February 19, 1942, Roosevelt signed Executive Order 9066 which set up designated military areas "from which any or all persons may be excluded." The most controversial part of the order included American born children and youth who had dual U.S. and Japanese citizenship.

In addition to the Japanese, thousands of civilian Germans and Italians were interned; some with their families, some taken from their families. They were given hearing, but had no representation of their own. These internees were picked up by the FBI based on records compiled prior to and at the beginning of the War.

In February 1943, when activating the 442nd Regimental Combat Team—a unit composed mostly of American-born American citizens of Japanese descent living in Hawaii—Roosevelt said, "No loyal citizen of the United States should be denied the democratic right to exercise the responsibilities of his citizenship, regardless of his ancestry. The principle on which this country was founded and by which it has always been governed is that Americanism is a matter of the mind and heart; Americanism is not, and never was, a matter of race or ancestry." In 1944, the U.S. Supreme Court upheld the legaiity of the executive order in the *Korematsu v. United States* case. The executive order remained in force until December when Roosevelt released the Japanese internees, except for those who announced their intention to return to Japan.

Italy was an official enemy, and citizens of Italy were also forced away from "strategic" coastal areas in California. Altogether, 58,000 Italians were forced to relocate. They relocated on their own and were not put in camps. Known spokesmen for Mussolini were arrested and held in prison.

The restrictions were dropped in October 1942, and Italy switched sides in 1943 and became an American ally. In the east, however, the large Italian populations of the northeast, especially in munitions-producing Centres such as Bridgeport and New Haven faced no restrictions and contributed just as much to the war effort as other Americans.

Wartime Politics

Roosevelt easily won the bitterly contested 1940 election, but the Conservative coalition maintained a tight grip on Congress.

Wendell Willkie, the defeated GOP candidate in 1940, became a roving ambassador for Roosevelt. After a series of squabbles with Vice President Henry A. Wallace, Roosevelt stripped him of his administrative responsibilities and dropped him from the 1944 ticket, choosing instead Senator Harry S. Truman. Truman was best known for investigating waste, fraud and inefficiency in civilian programs. In very light turnout in 1942 the Republicans made major gains. In the 1944 election, Roosevelt defeated Tom Dewey in a relatively close race that attracted little attention.

Propaganda and Culture

The media cooperated with the federal government in presenting the official view of the war. All movie scripts had to be pre-approved. World War II posters helped to mobilize the nation. Inexpensive, accessible, and ever-present, the poster was an ideal agent for making war aims the personal mission of every citizen. Government agencies, businesses, and private organizations issued an array of poster images linking the military front with the home front—calling upon every American to boost production at work and at home. Deriving their appearance from the fine and commercial arts, posters conveyed more than simple slogans.

Posters expressed the needs and goals of the people who created them. By definition, wartime posters are naturally propagandistic, but most posters were merely patriotically so. Some, however, resorted to extreme racial and ethnic caricatures of the enemy, sometimes as hopelessly bumbling cartoon characters, sometimes as evil, half-human creatures.

The National Archives, Northwestern University and the University of Minnesota all have extensive collections of World War II posters accessible online that contain many examples of posters of the era in regard to the use of propaganda, both subtle and patriotic, and blatantly anti-German and Japanese.

One of the most noteworthy areas of civilian involvement during the war was in the area of recycling. Many everyday commodities were vital to the war effort, and drives were organized to recycle such things as rubber, tin, waste kitchen fats (the predominant raw material of explosives and many pharmaceuticals) paper, lumber, steel and many others.

Popular phrases promoted by the government at the time were "Get into the scrap!" and "Get some cash for your trash" (a nominal sum was paid to the donor for many kinds of scrap items) and Thomas "Fats" Waller even wrote and recorded a song with the latter title.

Such commodities as rubber and tin remained highly important as recycled materials until the end of the war, while others, such as steel, were critically needed at first, but in lesser quantities as damaged war materiel were returned from overseas for scrapping, lessening the need for civilian scrap metal drives. Once again, war propaganda played a prominent role in many of these drives.

A strong aspect of American culture then as now was a fascination with celebrities, and many stars of Hollywood and radio gave service above and beyond the call in the donation of their time for everything from being Civilian Defence marshals to making personal appearances at War Bond drives. Bonds were the money that financed the war, and Bond drives where celebrities appeared were always very successful. Several stars were responsible for personal appearance tours that netted multiple millions of dollars in bond pledges—an astonishing amount in 1943.

The public paid 3/4 of the face value of a war bond, and received the full face value back after a set number of years. While this may have represented a rather unspectacular interest rate, the government has never defaulted on payment of any mature bond. People were challenged to put "at least 10% of every pay check into Bonds". Compliance was very high, with entire factories of workers earning a special "Minuteman" flag to fly over their plant if all workers belonged to the "Ten Percent Club". There were seven major War Loan drives, all of which exceeded their goals.

An added advantage was that citizens who were putting their money into War Bonds were not putting it into the home front wartime economy. There was a job for anyone who wanted one during the war, most of them well-paid. Personal income was at an all-time high, and more dollars were chasing fewer goods to purchase. This was a recipe for economic disaster that was largely avoided because Americans—cajoled daily by their government to do so—were also saving money at an all-time high rate, mostly in War Bonds but also in private savings accounts and insurance policies.

Hollywood studios also went all-out for the war effort, as studios allowed their major stars (such as Clark Gable and James Stewart) to enlist, and also created propaganda films to remind American movie goers of their heritage. Many of the finest films of the era are about the war, such as *Casablanca, Mrs. Miniver*, and *Going My Way*, while others, such as *Yankee Doodle Dandy*, focused on patriotism.

Cartoons and short subjects were a major sign of the times, as Warner Brothers Studios and Disney Studios gave unprecedented aid to the war effort by creating cartoons that were both wildly patriotic (and very funny), and also contributed to remind movie-goers of important wartime activities such as rationing and scrap drives, war bond purchases, and the creation of victory gardens.

Warner shorts such as Draftee Daffy, Russian Rhapsody and Daffy-The Commando are particularly remembered for their biting wit and unflinching mockery of the enemy (particularly Hilter, Tojo and Hermann Goering. Their cartoons of Private Snafu, produced for the military as "training films", served to remind many military men of the importance of following proper procedure during wartime, for their own safety. Hanna Barbara also contributed to the war effort with slyly pro US short cartoon The Yankee Doodle Mouse with "Lt." Jerry Mouse as the hero and Tom Cat as the "enemy".

China

China suffered the second highest number of casualties of the entire war. Civilians in the occupied territories had to endure many large-scale massacres, including the Nanking Massacre. In a few areas, Japanese forces also unleashed newly developed biological weapons on Chinese civilians leading to an estimated 200,000 dead. Tens of thousands are thought to have died when Nationalist troops broke the levees of the Yangtze to stop the Japanese advance after the loss of the Chinese capital, Nanking. Millions more Chinese died because of famine during the war.

Millions of Chinese moved to the Western regions of China to avoid Japanese invasion. Cities like Kunming ballooned with new arrivals. Entire factories and universities were often taken along for the journey. Japan captured major coastal cities like Shanghai early in the war; cutting the rest of China off from its chief source of finance and industry.

The city of Chongqing became the most frequently bombed city in history. Though China received aid from the United States, China did not have sufficient infrastructure to properly arm or even feed its military forces, let alone civilians. Much of the aid was also funnelled away through corruption.

Communist forces led by Mao were based mainly in Northern China and employed guerilla tactics against the Japanese. However, it is now felt that they were at most minimally involved in the Japanese resistance. In occupied territories under Japanese control, civilians were treated harshly.

Axis

Germany

Germany had not fully mobilized in 1939, nor even in 1941. Not until 1943 under Albert Speer did Germany finally redirect its entire economy and manpower to war production.

Economy

Although Germany had about double the population of Britain (80 million versus 40 million), it had to use far more labour to provide food and energy. Britain imported food and employed only a million people (5% of labour force) on farms, while Germany used 11 million (27%). For Germany to build its twelve synthetic oil plants with a capacity of 3.3 million tons a year required 2.4 million tons of structural steel and 7.5 million man-days of labour. (Britain imported all its oil from Iraq, Persia and North America). To overcome this problem, Germany employed millions of forced labourers and POWs; by 1944, they had brought in more than five million civilian workers and nearly two million prisoners of war—a total of 7.13 million foreign workers.

Rationing

For the first part of the war, there were surprisingly few restrictions on civilian activities. Most goods were freely available in the early years of the war. Rationing in Germany was introduced in 1939, slightly later than it was in Britain, because Hitler was at first convinced that it would affect public support of the war if a strict rationing program was introduced. The Nazi popularity was in fact partially due to the fact that Germany under the Nazis was relatively prosperous, and Hitler did not want to lose popularity or faith.

Hitler felt that food and other shortages had been a major factor in destroying civilian morale during World War I which led to the overthrow of the Kaiser and other German monarchies at the end of the war. However, when the war began to go against the Germans in Russia and the Allied bombing effort began to affect domestic production, this changed and a very severe rationing program had to be introduced. The system gave extra rations for men involved in heavy industry, and lower rations for Jews and Poles in the areas occupied by Germany, but not to the Rhineland Poles.

The Points System

"For every person, there were rationing cards for general foodstuffs, meats, fats (such as butter, margarine and oil) and tobacco products distributed every other month. The cards were printed on strong paper, containing numerous small "Marken" subdivisions printed with their value – for example, from "5 g Butter" to "100 g Butter".

Every acquisition of rationed goods required an appropriate "Marken", and if a person wished to eat a certain soup at a restaurant, the waiter would take out a pair of scissors and cut off the required items to make the soup and amounts listed on the menu. In the evenings, shop-owners would spend an hour at least gluing the collected "Marken" onto large sheets of paper which they then had to hand in to the appropriate authorities."

Rare Foods

The amounts available under rationing were sufficient to live from, but clearly did not permit luxuries. Whipped cream became unknown from 1939 until 1948, as well as chocolates, cakes with rich cremes etc..., and meat, of course, could not be eaten every day. Other items were not rationed, but simply became unavailable as they had to be imported from overseas: coffee in particular which throughout was replaced by substitutes made from roasted grains.

Vegetables and local fruit were not rationed; imported citrus fruits and bananas were unavailable. In more rural areas, farmers continued to bring their products to the markets, as large cities depended on long distance delivery. Because coffee was scarce, people created a substitute for it made from roasted ground down barley seeds and acorns. Many people kept rabbits for their meat when meat became scarce in shops, and it was often a child's job to care for them each day.

Labour

Women were idealized by Nazi ideology and work was not felt to be appropriate for them. Children were expected to go to houses collecting materials for the production of war equipment. The German industry used forced labour, called from the countries they occupied.

Japan

Please help improve this article by expanding it. Further information might be found on the talk page. *(June 2009)*

Japanese Rice Supply

Year	1937	1938	1939	1940	1941	1942	1943	1944	1945
Domestic Production									
	9,928	9,862	10,324	9,107	8,245	9,999	9,422	8,784	6,445
Imports	2,173	2,546	1,634	1,860	2,517	2,581	1,183	874	268
All rice	12,101	12,408	11,958	10,967	10,762	12,580	10,605	9,658	6,713

7

Social Welfare and the Art of Giving

Giving is growing, according to statistics published by the Australian Tax Office. In the 2003-04 year, gifts and donations for which taxpayers claimed tax deductions exceeded one billion dollars for the first time. The proportion of taxpayers claiming deductions for donations or gifts has risen from 31.5% to 35.3% over this period, while the average donation has risen from $175 to $301.

This upward trend in (tax-deductible) generosity partly reflects changes to the tax system, in particular the introduction in 2001 of Prescribed Private Funds (PPFs) of which there are now nearly 300. But it probably also stems from Australia's extended period of economic growth (the longest for over 100 years) and the substantial increase in personal wealth as a result of Australia's real estate and share market booms.

The economist John Maynard Keynes, who was the first Chairman of the Arts Council of Great Britain, feared that private patronage of the arts would be destroyed by the economic egalitarianism of his age (something of which he was, in general terms, a fervent advocate) and that government funding 'would be the only way of saving arts from extinction'.

Fortunately, it hasn't come to that, either in Britain or in Australia. Unfortunately, however, only a small proportion of the increased generosity of individual Australians benefits the arts. A survey conducted for the Commonwealth Department of Family and Community Services and the Prime Minister's Community Business Partnership-which defined 'giving' more broadly than the Tax Office-found that fewer than 5% of all individual donors gave money to arts or cultural associations, and that arts or cultural associations received just 2.3% of all donations. Religious and spiritual organisations, international aid and development organisations, community and welfare associations and medical research institutes account for nearly three-quarters of all individual donations. Arts and cultural organisations attract a larger share, around 10%, of business giving than they do from individuals.

Tasmanians are among the least generous donors in Australia. Only 30.6% of Tasmanian taxpayers claimed deductions for gifts or donations in 2003-04, less than in any other part of Australia except the Northern Territory. (By contrast, 38.1% of Victorians claimed deductions for gifts or donation). And those Tasmanians who did make gifts or donations gave an average of $204 each, again less than in any other part of Australia except the Northern Territory.

To a large extent, this reflects the fact that Tasmanians have, on average, lower incomes than other Australians. More affluent Australians can afford to give more generously-and they do. The top 0.03% of taxpayers-those earning $1 million or more-accounted for 13.3% of all tax-deductible gifts and donations in 2003-04. 63.2% of them gave something, and those who did gave an average of over $73,300. Put differently, taxpayers in this income group donated 2.4% of their income-well in excess of the average of just 0.28% of income donated by taxpayers as a whole.

Tasmania has fewer high-income earners (relative to its population) than any other part of Australia-which is the main reason why Tasmanian incomes are below the national average, not that low-income households in Tasmania have lower incomes than elsewhere in Australia or that they are relatively more numerous.

Thus, even though Tasmanians participate in cultural activities to a larger extent than residents of other States, arts and cultural organisations face greater challenges in funding their activities than their counterparts elsewhere in Australia. Moreover, the Tasmanian Government spends less per head on the arts than any other State or Territory Government except Queensland-although this is largely because of the absence in Tasmania of a large performing arts centre with an operating deficit funded by State government grants.

Individual philanthropic giving is motivated by a wide variety of considerations, including both altruism and an expectation of reciprocity (although the latter motive is more common among businesses), as a way of connecting with the community, with a view to achieving some desired outcome ('making a difference'), or as a way of expressing one's identity or reputation.

The Arts can be an Outlet for all of these Motivations

Traditionally, individual patrons of the arts have often expected something in return for their financial support, such as flattering depictions in portraits or performances. This is far less plausible in the modern world, with artists and arts organisations attaching greater importance to their independence, and a more cynical public capable of discerning advertising for what it is. Nonetheless, individual supporters of the arts do in most cases appreciate invitations to opening night performances, book launches, and other tokens of recognition for their support. And some donors do look upon their support for emerging artists as a form of investment-albeit a high-risk one-which may eventually yield a financial return. For others, the need for a form of 'reciprocity' is satisfied by the intrinsic pleasure they derive from being associated with the creation of a work of art, or the development of an artist.

But for many individuals, the motivation for the support which they provide to the arts has been and is today beyond personal pleasure or material reward.

The arts can be, and often are, a means of calling attention to issues of concern or a vehicle for protest. The arts can provide a means for people otherwise voiceless to express themselves. They can provide a channel for emotions and feelings which might otherwise be vented in destructive ways. Support for the arts can, in other words, provide individuals with a way of 'making a difference' no less effectively than support for organisations and institutions with an explicit agenda. In commenting upon my appointment as Chair of the Tasmanian Arts Advisory Board,

Tasmanian poet Tim Thorne suggested that I ponder a quote he attributed to the Czech activist Egon Kisch, that 'all real art is a danger to those in power'. Kisch himself was of course famously seen as a danger by those in power in Australia at the time of his attempt to visit this country in 1934; the immigration authorities sought (in the end, unsuccessfully) to preclude his entry into Australia by giving him a dictation test in a European language other than the eleven in which he was fluent.

Having taken Thorne's advice, and pondered his quote, I am unconvinced that art can be dismissed as 'unreal' simply because it is apolitical, or even if it suits the agenda of those who happen to be in power at the time. To do so would, for example, be to detract from the many great pre-Renaissance works of art which portrayed and conformed to the accepted religious norms of the time; or from Shakespeare's plays which, though often dealing with political issues, nonetheless did so in ways which supported the Tudor and Stuart establishments.

But I accept without demur that art can be challenging and confronting, politically and in another ways; and that 'great' art often is.

The first work of art that I ever bought (apart from vinyl recording) was a reproduction of a painting by Valery Whatley of the Franklin River, at the height of the debate over the Gordon-below-Franklin dam. That painting, and Peter Dombrovskis's iconic photograph of Rock Island Bend in the Gordon River, were for many people catalysts in their thinking about the most contentious environmental issue of the early 1980s.

As Jane Stewart, the Director of the Devonport Regional Art Gallery, noted in her introduction to *From An Island South,* the eight artists whose work was toured by Asialink in an exhibition of the same name last year have 'inevitably... begun to breathe the politics, history and traditions of the island, aspects of which have unavoidably found a way into their artwork'. Richard Wastell's paintings, two of which were featured in this exhibition, speak directly to the contentious political issue of forestry in Tasmania. Nigel Jamieson's dance and theatre piece, *Honour Bound,* contributed to a shift in Australian public opinion over the continuing incarceration without trial of David Hicks. Richard

Flanagan's *The Unknown Terrorist* may (and I hope will) heighten public awareness of the erosion of civil liberties and legal rights in the name of 'national security'.

While the arts can serve to heighten awareness of major political issues, they may also be an effective vehicle for activism on a much smaller scale as well, in ways which allow individuals to 'make a difference' in a meaningful and positive manner.

For example the Besen Family Foundation and the Myer Foundation have, through their support for the Torch Project, enabled Indigenous communities and individuals in a number of locations across regional Victoria and in Melbourne to explore themes such as education, substance abuse, reconciliation and domestic violence through drama, dance and visual art. The Mercy Foundation, associated with the Sisters of Mercy, last year funded art projects to enable Indigenous communities to express their sense of injustice in relations between themselves and mining companies, and to develop the skills and confidence to plan and implement their own activities in future.

None of which is to say that everyone who pays to see, or buys a work of art, or who attends a performance, which deals with a controversial subject, is making a political statement. But for many people, support for the arts and for cultural activities, through patronage or philanthropy, is a form of activism. For its own sake, and to the extent that it draws additional funds into the artistic and cultural sphere, that is a Good Thing.

Charity

In modern usage, the practice of charity means the giving of help to those in need who are not related to the giver.

Etymology

The word *"charity"* entered the English language through the Old French word *"charite"* which was derived from the Latin *"caritas"*. Originally in Latin the word *caritas* meant preciousness, dearness, high price. From this, in Christian theology, *caritas* became the standard Latin translation for the Greek word *agapc,* meaning an unlimited loving-kindness to all others, such as the love of God. This much wider concept is the meaning of the word charity in the Christian triplet "faith, hope and charity", as used by the King

James Version of the Bible in its translation of St. Paul's Letter to the Corinthians. However the English word more generally used for this concept, both before and since (and by the "King James" Bible at other passages), is the more direct *love.*

St. Paul's *agapc* was *not* primarily about good works and giving to the poor (*And though I feed the poor with all my goods, and though I give my body, that I be burned, and have not love, it profiteth me nothing*-1 Cor 13:3, Geneva translation, 1560), although in English the word "charity" has steadily acquired this as its primary meaning, wherein it was first used in Old French at least since the year 1200 A.D..

Practice

Charitable giving is the act of giving money, goods or time to the unfortunate, either directly or by means of a charitable trust or other worthy cause. Charitable giving as a religious act or duty is referred to as almsgiving or alms. The name stems from the most obvious expression of the virtue of charity is giving the objects of it the means they need to survive.

The poor, particularly widows and orphans, and the sick and disabled, are generally regarded as the proper objects of charity. Some groups regard charity as being properly directed toward other members of their group. Although giving to those nearly connected to oneself is sometimes called charity—as in the saying "Charity begins at home" — normally charity denotes giving to those not related, with filial piety and like terms for supporting one's family and friends. Indeed, treating those related to the giver as if they were strangers in need of charity has led to the figure of speech "as cold as charity" — providing for one's relatives as if they were strangers, without affection.

Most forms of charity are concerned with providing food, water, clothing, and shelter, and tending the ill, but other actions may be performed as charity: visiting the imprisoned or the home bound, dowries for poor women, ransoming captives, educating orphans. Donations to causes that would benefit the unfortunate indirectly, as donations to cancer research hope to benefit cancer victims, are also charity. The recipient of charity may offer to pray for the benefactor; indeed, in medieval Europe, it was customary to feast the poor at the funeral in return for their prayers for the deceased. Institutions may commemorate benefactors by displaying their names, up to naming buildings or even the institution itself after the benefactors. If the recipient makes material return of more than a token value, the transaction is normally not called charity.

Originally charity entailed the benefactor directly giving the goods to the receiver. People who could not support themselves—or who feigned such inability—would become beggars.

Institutions evolved to carry out the labour of assisting the poor, and these institutions are called charities. These include orphanages, food banks, religious orders dedicated to care of the poor, hospitals, organizations that visit the home bound and imprisoned, and many others. Such institutions allow those whose time or inclination does not lend themselves to directly care for the poor to enable others to do so, both by providing money for the work and supporting them while they do the work. Institutions can also attempt to more effectively sort out the actually needy from those who fraudulently claim charity. Early Christians particularly recommended the care of the unfortunate to the charge of the local bishop. In Islam this is called Zakat, and is one of the five pillars upon which the Muslim religion is based.

There have been examinations of who gives more to charity. One study conducted in the United States found that as a percentage of income, charitable giving increased as income decreased. The poorest fifth of Americans, for example, gave away 4.3% of their income, while the wealthiest fifth gave away 2.1%. In absolute terms, this was an average of $453 on an average income of $10,531, compared to $3,326 on an income of $158,388.

Philanthropy

Philanthropy is the effort or inclination to increase the well-being of humankind, as by charitable aid or donations.

Etymology

It is generally agreed that the word was coined 2500 years ago in ancient Greece, by the playwright Aeschylus, or whoever else wrote *Prometheus Bound*. There the author told as a myth how the primitive creatures that were created to be human, at first had no knowledge, skills, or culture of any kind—so they lived in caves, in the dark, in constant fear for their lives. Zeus, the tyrannical king of the gods, decided to destroy them, but Prometheus, a Titan whose name meant "forethought," out of his "*philanthropos tropos*" or "humanity-loving character" gave them two empowering, life-enhancing, gifts: fire, symbolizing all knowledge, skills, technology, arts, and science; and "blind hope" or optimism. The two went together—with fire, humans could be optimistic; with optimism, they could use fire constructively, to improve the human condition.

The new word, *philanthropos*, combined two words: *philos*, "loving" in the sense of benefitting, caring for, nourishing; and *anthropos*, "human being" in the sense of "humankind", "humanity", or "human-ness". Prometheus did not "love" the proto-humans individually, because at that mythical point in time individuality did not yet exist—that requires culture. What he evidently "loved", therefore, was their human potential—what they could accomplish and become with "fire" and "blind hope". The two gifts in effect completed the creation of humankind as a distinctly civilized animal. 'Philanthropia'—loving what it is to be human—was thought to be the key to civilization.

The Greeks adopted the "love of humanity" as an educational ideal, whose goal was excellence (*arete*)—the fullest development of body, mind and spirit, which is the essence of liberal education. The Platonic Academy's philosophical dictionary defined *Philanthropia* as: "A state of well-educated habits stemming from love of humanity. A state of being productive of benefit to humans." *Philanthropia* was later translated by the Romans into Latin as, simply, *humanitas*—humane-ness. And because Prometheus' human-empowering gifts rebelled against Zeus' tyranny, *philanthropia* was also associated with freedom and democracy. Both Socrates and the laws of Athens were described as "philanthropic and democratic"—a common expression, the idea being that philanthropic humans are reliably capable of self-government.

Putting all this together in modern terms, there are four relatively authoritative definitions of "philanthropy" that come close to the Classical concept: John W. Gardner's "private initiatives for the public good"; Robert Payton's "voluntary action for the public good"; Lester Salamon's "the private giving of time or valuables...for public purposes" and Robert Bremner's "the aim of philanthropy...is improvement in the quality of human life". Combining these to connect modern philanthropy with its entire previous history, "philanthropy" may best be defined as, "private initiatives for public good, focusing on quality of life."

This distinguishes it from government (public initiatives for public good) and business (private initiatives for private good). Omitting the definite article "the" with "public good" avoids the dubious assumption that there is ever a single, knowable public good, and in any case people rarely if ever agree on what that might be; rather, this definition merely says that the benefactor intends a "public" rather than an exclusively "private" good or benefit. The inclusion of "quality of life" ensures the strong humanistic emphasis of the Promethean archetype.

The Classical view of philanthropy disappeared in the Middle Ages, was rediscovered and revived with the Renaissance, and came into the English language in the early 17th century. Sir Francis Bacon in 1592 wrote in a letter that his "vast contemplative ends" expressed his "philanthropia", and his 1608 essay *On Goodness* defined his subject as "the affecting of the weale of men... what the Grecians call philanthropia." Henry Cockeram, in his English dictionary (1623), cited "philanthropie" as a synonym for "humanitie" (in Latin, humanitas) — thus reaffirming the Classical formulation.

Philanthropy in the USA

"Voluntary Associations"

What emerged in this way was a culture of collaboration. Colonial society was built by volunteers, or as Alexis de Tocqueville later referred to them, "voluntary associations" — which is to say, "private initiatives for public good, focusing on quality of life". He observed that they permeated American life, were a distinguishing feature of the American character and culture, and a key to American democracy. Americans, he said, did not rely on others — government, an aristocracy, or the church — to solve their public problems; rather, they did it themselves, through voluntary associations, which is to say, philanthropy, which was characteristically democratic. One of the first, if not the first of these, was also one of the first American governments: the Mayflower Compact of 1620. The Pilgrims, still offshore but in American waters as it were, declared that they "solemnly and mutually, in the Presence of God and one another, combine ourselves together into a civil Body Politick, for our better Ordering and Preservation." The first corporation, Harvard College (1636), also in the Massachusetts Bay Colony, was a philanthropic voluntary association created to train young men for the clergy.

As was typical in that period, American philanthropic associations had ideological dimensions. Three of the leading English colonies—Massachusetts, Pennsylvania and Virginia—were styled "Commonwealths", which meant a purportedly ideal society in which all members contributed to the "common weal"—the public good.

A leading promoter of this Classical and Christian ideal was the preacher Cotton Mather, who in 1710 published a widely read American classic, *Bonifacius, or an Essay to Do Good*. Mather seems to have been concerned that the original idealism had eroded, so he advocated philanthropic benefaction as a way of life. Though his context was Christian, his idea was also characteristically American and explicitly Classical, on the threshold of the Enlightenment.

"Let no man pretend to the Name of A Christian, who does not Approve the proposal of A Perpetual Endeavour to Do Good in the World.... The Christians who have no Ambition to be [useful], Shall be condemned by the Pagans; among whom it was a Term of the Highest Honour, to be termed, A Benefactor; to have Done Good, was accounted Honourable. The Philosopher [i.e., Aristotle], being asked why Every one desired so much to look upon a Fair Object! He answered That it was a Question of a Blind man. If any man ask, as wanting the Sense of it, What is it worth the while to Do Good in the world! I must Say, It Sounds not like the Question of a Good man."

Mather's many practical suggestions for doing good had strong civic emphases—founding schools, libraries, hospitals, useful publications, etc... They were not primarily about rich people helping poor people, but about private initiatives for public good, focusing on quality of life. Two young Americans whose prominent lives, they later said, were influenced by Mather's book, were Benjamin Franklin and Paul Revere.

Benjamin Franklin

Regarded in his own time as "the first great American," lionized in 18th-century Europe and America as a model of American values, and especially of the Enlightenment in America, the key to his life was his Classical, and classically American, philanthropy. He self-consciously and purposefully oriented his life around volunteer public service. Even his political rival in France, John Adams, avowed that "there was scarcely a peasant or citizen" who "did not consider him as a friend to humankind." Immanuel Kant, the leading philosopher of the German Enlightenment, called Franklin the "new Prometheus" for stealing fire from the heavens in his scientific experiments with lightning as electricity, for the benefit of mankind. Franklin had direct connections with the Scottish Enlightenment; he was called "Dr. Franklin" because he had been awarded honorary degrees from the three Scottish Universities—St. Andrews, Glasgow and Edinburgh—and while travelling there he had personally befriended the leading Scottish Enlightenment thinkers.

In Philadelphia, Franklin created perhaps the first personal system of civic philanthropy in America. As a young tradesman in 1727, he formed the "Junto": a 12-member club that met on Friday evenings to discuss current issues and events. One of the four qualifications for membership was the "love [of] mankind in general". Two years later (1729) he founded the *Philadelphia Gazette*, and for the next thirty years he used the Junto as a sort of think-tank to generate and vet philanthropic ideas, and the *Gazette* to test and mobilize public support, recruit volunteers, and fund-raise. This system was heroically productive and beneficial, creating America's first subscription library (1731), a volunteer fire association, a fire insurance association, the American Philosophical Society (1743-4), an "academy" (1750—which became the University of Pennsylvania), a hospital (1752—through fundraising with a challenge grant), the paving and patrolling of public streets, the finance and construction of a civic meeting house, and many others.

In 1747 the Pennsylvania Colony was disrupted by violent conflicts with Indians in the west, and with French-Canadian privateers in the lower Delaware River. The government in Philadelphia was Quaker, hence pacifist, and did nothing. Franklin, increasingly frustrated with this inaction, consulted his Junto, and published a pamphlet, *Plain Truth,* declaring that Pennsylvania was defenseless unless the people would take matters into their own hands. He proposed a "military association" to raise funds and a private militia, and within a few weeks it had recruited more than a hundred companies, with over 10,000 men-at-arms, and raised over £6,500 in a public lottery. This was a prototype of the American Revolution.

The American Revolution

The Classical view of philanthropy provided the conceptual model, and voluntary associations the procedural model, for the American Revolution. The Revolution began in Concord, Massachusetts—arguably one of the epicentres of American philanthropy. "Here once the embattled farmers stood,/And fired the shot heard 'round the world."-Ralph Waldo Emerson's "Concord Hymn"

The 'farmers' referred to in this line were the "Minutemen", voluntary associations of farmers who would be ready to leave their farms and take up arms against the British. They were warned by observers and riders, most famously by Paul Revere, an avid and leading volunteer in many civic causes, who had organized a voluntary association of troop observers and riders like himself to rally the towns around Boston.

The Continental Army was manned by volunteers, and financed by private donations; its Commanding General, George Washington, served without pay as a volunteer for three years until his wife gave child birth to their son george, explicitly *pro bono publico*—for the public good. He often signed his letters, "Philanthropically yours".

Throughout the Colonies, the commitment to independence had been cultivated by innumerable voluntary political associations, such as the Sons of Liberty. The Founders at Independence Hall in Philadelphia acted as a philanthropic voluntary association.

The *Declaration of Independence* was the first instance in history in which the creation of a national government was formally preceded by an idealistic mission statement—routine in voluntary associations—addressed to, on behalf of, and for the benefit of, all mankind. The *Declaration* concludes with a voluntary pledge by the Founders as individuals "to each other" of their personal lives, fortunes, and sacred honour.

The first form of government proposed for the new nation was called an "Association". The final form, the United States Constitution, proceeded as a voluntary association, also beginning with a mission statement and—another "first" in history—ratified by vote of its individual members, "The People". The Constitution's "Preamble" featured private initiative, public good, and quality of life:

"We The People of the United States, in Order to form a more perfect Union, establish Justice, insure domestic Tranquility, provide for the common defence, promote the general Welfare, and secure the Blessings of Liberty to ourselves and our Posterity, do ordain and establish this Constitution for the United States of America."

Finally, in the very first *Federalist Paper*, page 1, paragraph 1, Alexander Hamilton launched the Founders' argument for the Constitution's ratification, by noting that "it is commonly remarked" that in creating this new nation, Americans were acting on behalf of, and for the benefit of, all mankind. "This" he wrote, "adds the inducements of philanthropy to those of patriotism."

And "commonly remarked" it was—: In 1776, Thomas Paine had written in *Common Sense*, his very popular and influential tract for independence:

"The cause of America is in a great measure the cause of all mankind. Many circumstances have, and will arise, which are not local, but universal, and through which the principles of all Lovers of Mankind (emphasis here) are affected, and in the Event of which, their Affections are interested."

As Ben Franklin had said to the French about the American Revolution: "We are fighting for the dignity and happiness of human nature."

The "philanthropy" Hamilton was talking about was not "rich helping poor", but private initiatives for public good, focusing on quality of life. Classical philanthropy had become classically American. The United States was not only created by philanthropy, but also for philanthropy—to be a philanthropic nation, a gift to humanity, squarely in the Promethean tradition.

19th Century: Disintegration

The Founders' synthesis, of the Classical view of philanthropy with American patriotic voluntary associations, did not sustain its cultural leadership. The Enlightenment, of which it was the quintessential American expression, was swept away in Europe by the French Revolution, Napoleon, and Romanticism. In America, the early history of the Republic saw rapid, tumultuous, growth and a sorting-out of what had been accomplished. The onset of the Industrial Revolution, waves of immigration, urban growth and westward expansion, together with shifting political practices and a new cast of characters in political leadership, combined to dissolve the philanthropic culture and spirit of its founding.

That disintegration was noticed and regretted. The blossoming of American literature in the 19th century, with Hawthorne, Emerson, Thoreau, Melville and others, was essentially a protest against the disruptive forces of technology, urbanization, and industrialization, and in their wake the perceived loss of classical American values. On the other hand, this movement was evidence that the flame of philanthropic, practical, idealism had not died with the Founders. In 1837, Ralph Waldo Emerson celebrated the philanthropic spirit of the Revolution in his "Concord Hymn," quoted above, and in his 1844 essay "The Young American," he wrote,

"It seems so easy for America to inspire and express the most expansive and humane spirit; new-born, free, healthful, strong, the land of the labourer, of the democrat, of the philanthropist, of the believer, of the saint, she should speak for the human race. It is the country of the future."

The flame was still alive in 1863, whens, as Garry Wills has shown, President Abraham Lincoln codified and enshrined the classic conceptualization of our country's mission in his Gettysburg

Address, speaking of "a new nation, conceived in Liberty, and dedicated to the proposition that all men are created equal".

Philanthropy's Contributions to American Life

The philanthropic spirit and practical necessity of voluntary associations and their attendant collaborative culture moved west with the frontier throughout the 19th century, thus reinforcing the "philanthropic and democratic" development of the American character. All of private education and of religion in America have been necessarily philanthropic, but beyond those every reform movement in the history of the United States—e.g., anti-slavery, women's suffrage, environmental conservation, civil rights, feminism, and various peace movements—began as philanthropic voluntary associations. Many were, or were regarded as, counter-cultural and even outrageous when they first arose, but all were "private initiatives for public good, focusing on quality of life".

American philanthropy has met challenges, and taken advantage of opportunities, that neither government nor business ordinarily address. The other sectors certainly affect American quality of life, but philanthropy focuses on it.

Philanthropy is a major source of income for fine arts and performing arts, religious, and humanitarian causes, as well as educational institutions.

Modern Philanthropists

In 1982, Paul Newman co-founded the Newman's Own food company and donated all after-tax profits to various charities. Upon his death in 2008, the company had donated over US$250 million to thousands of charities.

During the past few years, some high profile examples of philanthropy include Irish rock singer Bono's campaign to cancel Third World debt to developed nations; the Gates Foundation's massive resources and ambitions, such as its campaigns to eradicate malaria and river blindness; billionaire investor and Berkshire Hathaway Chairman Warren Buffett's donation in 2006 of $31 billion to the Gates Foundation; Ronald Perelman's $70 million in charitable donations in 2008 alone, including $50 million to finance the Ronald O. Perelman Heart Centre at New York Presbyterian Hospital and Weill Cornell Medical Centre.

Philanthropy is facilitated by development professionals and fundraisers. Donor relations and stewardship professionals support the development profession by recognizing and thanking donors in a fashion that will cultivate future giving to nonprofit organizations. The Association of Donor Relations Professionals (ADRP) is the first community of stewardship and donor relations professionals in the United States and Canada.

Views

Philosophy : The purpose of philanthropy is also debated. Some equate philanthropy with benevolence and charity for the poor. Others hold that philanthropy can be any altruistic act that fulfills a social need that is not served, is under-served, or is perceived as such by the market. Some believe that philanthropy can be a means to build community by growing community funds and giving vehicles. When communities see themselves as being resource rich instead of asset poor, the community is in a better position to solve community problems. Philanthropy responds to either the present or the future needs. The charitable response to an impending disaster is an action of philanthropy. It offers immediate honour for the philanthropist, yet requires no foresight. Responding to future needs, however, draws on the donor's foresight and wisdom, but seldom recognizes the donor. Prevention of future needs will often avert far more hardship than a response after the fact. For example, the charities responding to starvation from overpopulation in Africa are afforded swift recognition. Meanwhile, philanthropists behind the U.S. population control movement of the 1960s and 1970s were never recognized, and are lost to history.

Politics : Philanthropists are often popular and become known to the public as "good" or even "great." Some governments are suspicious of philanthropic activities as possible grabs for Favour, but still allow special interest groups to form non-governmental organizations.

Uses of the Word

Conventional Usage

By the conventional definition of philanthropy, donations are dedicated to a narrowly defined cause and the donation is targeted to effect a recognizable change in social conditions. This often necessitates large donations and financial support sustained over time.

The need for a large financial commitment creates a distinction between philanthropy and *charitable giving*, which typically plays a supporting role in a charitable organization initiated by someone else. Thus, the conventional usage of *philanthropy* applies mainly to wealthy persons, and sometimes to a trust created by a wealthy person with a particular cause or objective targeted.

Many non-wealthy persons have dedicated – thus, donated – substantial portions of their time, effort and wealth to charitable causes. These people are not typically described as philanthropists because individual effort alone is seldom recognized as instigating significant change. These people are thought of as charitable workers but some people wish to recognize these people as philanthropists in honour of their efforts.

Truth in Giving: Experimental Evidence on the Welfare Effects of Informed Giving to the Poor

The willingness to redistribute income varies significantly across persons and countries for many reasons, including differences in income, variation in the price of giving, and donor attitudes. One well-documented regularity in the literature on income redistribution is that individuals prefer to assist recipients who are not responsible for their predicament. A person who fell because he is sick, for instance, is more likely to receive support than a person who fell because he is drunk (Piliavin, Rodin and Piliavin, 1969). Similarly, students are typically willing to help a classmate who was in an accident, but they often refuse to support a colleague who needs help because he was out partying (Betancourt, 1990). Variation in the beliefs about why the poor need support can help explain differences in redis tributive policy across democratic countries and between types of recipients.

While there is substantial evidence that individuals use information about recipients to decide how generous a donation to make, we know surprisingly little about how much donors care to help their preferred types. The observation that donors adjust their transfers according to information and beliefs about recipients is only weak evidence that truth in giving matters because these observations are consistent with donors being almost indifferent between giving to the "right" persons and giving randomly.

The graph shows the utility of a dictator in four situations: paired with a disabled person (*U*disability); paired with someone taking drugs (*U*drugs); when the recipient's type is unknown (*U*expected); and when the dictator maximizes his own income. Note that *U*disability and *U*drugs cross. The idea is that our dictator, if forced to make a zero transfer, would prefer to give nothing to a drug addict. The graph also assumes that the dictator would not wish to make an "insultingly low transfer" to his preferred type, the disabled recipient. One can think of these transfers as the ones that would typically be rejected in an ultimatum game. Knowing whether donors wish to learn about who they are assisting is important for the design of transfer programs. If governments and NGOs spend resources on monitoring recipients and detecting fraud, this will only increase donations and the political support for transfers if donors do in fact care to learn about the effectiveness of assistance. And even if some donors demand additional information, policy makers still face an interesting trade-off: resources spent on monitoring are no longer available as transfers, possibly reducing the welfare of those who deserve to be helped. Resolving this trade-off in an optimal manner requires administrators to understand whether donors demand information about recipient type and how those who give would adjust their transfers if they knew more.

History seems to suggest that uncertainty about the effectiveness of transfer programs can undermine the political support for income redistribution. For instance, the U.S. welfare debate of the 1980's was spurred by beliefs that welfare recipients took advantage of the former welfare program, Aid for Families with Dependent Children. The debate was not about cost, but about making sure assistance went to the "right" groups (Farkas et al.). Of course, claims such as 'I would be happy to give more, if only I knew that aid went to the right persons' are difficult to evaluate. These concerns might be real, indicating that improved information would increase transfers, or they might mask a categorical unwillingness to give.

8

Universal and Selective Social Services

Comprehensive Versus Selective Primary Health Care: Lessons for Global Health Policy

Primary health care was declared the model for global health policy at a 1978 meeting of health ministers and experts from around the world. Primary health care requires a change in socioeconomic status, distribution of resources, a focus on health system development, and emphasis on basic health services. Considered too idealistic and expensive, it was replaced with a disease-focused, selective model. After several years of investment in vertical interventions, preventable diseases remain a major challenge for developing countries. The selective model has not responded adequately to the interrelationship between health and socioeconomic development, and a rethinking of global health policy is urgently needed.

The health care systems of many developing countries emerged from colonial medical services that emphasized costly high-technology, urban-based, curative care. When these countries became independent in the 1950s and 1960s, they inherited health care systems modelled after the systems in industrialized nations. Public health programs of international development agencies during this period were also largely targeted at eradicating specific diseases such as smallpox, yaws, and malaria. Each disease eradication program operated autonomously, with its own administration and budget and very little integration into the larger health system. There were some successes during this period (for example, eradication of smallpox and a decrease in tuberculosis). However, these short-term interventions were not addressing poor populations' overall disease burden. Analysts realized that although one disease might be controlled or eliminated, recipients of that intervention might die of another disease or its complications. The situation worsened into the early 1970s, as populations continued to experience failing health outcomes with rising spending.

Recognizing that narrow targets were not the only option, countries attempted to implement comprehensive approaches to the provision of basic health services. Examples included the creation of the rural health Centre, staffed by medical and health assistants and supported by the Bhore Commission in India; the implementation of "community-based health programs" in Nicaragua, Costa Rica, Guatemala, Honduras, Mexico, Bangladesh, and the Philippines; and the barefoot doctor program in China. As part of the overall efforts to improve population health, these countries brought a new theme to international health discourse: commitment to social equity in health services. *Social equity* means that although different socioeconomic levels exist, the gaps between those levels are not insurmountable. Examples from these countries contributed to the optimism that inequity could be tackled to improve global health.

Introduction of "Health for All

" By the mid-1970s international health agencies and experts began to examine alternative approaches to health improvement in developing countries. The impressive health gains in China as a result of its community-based health programs and similar approaches elsewhere stood in contrast to the poor results of disease-focused programs. Soon this bottom-up approach that emphasized prevention and managed health problems in their social contexts emerged as an attractive alternative to the top-down, high-tech approach and raised optimism about the feasibility of tackling inequity to improve global health.

Thus, "health for all" was introduced to global health planners and practitioners by the World Health Organization (WHO) and the United Nations Children's Fund (UNICEF) at the International Conference on Primary Health Care in Alma Ata, Kazakhstan, in

1978. The declaration was intended to revolutionize and reform previous health policies and plans used in developing countries, and it reaffirmed WHO's definition of health in 1946: "a state of complete physical, mental, and social well being, and not merely the absence of disease or infirmity."

The conference declared that health is a fundamental human right and that attainment of the highest possible level of health was an important worldwide social goal.

To achieve the goal of health for all, global health agencies pledged to work toward meeting people's basic health needs through a comprehensive approach called primary health care. Primary health care as envisioned at Alma Ata had strong sociopolitical implications. It explicitly outlined a strategy that would respond more equitably, appropriately, and effectively to basic health needs and also address the underlying social, economic, and political causes of poor health. It was to be underpinned by universal accessibility and coverage on the basis of need, with emphasis on disease prevention and health promotion, community participation, self-reliance, and inter sectoral collaboration.

It acknowledged that poverty, social unrest and instability, the environment, and lack of basic resources contribute to poor health status. It outlined eight elements that future interventions would use to fulfil the goal of health improvement: education concerning prevailing health problems and methods of preventing and controlling them; promotion of food supply and proper nutrition; an adequate supply of safe water and basic sanitation; maternal and child health care, including family planning; immunization against major infectious diseases; prevention and control of locally endemic diseases; appropriate treatment of common diseases and injuries; and provision of essential drugs.

Selective Primary Health Care

One year after the Alma Alta declaration, Julia Walsh and Kenneth Warren presented "selective primary health care" as an "interim" strategy to begin the process of primary health care implementation. They argued that the best way to improve health was to fight disease based on cost-effective medical interventions. Although they acknowledged that the goal set at Alma Ata was "above reproach," they contended that its scope and resource constraints made it unattainable. They proposed that a selective attack on a region's most severe public health problems would maximize improvement of health in developing countries.

They identified four factors to guide the selection of target diseases for prevention and treatment: prevalence, morbidity, mortality, and feasibility of control (including efficacy and cost). Thus, rather than the envisioned emphasis on development and sustainability of health systems and infrastructures to improve population health, primary health care implementation in developing countries became focused on four vertical programs: growth monitoring, oral rehydration therapy, breast-feeding, and immunization (GOBI).

Family planning, female education, and food supplementation (FFF) were added later. These interventions targeted only women of childbearing age (15–45) and children through age five. This narrow selection of specific conditions for these population groups was designed to improve health statistics, but it abandoned Alma Ata's focus on social equity and health systems development. This transformation from the lofty goals set at Alma Ata to a selective approach sparked more than two decades of exhaustive debate.

Effectiveness of Comprehensive Primary Health Care

Some global health analysts argue that comprehensive primary health care was an experiment that failed; others contend that it was never truly tested. With only one year between the Alma Ata declaration and the shift toward a selective approach to its implementation, the transformative potential of comprehensive primary health care remained largely unexploited. Nevertheless, there were some important successes, particularly in the 1980s. Mozambique, Cuba, and Nicaragua, for example, expanded their primary health care coverage and greatly improved their population health indices. The keys to these accomplishments were the political will to meet all citizens' basic health needs, active popular participation in the effort to realize this goal, and increased social and economic equity.

Whereas the progress in Mozambique and Nicaragua was short-lived, Cuba has maintained steady progress even after the collapse of, and loss of support from, the Soviet Union and many years of embargo by the United States. Its success has been attributed to its model primary health care system. Under the Cuban constitution, health care is a right of citizens and a responsibility of government.

In addition, Cuba's Public Health Law outlines the principles of the National Healthcare System as follows: socialized medicine organized by government; basic services accessible to the whole population and free to all; preventive medicine as the hallmark of the system; public participation in health care; and a comprehensive approach to planned development of the health system. A 1997 report from the American Association for World Health, analyzing the U.S. embargo's effects on health in Cuba, concluded that a humanitarian catastrophe had been averted because the country maintained a high level of budgetary support for a health care system designed to deliver primary and preventive health care to all of its citizens.

Cuba's population health indices are on a par with those of developed countries that have several times its budget: Life expectancy is seventy-seven years, and the infant mortality rate is 7.7 per 1,000 live births, which ranks Cuba among the twenty-five countries in the world with the lowest infant mortality rates. As Cesar Chelala observed, Cuba's infant mortality rate for 1997 was half that of Washington, D.C.

Effectiveness of Selective Primary Health Care

While many factors ultimately affected the implementation of primary health care by national governments and aid agencies, selective primary health care and the resulting programs that were and are supported cannot fulfil the ideals of Alma Ata, including the emphasis on self-reliance, which is essential for communities to promote and sustain their own health.

Shortcomings

First, the selective approach ignores the broader context of development and the values that are imbued in the equitable development of countries. It does not address health as more than the absence of disease; as a state of well-being, including dignity; and as embodying the ability to be a functioning member of society.

In conjunction with the lack of a development context, the selective model does not acknowledge the role of social equity and social justice for the recipients of technologically driven medical interventions. The reality of the model is that vertical programs are Centreed in urban hospitals and health care facilities. Without the participation of communities, there is no avenue for change.

Second, the donor-driven, technocratic approach to determining priorities for interventions detracts from the grassroots approach that the Alma Ata declaration stated was necessary for health development. Third, the model tends to preserve the status quo of vertical objectives, fighting one disease at a time and not incorporating these efforts into a higher baseline of health status.

Fourth, there is little coordination among these vertical programs, leading to redundancy, overlap, and waste. Finally, the sole emphasis on women and young children, to the neglect of other segments of the population, is an important flaw. The high burden of HIV/AIDS among people ages 20–39 in many developing countries (an indication of infection during adolescence) is not surprising, given the long neglect of this population group in health policy and practice.

Improvements and Deficits in Global Health

In spite of the above shortcomings, selective primary health care has been lauded as having contributed greatly to improvements in global health. It is said, for example, that eight of every ten children in the world today receive vaccinations against the five major childhood diseases. Globally, between 1980 and 1993 infant mortality fell by 25 percent, while overall life expectancy increased by more than four years, to sixty-five years.

However, whereas the number of children under age five who died from vaccine-preventable diseases decreased by 1.3 million between 1985 and 1993, more than twelve million of these children died within this period nevertheless. Moreover, childhood diarrhea and malnutrition remain leading causes of impaired child health in developing countries, contributing greatly to the thirteen million deaths that occur annually among children under age five.

A 2003 United Nations report argues that international assistance aimed at helping poorer countries develop is failing; it calls for a reexamination of current strategies if the world is to meet targets for reducing poverty, hunger, and illness. According to the report, fifty-four countries are poorer now than they were in 1990, and life expectancy has regressed in thirty-four countries, mostly in Africa.

Lessons for Future Global Health Policy

Although disease-specific interventions are important, assuring real change will require attention to environmental, political, and social actions that target the root causes of disease as envisaged at Alma Ata. Alma Ata's comprehensive primary health care was a global recognition of some of the causes of unsatisfactory results in many programs. Studies during the 1970s revealed that lack of overall development was inextricably linked to health and that health discussed in a vacuum would never succeed. However, experimentation with comprehensive and selective approaches to global health policy have also revealed that discussion of health in the context of society, economics, politics, and development put many barriers in the way of success as well.

One of the ideological barriers was the concomitant challenge of social equity and social justice. Alma Ata made it the responsibility of governments and agencies to promote equity and ensure that certain citizens were not unduly suffering for the benefits received by others. Comprehensive primary health care combined many complex features into its definition of health and health care.

Various Sectors need to Work Together

First, because health does not occur in isolation, the various sectors, including those within a national government and among aid agencies, need to work together at every level of practice. The ministry of health is not the sole agency charged with production of health; departments of agriculture, housing, sanitation, and education, along with food distribution, are all involved in achieving health.

Interventions must come from needs of the Community

Second, the Alma Ata declaration requires that interventions come from the needs of the community, expressed and subsequently led by community members. Global health problems cannot be solved by distant policymakers and planners. Involvement of individuals and communities mobilizes local resources to deal with health problems. Implied in the concept of participation is decentralized physical location; programs need to be founded and researched in the locality in which they will be applied. The Alma Ata declaration also recognizes that the issue of accessibility to health services and resources has historically been a barrier to effective care and that placing emphasis on curative, tertiary care hospitals located in urban Centres often precludes access for a mostly rural population.

Fullest Potential Difficult to Achieve Without Supporting Infrastructure

These are some of the underpinning principles behind the Alma Ata declaration; unfortunately, key elements are lacking in the selective approach adopted for its implementation. Some developing countries continue to rely on vertical programs, with less emphasis on people's involvement and development of systems and infrastructures to sustain those programs. For example, although the current initiative on vaccines and immunization designed to help countries incorporate new vaccines into their national health systems surely has benefits for addressing specific communicable diseases, their fullest potential will be difficult to achieve in the absence of effective health systems and supporting infrastructures. Limited assessment of this initiative undertaken in Mozambique, Ghana, Lesotho, and Tanzania revealed that the infrastructural foundation needed for successful implementation and sustainability is inadequate.

Maintaining the cost of expensive new vaccines after donor support ceases also poses a serious challenge to sustainability. As with most vertical programs, analysts have expressed concern that raising poor countries' awareness of new vaccines and immunization programs without support in implementing such programs could end up creating markets for these vaccines while doing little to tackle major health problems.

Given that disease-focused models continue to be funded and promoted in developing countries, it is apparent that adequate lessons have not been learned from experimentation with selective, vertical approaches; that the notion of self-reliance, community participation, and health systems development proposed at Alma Ata have diminished in importance; and that inadequate consideration is given to the link between health and socioeconomic development. Global health policy for the twenty-first century should recognize that high-tech and expensive models to address diseases of poverty will not be sustainable where infrastructures needed for operationalization and institutionalization of those technologies scarcely exist.

Revitalizing Alma Ata's Tenets

Although the challenges of addressing the socioeconomic root causes of disease in developing countries may seem insurmountable, analyses of factors that contributed to health improvements in developed countries provide cause for optimism. For example, the appalling health conditions described in the *Report of the Sanitary Commission of Massachusetts* to the Massachusetts state legislature in 1850 were similar to those that prevail in developing countries today.

The recommendations embodied the essential elements of comprehensive primary health care—communicable disease control, promotion of child health, housing improvement, sanitation, training of community health workers, public health education, promotion of individual responsibility for one's own health, mobilization of community participation through sanitary associations, and creation of multidisciplinary boards of health to assess needs and plan programs.

Recognizing the importance of political commitment, the report called for establishment of a strong public health constituency and addressed inequity by highlighting major differences in life expectancies between U.S. rural and urban areas. Thus, many of the improvements in Americans' health have been attributed to the ensuing political commitment and emphasis on public health and to social and economic interventions.

Similarly, in reviewing factors that contributed to improvements in health in England, Thomas McKeown demonstrated that population health improved more because of investments in "environmental public health," political, economic, and social measures than from specific medical or therapeutic interventions. Decline in deaths from tuberculosis and from respiratory and water-and foodborne diseases had already occurred before any effective immunizations or treatments were available.

Concrete Strategies and Processes

Thus, to improve the health status of people in developing countries and to ensure sustainability, a revitalization of the tenets of Alma Ata's primary health care is needed. Of critical importance is the need to establish concrete strategies and processes, with clear targets, to reduce inequities in the allocation of resources for primary health care, and with a focus on both horizontal and vertical equity. The value of this proposal is illustrated by the striking success that has been achieved in social development and health by a few poor countries, notably Sri Lanka, Costa Rica, Cuba, China, and Kerala state in India.

Mortality and malnutrition rates are much lower and life expectancy much higher in these countries than in other countries with similar economic characteristics and indeed some wealthier countries. In this regard, it is important to stress that the nature of the political system, its values, and its processes for participation define the frontiers of opportunity for health equity. Systems characterized by the absence of democracy and by pervasive corruption, violence, and sex discrimination are breeding grounds for inequities in health and in other social spheres.

Social Policies

Health policymakers should be aware that macroeconomic, labour, and social policies have the potential to limit or enhance health opportunities for different groups in the population. International aid agencies and governments in developing countries should be aware that the pursuit of liberal macroeconomic progrowth policies has the tendency to provide better opportunities to those with resources and high levels of education while large segments of the population without these assets are unlikely to benefit and may in fact become casualties of economic transition. Thus, it is the duty of health policymakers to signal when other policies may undermine efforts to promote health equity.

Inter sectoral Forums

Countries also need to strengthen their primary health care

through the development of inter sectoral forums at every level. Human health should be a cross-cutting issue throughout the decision-making process in different sectors and at different levels. Health policy development should involve those sectors, agencies, and social groups that are critical to achieving better health. This can be achieved through advocacy for health objectives as integral to socioeconomic development and through engagement of different sectoral partners and community structures in the consensual process.

Funding Commitment

Developing countries' governments must be committed to funding and budgets for sustaining community involvement in health. This can be achieved through, for example, private-sector involvement and through hosting village, district, or regional people's health assemblies so that the voices and opinions of the people can be represented in the design and implementation of health policies.

Trained Health Personnel

Most importantly, to ensure the quality of primary health care, reform of the health sector under primary health care should include coherent human resource development plans at the village, district, state/regional, and national levels and strategies for retention of trained personnel in remote and rural areas. Primary health care systems in developing countries provide interventions that are already known to be effective. This means that achievement of quality in primary health care facilities requires the proper performance of these interventions according to prescribed standards to reduce mortality, morbidity, and disability. However, the most common challenge is that often these interventions are not properly executed.

A recent study in southeast Nigeria, for example, revealed that inadequacy in the quality of services provided by community-based primary health care workers is a product of failures in a range of quality measures: structural, process failings, and lack of a protocol for systematic supervision of health workers. Thus, quality improvement in this context is not simply a matter of providing infrastructural resources but, rather, one of paying attention to improvement in process, especially through training and supervision.

Long-term Social Interventions

Finally, although short-term measures do not necessarily undermine the contributions of vertical therapeutic interventions to public health, it is apparent, as this paper has shown, that they are not sufficient to greatly alleviate the overall burden of disease in developing countries unless the socioeconomic, political, and health system factors that underpin health and disease in these countries are challenged. The remedy, as we have argued, lies in a fundamental shift in emphasis from vertical, short-term measures to a revitalization of Alma Ata's primary health care, with emphasis on poverty alleviation, community participation, and the development of health systems and infrastructures to create and sustain health.

The Universal Welfare State as a Social Dilemma

The Welfare State – A Private or Public Good?

From a mainstream neoclassical economist perspective, most of the things provided by modern welfare states are essentially *private goods*. Such goods, health care, social insurance and education, for example, can be privately consumed. This means that A, who owns the good, can exclude B from consuming the good in question. So in order for the welfare state to be understood as bundle of publicly provided private goods, it would not be a suitable candidate for the social dilemma/collective action approach in political science (Ostrom 1998). The reason for this is that this approach, by definition, only relates to *public goods,* that is, goods where it is not possible for the individual to exclude others from using the good.

The existence of the welfare state is understood by many mainstream economists as an anomaly because, what the welfare state provides should instead be left to market decisions where, as for other private goods like food, cosmetics and clothes, individual demand would meet its supply (Baumol 1965). Moreover, if left to the market, standard economic theory states that the things the welfare state provides would be produced with much greater efficiency than if provided by the government and paid for by taxes. The occurs because competing producers of such private goods would have a strong incentive to rationalize production, while such incentives are of course lacking in a state-monopoly system. For economists and political scientists adhering to the "public choice" approach, the existence of the modern welfare state is explained by the existence of so called normative irregularities. These include the murky activities of "rent-seeking" bureaucrats wanting to expand their power and budgets, or likewise "rent-seeking" interests groups which, by an improperly functioning political process have succeed in derailing public decisions from what is in the "general interest" (Mueller 1989).

Recent developments in non-cooperative game-theory, stressing the problem of incomplete and/or as symetric information, have challenged this view of the welfare state. The result from this line of research is that, because of these information problems, the market will either not fill the demand for many forms of social insurance, health care and education, or it will do so less efficient than the state. Summarizing both the theoretical and empirical research in this field, Nicholas Barr has shown that for unemployment insurance, basic education, health care and pensions, market forces can not supply what the consumers/voters demand.

More specifically, there are three main problems that the market, according to this approach, can not handle. One is what is called "adverse selection", it will be in the interest of competing insurance companies to get rid of "bad risks". Consequently, such "bad risks" will try to conceal that they are in fact "bad risks" because they know that if they revealed this information, they would either not be accepted as customers at all or they would have to pay a higher premium. It should be added that with the advances in gene-technology, the possibilities for insurance companies to identify such "bad risks" is likely to increase dramatically.

The second information problem in most social insurance system is known as "moral hazard", which are difficulties for private insurance companies to get information when an involuntary injury giving right to benefits has occurred. In some cases, such as health care, this problem can be ameliorated by the use of some knowledgeable profession (read: doctors), while for unemployment or social assistance it is much more difficult, if at all possible, to get such information. The third problem why private insurance will not be provided is that in some cases, injuries hit very large parts of the population at the same time, so called interdependent risks (for pensions this is periods with high inflation, for unemployment insurance this is extended economic downturns).

Thus, if what the welfare state provides is left to market provision, three things are likely to happen. One is that in order to force insurance companies to refrain from dumping "bad risks" and guaranteeing for the problem of interdependent risks, the state must enforce regulation to such a level that the system, in practice, becomes a public system. Another scenario is that the costs for surveillance to handle these problems become very high. The third is that transaction costs, i.e., costs for consumers and producers to enter and monitor contracts, are likely to be very high, especially in the area of health care where there are many parties involved (patients, doctors, hospitals, insurance companies, medical labouratories, etc...). Nicholas Barr has summarized the consequences of these information problems and the problem of interdependent risks as follows:

Information problems provide both a theoretical *justification of* and an *explanation for* a welfare state which is much more than a safety net. Such a welfare state is justified not simply by redis tributive aims one may (or may not) have, but because it does things which private markets for technical reasons would either do inefficiently, or would not do at all.

The implication is that most parts of what is known as the modern welfare state is in fact a *public good* and thus a candidate, as good as any, for the problems we know as social dilemmas and collective action (Putterman, Roemer, and Silvestre 1998). This conclusion rests, of course, on the idea that there is a general demand for such things as social and health insurance, and education, whether provided by the government or not. If this is correct, the existence of such services can not be understood as primarily a result from the activities of "rent-seeking" public bureaucrats and/or interests groups, squeezing out special benefits for their members from the general taxpayer. Empirical studies show very little, if any, support for this view (Lewin 1991). To the contrary, as I will show below, the existence of a broad demand for universal social programs finds strong support in survey data.

It should be added that there is a social dilemma problem here, apart from what is said above about social insurance. If we simply understand the welfare state as "the rich helping the poor" for pure altruistic reasons, "the rich" still face a collective action problem in order to accomplish this. As stated by Milton Friedman in 1962, every rich person may want to get rid of poverty in society, but, if rational, will do so on the condition that enough other rich persons are also willing to contribute to such a noble cause (Friedman 1962).

Let's call this conditional altruism. The reason this altruism is conditional is that the poor as a social category (and poverty as a social problem) will only be effectively dealt with if enough rich persons contribute enough money. (This may be the reason why "the rich" when organizing help for the poor, often meet in semi-public settings such a charity gala dinners, where each individuals contributions is made in public.) Without some form of guarantee that enough other rich persons will contribute, each rich altruistic person may rationally abstain from making a contribution reasoning that small efforts can not redress big problems. One such guarantee could be the institutionalization of a properly organized tax system that taxes all rich people and a welfare state administration that makes sure the resources also reach the poor (Rothstein 1998).

Before proceeding, there is need to say something about the standard efficiency argument that market provision is more efficient than government provision. In face of the information problems in social insurance mentioned above, mandatory insurance for all increases efficiency because it pools the risks as broadly as possible. A related reason for the increased efficiency of compulsory insurance is that the costs competing private insurance companies would incur, trying to handle the information problems above (known as transaction costs), tend to be very high (Gerdtham and Lothgren 1998).

The empirical evidence is also for once very clear, it can not be shown that countries with high public spending have lesser economic growth rates than countries with low public spending. At the micro-level, increased wage-taxes does not have a general negative effect on the provision of wage-labour. The empirical evidence shows that if income taxes are lowered, some work less because they get the income they want with less work. Others will work more because it pays more to work. The major message from the empirical research is that the net result of these two different effects is close to zero (Pencavel 1986).

The Puzzle of Increased Variation

In the comparative welfare state literature, two major findings are of interest from a social dilemma perspective. The first is the well-known differences that exist in the quality and scope of welfare state programs among the industrialized western democracies. Quantitatively, the Scandinavia countries spend about twice as much as a percentage of GDP on social insurance and social assistance than the United States, Most other European countries' spending falls somewhere in between. The other finding is less well known, this huge difference in welfare state ambitions is a rather recent phenomenon. If we go back to the early 1960s, these countries spent almost the same as a percentage of GDP on welfare policies (OECD 1994). Given the internationalization of values, increase in trade, globalization of capital, etc..., this is a rather unexpected development. After all, these are countries with basically the same type of social, economic and political structures, that is, they are all western democratic capitalist market economies. Most social scientists working in the early 1960s would probably, without our benefit of hindsight, have predicted convergence in social policy between these countries, not such a dramatic divergence.

It should be reminded that behind these macroeconomic figures are the lives of real people. Comparing the economic situation of single parent families in the mid-1980, 54 percent in the U.S and 46 percent in Canada lived in severe poverty (defined as having less than half of the median income) compared to 6 % in the Ne'herlands and 7 in % (McFate, Smeeding, and Rainwater 1995). Of 100,000 persons, 580 are in prison in the United States compared to an average of 40 in the Scandinavia countries (Wacquant 1998). There are of course many different reasons behind crime and imprisonment, but poverty would clearly count as one.

One way to explain the differences in welfare state programs would be through standard political variables; the ideological orientation of dominant political parties in Scandinavia are different (read: more Social Democratic) from those in the United States or Canada. This is of course true, but then it should also be said that all the Scandinavia countries have had extended periods with non-socialist/conservative parties in government during this period. Moreover, these have been periods marked more by expansion than contraction of welfare state spending (Rothstein 1998). A second type of explanation would point to general norms and values, for example, Scandinavians, for whatever historical and cultural reasons, are more inclined to embrace norms such as equality and social justice. The problem, however, is that comparative studies based on survey data find little support for this type of explanation. In contrast, findings from such studies report a striking similarity in such basic values and norms about justice and equality between countries with very different ambitions in welfare state measures (Svallfors 1997). So, we are left with a puzzle; standard theories about economic development, political power or social norms don't seem to be able to explain the differences in welfare state programs.

Here, I will propose an explanation that this puzzle can be understood from a social dilemma perspective. My argument is that the solution to how this dilemma has been solved in different countries is related to the way in which the institutions of the welfare state programs have been historically established. In order to highlight the differences, I will concentrate the analysis on one of the so called outliers, namely Sweden, which in various studies has been shown to be the most expansive welfare state.

Speaking from an institutionalist perspective, what best characterizes the Swedish and the other Scandinavia (and some other North European) welfare states, is most programs are universal, not selective. This means that social programs such as old-age pensions, health care, child-care, education, child allowances, and health insurance, are not targeted to "the poor", but instead cover the entire population without consideration of their ability to pay.

Many scholars have maintained, since benefits and services are distributed in roughly equal shares to everyone, and since the tax system is proportional on the whole, no real redistribution between income groups takes place in universal welfare states. Some economists have even claimed that a universal welfare system amounts largely to a costly bureaucratic roundabout with very little redis tributive effects (Tullock 1983). Nothing could be further from the truth. The table below illustrates why:

Table 1. The Redis Tributive effect of the Universal Welfare State.

Group	*Average Income*	*Tax (40%)*	*Transfers*	*Income after taxes and transfers*
A (20%)	1000	400	240	840
B (20%)	800	320	240	720
C (20%)	600	240	240	600
D (20%)	400	160	240	480
E (20%)	200	80	240	360
Ratio between groups A & E	5/1	(= 1200)	(1200/5=24)	2.33/1

The redis tributive logic of the model is as follows. In the first column, income earners are divided for the sake of simplicity, into five groups of equal size, according to average income. We assume the average income of the group earning most is five times that of the group earning least. This difference, which we may call the inequality quotient, is 5/1. We further assume, *nota bene,* not a progressive but rather a strictly proportional system of income taxes.

We set the tax rate at 40%, which corresponds roughly to that part of the Swedish public sector's presently 56.2% of GNP that is spent on social, educational, and other welfare policy. Finally, we assume that all public benefits and services are universal, which means that the individuals in each group receive *on average* the same sum in the form of cash benefits and/or subsidized public services.

The level of inequality has thus been reduced by more than half in this model of how the universal welfare policy works. Note that this redis tributive logic works the same if you take the groups' (or person's) income over a life-time, as well as if you compare at one single point in time. It is only if you can argue that over time, the persons in groups A and B will switch with the persons in groups D and E, that the redis tributive effect decreases.

This model has, in fact, a strong support in empirical data of how different welfare states redistribute income (McFate, Smeeding, and Rainwater 1995). It turns out that, perhaps contrary to one's intuition, it is the states which tax everyone "the same" and gives everyone "the same". This means the universal systems usually end up effectively redistributing economic resources, while the ones which intend to tax the rich to give to the poor, end up with much less redistribution.

The reason for this paradox of redistribution is that while taxes usually are relative (a fixed percentage of income for example), benefits or services are usually nominal. The extent of redistribution depends, in other words, not just on accuracy of aim but also on the sums transferred. To put it in other words: if you tax the rich and give to the poor, the rich will not accept high taxes.

Rationality, Information and Support for the Universal Welfare State

The model can not predict what will be the likely outcome if agents act solely out of self-interest. The reason is that while group E and D will clearly be in Favour of a universal system because they get more benefits than what they pay in taxes, group A and B will be against a universal system for the opposite reason (they contribute more than they get). This means that the group, which in the model determines if a universal welfare state will persist or not, is group C (i.e., "the middle class").

The reason for this is twofold. First, for this group, the system is cost neutral, that is, they pay in as much as they get out from the system. Second, in a democratic polity, and again following the standard economic theory of self-interested behaviour, groups C (henceforth "the middle class") will be what in political science are known as the "swing voters", that is, they will decide what the majority will be. Swedish survey data confirms this picture, i.e., that support for the universal welfare state decreases with higher social class (Svallfors 1996).

From an electoral perspective, it is only if the middle class opts for a political alliance with groups D and E that the universal welfare state will be stable. This means that from a standard economic utility maximizing point, we can not predict what will happen in this model, that is, if the universal welfare state is stable or not. This is, as stated above, also the empirical case. Some modern capitalist democracies have more universal welfare systems, while others have more selective arrangements, and this follows to a large extent from the electoral behaviour of the middle class.

However, if we relax the assumption about the individual tax payer's/voter's/social insurance recipient's economic rationality, in three ways, another picture comes through. First, following the work by Kahnemann and Tversky, we know from experimental data that people tend to be risk adverse. Given the guarantees that government insurance can provide compared to a private insurance company, the middle class may be more prone to support universal public social insurance. However, this depends on if the government is perceived as trustworthy or not.

Second, it is very difficult in this case for the (middle class) individual to get accurate information about the gains and losses when she compares taxes and benefits. The lack of information, and if we add to that, uncertainty about the future, are very likely change the basis upon which people act. Following a recent argument by Arthur Denzau and Douglas North, as well as John Scholz, in such situations marked by uncertainty and lack of information, people do not act as if they have computers in their head solving equations about possible gains and losses. Instead, shared mental maps, heuristics, ideological persuasions and moral standards are used when agents form decisions.

This implies that, in particular for group C in our model, the decision to support a universal system (or not) is very likely to be a *combination* of rational utility maximizing calculation (so far as it can be made) *and* ideological/normative orientations. This has recently been stated in the approach named "evolutionary game theory" as follows: agents are not perfectly rational and fully informed about the world in which they live. They base their decisions on fragmentary information, they have incomplete models of the process they are engaged in, and they may not be especially forward looking. Still, they are not completely irrational: they adjust to their behaviour based on what they think other agents are going to do, and these expectations are generated endogenously by information about what other agents have done in the past.

Third, we know from experimental studies of collective action problems that a considerable number of individuals do not follow the self-interested utility maximizing script at all. Especially if given the possibility to communicate, people do not free ride as much as standard rational choice theory predicts (Tyler 1998). To quote one recent survey of the results form this experimental research: *"hard-nosed game theory cannot explain the data"* (Ledyard 1995). The willingness to act out of norms of solidarity is simply much higher and more widespread than the standard economic theory about human behaviour predicts (Sally 1995). If democracy is considered not only as system for the simple aggregation of preferences, but also as a deliberative and discursive process, the results about the importance of communication from experimental studies should have implications for how agents behave (Mackie 1998).

As we are dealing with electoral behaviour, it should be underlined that the negative results for the public choice theory are confirmed in survey studies about how people vote. Empirical studies about voting behaviour have refuted the economic logic of voting put forward by the public choice school in political science. Instead of voting out of pure self-interest, citizens take the overall well-being of the society into account. In electoral research, this is known as *sociotropic* voting (Lewin 1991).

Empirical results about political behaviour and behaviour in experimental social dilemma situations have led a couple of political scientists to suggest that we must build our analyses on a more realistic foundation of what type of utility functions people act. From a social dilemma perspective, it should be clear that most people do not act out of one single rational utility maximizing utility function because, in that case, most social dilemmas would end up in pathological social traps.

One way to solve this problem is to start the analysis that most people do not have a single, but (at least) two different utility functions. Margaret Levi, who has done research under what conditions young men volunteer for war, has put this as follows, there are segments of the citizenry whose utility function is unitary; they are purely income maximizes or purely moral. A large proportion, however, appear to have *dual utilities.* They wish to contribute to the social good, at least as long as they believe a social good is being produced. They also want to ensure that their individualistic interests are being satisfied as far as possible.

This idea of a *dual utility function* can serve as a useful tool when we try to understand how social dilemmas can be solved. In line with the experimental studies mentioned above, it shows that most people do want to contribute to solve collective action problems instead of acting as free riders What they do not want to be is "suckers", contributing when "the others" are not contributing.

Thus, one of the things needed to solve social dilemmas is trust and other such norms of reciprocity, which insure the individual that enough others will behave cooperatively. What complicates the problem in our case is that when it comes to social insurance, the individual citizen is clearly in *two different* social dilemma situations where trust is important. The first is with the government: will the state actually, when the day comes, deliver what it has promised to deliver. For the individual, many things provided for by the welfare state have long time horizons (pensions, college education for ones children, old-age and old-age health care). So, the individual does not only have to consider if the current government can be trusted, but also any government likely to hold power in the future.

The second dilemma is with all other citizens – will they financially support the system or are they more likely to cheat and avoid paying taxes. And will they try to undermine the system by claiming benefits they are not entitled to, or will they play by the rules. In many social insurance cases, "moral hazard" is a problem, i.e., it is difficult to know if the unemployed are really unable to find work, etc... This means that even if an individual in principle, out of some moral conviction, would Favour a universal welfare state system, he or she may nevertheless withhold support because mistrust of either the government or of fellow citizens. Thus, these two strategic situations (citizen vs. the government and citizen vs. all other citizens) can be understood as two "nested games".

Margaret Levi has conceptualized this as the problem of *contingent consent*. The idea is that citizens will consent under certain conditions to collective (in this case government organized) action to produce *public goods*. The starting point is that citizens will try to balance their wish to act according to the norm of contributing to "the common good" with their rational self-interest. The theory of contingent consent entails the following: we imagine a situation in which citizens attach positive moral value to the object sought by collective measures, for example some form of social insurance.

In the face of problems of free riding, achieving sufficient support for such measures presupposes that three conditions be fulfilled. These are the following: (1) citizens regard the good to be produced in itself as valuable. We will call this the question about *substantial justice;* (2) citizens consider the administrative process needed to implement this value to be organized in keeping with *procedural justice*, i.e., that the government will deliver what it has promised to deliver in a fair and impartial way; and 3) citizens believe their fellow citizens also contribute to the program on a solidaristic basis (non or insignificant "free-riding").

Most discussions of social policy concern only the first normative condition of substantial justice.

The second condition is adding because studies show, in addition to substantial justice, people seem to care a lot about procedural justice (Tyler 1998). The reason for adding the second and third conditions stems from the literature on non-cooperative game theory and social dilemmas, which stress the importance of trust in institutions and trust in other agents. Below, I will discuss the institutional implications of each of these three conditions.

Substantive Justice

The first condition of contingent consent has to do with the normative question of *substantive justice.* That is, can one argue that the goals of a particular social policy measure are just? This first principle lies, we might say, at the heart of a universal welfare policy (Titmuss 1968). Indeed, the whole point of a universal welfare policy is not to discriminate between citizens, not to separate "the needy" and "the poor" from other citizens and to treat them differently. Social policy should seek instead to a moral obligation to furnish all citizens with, in Amarty Sen's words, *basic capabilities.*

In contrast to the situation under a selective system, the public discourse about social policy in a universal system cannot be conducted in the terms indicated by the question: "what shall we do about these deviant groups/individuals?" Or as former US Vice-President Dan Quayle put it in a debate: "those people." The public discussion of social policy in a selective system often becomes a question of what the well-adjusted majority should do about "the others", i.e., the socially marginalised minority. The *substantial justice* of the system can thereby come under question by the majority, who might start asking (a) where the line between the needy and non-needy should be drawn, and (b) whether the needy ("the others") themselves are not to blame for their predicament (and so cannot legitimately claim assistance). We may refer to the first as the general, and the second as the individual boundary-drawing problems.

In the selective model, the discussion often focuses on how to separate the "deserving" from the "undeserving" poor (Katz 1989), which translates into a seemingly unending debate about how and where to draw these two boundary lines. Leading politicians are therefore likely to find themselves in a situation where it becomes increasingly difficult to argue that the selective programs are normatively fair. Public consent to the system is undermined, because the social policy debate comes to turn not on what is *generally fair,* but rather what is *specifically necessary for "the others".*

Moreover, in a selective system, the moral logic of the discourse tends in itself to undermine the legitimacy of the system. This occurs because most selective types of policies that are structured to integrate a specific group with the rest of society, seem to entail a paradox of the following kind: To motivate selective measures, like affirmative action, the targeted group must first to be singled out as inherently *different* from ordinary citizens. But if the group is that different, how can they ever by any social policy initiative, become like "ordinary citizens". If the selective policy has only marginal effects, the usual strategy for those advocating it is to argue that the group is even more different (and thus have even more special needs) than what had initially been presumed, and therefore needs more selective/targeted policies.

Under a universal system, in which the state furnishes all citizens with *basic capabilities,* the moral logic is altogether different. Since the universal welfare policy embraces all citizens, the debate assumes quite another character: social policy is now thought to concern the entire community, and the question becomes *what, from a general standpoint,* is a fair manner in which to organize social policy. No discussion of the type above, concerning how and where to draw the two boundary lines for "the others", need ever take place, simply because no such lines need be drawn. Welfare policy does not, therefore, turn into a question of what should be done about "the poor" and "the maladjusted," but rather a question of what constitutes *general fairness* in respect to the relation between citizens and the state. The question becomes not "how shall we solve *their* problem?" but rather "how shall we solve *our common* problems with social insurance?

Procedural Justice

Condition number two concerns the implementation of policy. Can welfare policy be *carried out* in a fair manner? How does the choice of a universal or selective welfare policy affect the public's view of state capacity? Beginning with the former, one should bear in mind that a typical universal welfare program, like flat-rate pensions or child allowances, is a great deal simpler, cheaper, and easier to implement than its selective counterpart. This is largely because there is no need, in a program of a universal type, for an administrative apparatus charged with carrying out the *two* types of eligibility tests which are a necessary concomitant of a selective program.

These test must ascertain (1) whether a given applicant is entitled to support, and (2) if so, to how much. Social policy can be given the form of specified citizen rights, and the social duties of the state can be rigorously defined in order to respect the integrity of citizens. The point is, depending on the institutions we select for furnishing citizens with *basic capabilities,* we create different types of moral logic in the social policy discourse. In the case of a selective policy, the state separates out those citizens unable to provide such basic *capabilities* for themselves, and furnishes them with said *capabilities.*

To do this, however, it must first determine whether or not they belong to the needy group, and if so, how much they need. The problem that arises is that it is very hard to do these things without violating the principle that the state should treat all citizens with, as stated by Ronald Dworkin, "equal concern and respect." The very act of separating out the needy almost always stamps them as socially inferior, as "others" with other types of social characteristics and needs, and results most often in stigmatization. In his important book "Spheres of Justice", Michael Walzer argues that social policy of this sort is incompatible with the maintenance of recipients' self-respect.

Selective programs present serious problems of procedural justice because they must allow local administrators a wide field for discretionary action. The difficulty of finding usable criteria for selecting recipients can often become unmanageable. This creates a "black hole of democracy," in which citizens find themselves faced with an administration or system of rules which no one really understands, and in which no one can be held responsible. In sum, the selective model leads, as Robert Goodin has stated to "unavoidable," "insurmountable," and "insoluble" problems in respect to the arbitrary treatment of citizens seeking assistance.

The difficulty of handling the discretionary power of administrators in selective programs has two important consequences. These consequences are often thought to be opposites, but in fact they are two sides of the same coin. They are the bureaucratic abuse of power, and fraud on the part of clients. Applicants in a selective system, if rational, will claim that their situation is worse than it actually is, and to describe their prospects for solving their problems on their own as small to nonexistent. The administrators in such a system, for their part, often have incentives from their superiors to be suspicious of clients' claims. In game theory, this is known as "the control game", a rather sad game because it has no stable equilibria and thus no solution. Fraud by a few clients feeds into increased control which, in its turn feeds into increased fraud by more clients, and so on (Hermansson 1990).

The question of procedural justice therefore looms large in selective systems. Even if cases of cheating, fraud, and the abuse of power are in fact relatively rare, the sensationalistic logic of mass media means that such cases will receive great attention, thereby influencing the majorities' "cognitive maps" on which social policy is based. It's very difficult to combine means-testing with procedural justice, for means-testing itself entails a violation of citizens' integrity-either in the means-test itself, or in the verification checks which often follow.

The Just Distribution of Burdens

Condition number three in the theory of contingent consent has to do with whether or not all citizens bear their share of the costs of a given policy, i.e., it concerns *the just distribution of burdens.* Citizens are portrayed here as players in a so-called assurance game, i.e., they are prepared to support the program in question, even if they cannot be sure they will themselves directly gain by it, as long as they can be convinced that all (or almost all) other citizens will also contribute to carrying it out. The willingness to contribute depends, that is, not just on the fulfillment of the requirements of procedural and substantive justice; it also assumes a credible organization of the collective efforts (so that such efforts are, in truth, *collective).* The other side of the question, of course, is how to discourage the unsolidaristic use of the benefits the welfare policy brings.

The universal model differs from the selective on this point as well. Typical for the latter is that assistance is granted only to those citizens who cannot in some other way provide for themselves or meet their "basic needs." This means as a rule that such citizens have no income, and therefore pay no tax. They constitute a category, then, which does not contribute economically. In a universal system, the vast majority of those who are recipients do work and thus do pay taxes.

In sum, to the extent the welfare system is designed so that even net beneficiaries can play a role as partners who contribute, according to their ability, to the defraying of costs, the legitimacy of welfare policy will increase. It becomes a question of how citizens shall undertake to solve their common problems, rather than a question of what "we" shall do about "them".

We observe here, then, two wholly distinct moral logics. The difficulty of implementing selective programs in such a way that their objectives are attained, and their processes considered fair, undermines public support for social policy in general. For example, the majority might be open to supporting social policy in principle, but constant reports of cheating, fraud, bureaucratic abuse of power, waste, inefficiency, and other irregularities lead to their taking the view that the policy's implementation is so deficient as to make the whole affair a waste of time and money.

It is very hard to imagine, moreover, that a population with such a negative view of welfare policy would be receptive to proposals to give it a more universal form (for this would involve *expanding* social policy). Instead, a suspicion of state measures becomes the dominant attitude. A state that fails to take care of "the poor" cannot of course be entrusted with the larger task of attending to the welfare of the entire population. Citizens are more willing, on the other hand, to agree to collective undertakings of this kind if they have confidence in the state as an institution.

9

Attitudes Toward Different Types of Social Programme

One consequence that modern social science has brought is that citizens are asked now and again about their attitudes towards various matters, including welfare policy. How does the empirical evidence look, then, in relation to the theory of contingent consent? Can empirical support be found for the proposition, that if the institutions of social policy are structured according to the principles of this theory, they will create norms forming a basis for the reproduction of the policy? Axel Hadenius in 1986 and Stefan Svallfors thereafter have conducted survey research which speak to this problem. They have asked identical questions of representative samples of the Swedish population about their support for different welfare state programs.

Attitudes Towards Public Expenditures

Answers to following question: "Taxes are used for various purposes. Do you think the revenues spent on the purposes mentioned below should be increased, held the same, or reduced?" The figures in the table represent the percentage of those wishing to increase expenditures minus the percentage of those wishing to reduce them.

At least two results of these studies are worthy of note. The first is the marked and stable difference in support for different types of programs over time. Support for the universal programs is unambiguously strong and stable, while the opposite is true for the two selective programs (housing allowances and social assistance). This seems to support our model of how people behave combining self-interest, uncertainty, risk-aversion, and solidarity. First, considering self-interest, these universal programs can be expected to have strong support because large segments of the population benefit from them. But, as showed in our model above, the crucial middle segment of the population might still opt out, if action is understood from a strict rational self-interested perspective.

Year	*1981*	*1986*	*1992*	*1997*
Health care	+42	+44	+48	+75
Support for the elderly	+29	+33	+58	+68
Support to families with children	+19	+35	+17	+30
Housing allowances	-23	-23	-25	-20
Social assistance	-5	-5	-13	+-0
Primary and secondary education	+20	+30	+49	+69
Employment policy	+63	+46	+55	+27
State and municipal administration	-54	-53	-68	-65

Sources: (Hadenius 1986; Svallfors 1996; Svallfors 1998).

Secondly, the programs with strong support above are all within the model of contingent consent, while the two programs with weak support, are clearly outside this model. The most crucial difference is that both housing allowances and social assistance are means-tested programs and thus difficult to implement with respect to procedural justice. There is also an argument that these are programs serving citizens who either do not pay taxes at all, or pay very little.

One program that stands out is employment policy which is, for most part, selective. Nevertheless, it has fairly strong support, although it has declined somewhat in the latest survey. One reason may be that this is a program which, at least in Sweden, does not only serve "the poor", but for historical reasons has a much broader range in what is known as "active labour market policy". Not only unemployed workers, but also workers who in the future risk unemployment, including many white-collar workers, attend job-counselling and vocational training. Secondly, this is a program in which, historically, the ruling Social Democratic Party has paid special attention to the problems of legitimacy in the implementation process. One example is that decisions about who is eligible for unemployment insurance are made by union representatives (Rothstein 1996).

There is reason to compare with the US on this point. As Margaret Weir has noted, it is striking that no form of active labour market policy has been successfully established in the US, despite the fact that a strong work ethic pervades American society (Weir 1992). The attempt made beginning in the 1960s-CETA (Comprehensive Employment and Training Act)-was that social program which the Reagan administration found easiest to dismantle upon assuming office in 1981. This was because CETA was equated, in public opinion, with waste, bureaucracy, and a focus on helping just certain socially distinct minority groups; it was, in short, a program exhibiting all the problematic features of selective policies. An American scholar puts it this way:

The legitimacy of CETA was seriously eroded by the stream of "bad press" it was receiving-adverse publicity on waste, nepotism, patronage and corruption. Perhaps nothing contributed more to the loss of confidence and legitimacy in CETA and, ultimately, to its demise.

Conclusion

I started out by making a case for defining many welfare state programs as public goods and thus a candidate as good as any for the social dilemma approach. Secondly, I presented the empirical puzzle that structurally similar countries have produced very different types of welfare states, and that these differences have been increasing since the 1960s. If the welfare state is a public good, then it is obvious that the Western countries have had different success in finding solutions to this social dilemma. Thirdly, I have presented a model of how universal social programs works which also shows that if voters/taxpayers act out of self-interest, both a selective and a universal welfare state are likely outcomes, which means that we face a situation with multiple equilibria. Forthly, I have argued that the different outcomes can not be traced back to the fact that citizens in these different countries have different basic values or norms about what is social justice. Neither can they easily be accounted for by standard explanations in political science about the importance of the ideology of ruling political parties. Instead, my argument is that the empirical puzzle, why structurally similar states manage to solve this social dilemma in very different ways, can be solved by institutional theory, specified as the theory of contingent consent.

While part of this explanation is ideological, i.e., what political leaders hold forth as substantially just, the two other parts (*procedural justice* and the *fair sharing of burdens*) has to do with how the government arranges the administrative institutions of the welfare state. The evidence from the Swedish system of welfare policies provides empirical support for the theory of contingent consent as a way to solve large social dilemma problems. It is precisely the universal programs, which fulfil the institutional conditions specified in this theory, that command widespread support in the population.

At the same time, it is the two programs (social assistance and housing allowances) which appear most clearly to violate the principles of this theory which enjoy the least support. It is hard to argue on behalf of these programs by appeal to a conception of substantive justice. Moreover, these programs are difficult (not to say impossible) to implement in a procedurally fair manner. They make it easy, finally (at least in the case of public assistance), to argue that those receiving benefits do not contribute according to ability to defraying the costs of the program, i.e., the benefits generally go to people who do not work and therefore do not pay income tax. In other words, citizens have reason to distrust both the government institutions and their fellow citizens.

It may be added that in the Swedish case, the construction of the institutions which made it possible to solve the social dilemma in this case, by no means came into existence by chance or as unintended consequences of other political decisions. Instead, they were deliberately crafted by centrally placed political actors, very much with the social dilemma problem in mind. But this is, by its very nature, a longer, yet very interesting, story.

Comparing Welfare States

Deborah Mitchell identifies five main approaches to the comparison of welfare systems:

- *Comparison of policy*, comparing the explicit terms in which actions are taken. Flora and Heidenheimer review the historical development of welfare in Europe and America. They find that welfare in different countries often develops on similar lines.
- *Comparison of inputs*. Inputs are the resources which go into welfare provision. For example, Wilensky's work on welfare spending shows that the main determinants are the age of the system and the structure of the population.
- *Comparing production*. Different states operate different kinds of rules and structures. Esping-Andersen uses evidence on the organisation and delivery of specific services to define positions adopted by different welfare states.
- *Comparing operations*. This is done by considering the detailed operation of benefits and services-what they do, how they are paid for, and who runs them.
- *Comparing outcomes*. The case can be made that what matters about welfare is not what is intended, nor what the process is, but whether or not people benefit from it. This is the basis of the work done by the Luxembourg Income Study in assessing and comparing social security systems in different countries.

The United Kingdom: The Welfare State

Asa Briggs, in a classic essay on the British welfare state, identified three principal elements. These were

- a guarantee of minimum standards, including a minimum income;
- social protection in the event of insecurity; and
- the provision of services at the best level possible.

This has become identified, in practice, with the 'institutional' model of welfare: the key elements are social protection, and the provision of welfare services on the basis of right. In practice, social welfare in the United Kingdom is very different from this ideal. Coverage is extensive, but benefits and services are delivered at a low level. The social protection provided is patchy, and services are tightly rationed.

Germany: The Social Market

The post-war German settlement was based on the idea of a 'social state', sometimes rendered as a 'social market economy'. The first, central principle was that economic development was the best way to achieve social welfare. The structure of social services had to reflect this priority. The principle is represented most clearly in the close relationship of services to people's position in the labour market. Social benefits are earnings-related, and those without work records may find they are not covered for important contingencies. Less clear, but probably even more important, is the general concern to ensure that public expenditure on welfare is directly compatible with the need for economic development and growth.

Second, the German economy, and the welfare system, developed through a corporatist structure. This principle was developed by Bismarck on the basis of existing mutual aid associations, and remained the basis for social protection subsequently. Social insurance, which covers the costs of health, some social care and much of the income maintenance system, is managed by a system of independent funds.

Third, there is a strong emphasis on the principle of "subsidiarity". This principle is taken in Germany to mean both that services should be decentralised or independently managed, and that the level of state intervention should be residual-that is, limited to circumstances which are not adequately covered in other ways. Higher earners are not covered by the main social insurance system, but are left to make their own arrangements.

France: Solidarity and Insertion

Social protection in France is based on the principle of solidarity: the commitment is declared in the first article of the French Code of Social Security. The principle is used in a number of different senses. The idea seems, at first sight, to refer to cooperative mutual support. Some writers apply the term in relation to 'mutualist' groups (friendly societies) and emphasise that people insured within national schemes *(les assures sociaux)* are called to contribute and benefit on an equal footing. Others stress that relationships of solidarity are based in interdependence. Solidarity is usually understood, in this context, in terms of common action, mutual responsibility and shared risks.

The pursuit of 'national solidarity' was undertaken in the first place by attempting progressively to extend the scope of existing solidarities, most notably through the creation of a 'regime general' for health and social security, and subsequently through its progressive expansion. Since the 1970s this pattern of solidarities has been supplemented by additional measures designed to bring 'excluded' people into the net. The most important of these measures is the *Revenu Minimum d'Insertion* (RMI), introduced in 1988, which combines a basic benefit with a personal contract for 'insertion' or social inclusion.

The French system of welfare is a complex, patchwork quilt of services. This kind of arrangement is relatively expensive, and much of the focus of social policy in recent years has fallen on the control of expenditure-filling 'the hole in the social', *le trou de la Secu*. The main areas of concern are not dependency or unemployment, but pensions, because of the special privileges accorded to particular occupational groups, and spending on health care, where the stress on independent, market-led services (*la medicine liberale*) presents considerable problems in cost control.

Sweden: The Institutional-Redistributive Model

The Swedish model can be seen as an ideal form of 'welfare state', offering institutional care in the sense that it offers universal minima to its citizens. It goes further than the British model in its commitment to social equality.

Titmuss's 'institutional-Redistributive' model combines the principles of comprehensive social provision with egalitarianism. This is an "ideal type", rather than a description of reality. Social protection is not necessarily associated with equality; the French and German systems offer differential protection according to one's position in the labour market. The Swedish system, looked at in greater detail, has many of the same characteristics: Ringen describes the system as "selective by occupational experience". However, the importance of equality-sometimes identified with 'solidarity', in the sense of organised co-operation-is considerable. The model of this is the 'solidaristic wage policy' advocated by the labour movement, which emphasised improving standards, limited differentials, and redistribution.

The United States: A 'Liberal' Regime?

The United States is sometimes described as a 'liberal' welfare regime, in the sense that it represents individualism, laissez-faire, residualism and a punitive view of poverty. These issues often seem to dominate US debates on welfare: examples are the introduction of 'workfare', the exclusion of long-term benefit dependents, and the criticism of the 'underclass'.

The US does not, however, have a unified welfare system. Federalism has meant that many important functions are held by the States, including public assistance, social care and various health schemes (Minnesota and Hawaii have state-funded health systems). By comparison with other developed countries, central government has had a limited role in social welfare provision: the main developments of federal provision were during the Roosevelt administration of the 1930s, which laid the foundations for the social security system, and the "War on Poverty" of the 1960s, which provided some important benefits (notably health care for people on low incomes) and engaged the federal government in a wide variety of projects and activities at local level.

In practice, the US is pluralistic, rather than liberal. There are significant departures from the residual model-e.g. state schooling, social insurance, or the Veterans' Administration, which provides health care for nearly 40 million people. In addition to federal and state activity, there are extensive private, mutualist and corporate interests in welfare provision. The resulting systems are complex (and expensive): the guiding principle is less one of consistent individualism than what Class has called "decentralised social altruism".

International Aspects of Social Policy

The Social Policy of the European Union

The European Community was founded for political and economic reasons. The central political aim was less European Union than the maintenance of peace in Europe. The principal economic aim was the establishment of a European free market.

By contrast, there were no clear social aims; such social measures as there were followed from the pressures of economic policy. During the 1970s, the emphasis of Community social policy changed towards improving 'living and working conditions' in the community, and the idea of the 'worker' was extended to include those who were not part of the labour force. Once it was accepted that the Community had social objectives distinct from the economic objectives, it became possible to expand the role of the Community in social policy.

The powers of the Union have developed through incremental development of marginal, relatively innocuous measures in order to establish precedent and competence. For example, provisions covering cigarette packets, bus passes or language teaching sought to establish competence in relation to public health, old people, transport and education. This has been resisted through the idea of 'subsidiarity', by which action should always be taken at the lowest possible level.

The Commission's approach to the development of policy is based on the incremental development of services, the progressive expansion of solidarity, and the insertion of those who are excluded. Powers have been taken to deal with the problems of exclusion.

Social Policy in Developing Countries

The central problem of the developing countries is poverty. According the World Bank, half the world's population lives on less than $2 a day. For Amartya Sen, poverty stems not just from a lack of resources, but from lack of entitlement: famines happen, not because there is not enough food, but because poor people are not allowed to eat the food that is there.

Economic development is essential to welfare. It produces material goods. It promotes integration and interdependence, and extends people's entitlements. It has clearly beneficial effects on social welfare: the last 30-40 years have seen spectacular improvements in longevity, infant survival, access to basic amenities like water supplies and fuel, and the provision of services like health care and education. At the same time, development produces casualties. It makes poor people vulnerable; it uproots traditional lifestyles; it can lead to social polarisation. The 'structural adjustment' favoured by international organisations-moving developing countries towards a formal market economy-has been criticised for pushing developing countries into a situation where their poor will be unprotected.

Although economic development is fundamental, it does not guarantee social protection. Several countries have introduced social security schemes, often tied to the status of particular categories of workers. In some of these only a small minority receive effective protection, but a few countries have made considerable advances in covering their populations, often over a relatively short period of time.

Globalization and Welfare

The development of a global economy has implications for national welfare policies. The nation state is being 'hollowed out', with power being dispersed to localities, independent organisations, and supra-national bodies (like NAFTA or the European Union). Mishra argues, in *Globalization and the Welfare State*, that globalization limits the capacity of nation-states to act for social protection. Global trends have been associated with a strong neo-liberal ideology, promoting inequality and representing social protection as the source of 'rigidity' in the labour market. International organisations like the World Bank and International Monetary Fund have been selling a particular brand of economic and social policy to developing countries, and the countries of Eastern Europe, focused on limited government expenditure, selective social services and private provision. This case is perhaps overstated. It is true that there has been retrenchment in many countries, and an increased focus on selective social services. At the same time, most developed countries have moved towards general coverage of the costs of hospital care and more inclusive social protection policies. There has been a greater diversification of the basis of coverage, through a combination of governmental and non-governmental provisions. There is no consistent trend to greater inequality.

Should Welfare benefits be Provided on a Universal or Selective Basis?

Welfare benefits and services are services provided for the

fulfillment of the needs of the populace. The question itself is broad, so to answer adequately I interpret it as whether welfare benefits and services provided by the state should be delivered on a universal or selective basis.

There are several methods of welfare provision. There is welfare based on contributions, where the amount one contributes to the market and government in terms of taxes and "usefulness" determines the amount one receives from the government. There is also the view that welfare should only be provided to the most needy, and finally the view that welfare should be provided to an equal level, regardless of actual need.

Selectivity versus universal provision has been contentious for a while now, with constant references to "the benefit culture" in news. The prevailing attitude that causes favouritism of selectivity is the belief that "a society where the state assists people to improve themselves we will never be able to eliminate poverty.". This is widely shared in Britain, where many see the incentives not to work as far greater than the incentives to work.

The case of Nadia Suleman in the US, who recently gave birth to octuplets, having already had six children, intensifies the debate. Claiming benefits for previous children, with which she has had IVF treatment to have more, increasing the burden on the ordinary taxpayer, comes across as ludicrous and unachievable if there was regulation rather than universality of benefits. This is a prime example of "the middle classes being impoverished to finance benefits for (people) who don't really need them".

In this paragraph I will discuss selective benefits based on the amount contributed to society by workers, as is the case in Germany and France.

There is a belief that the welfare state was established to quickly and broadly, which we have struggled to adjust since its founding. Ideally welfare provision exists, but within the bounds of what is possible. Achieving a universal level of welfare is nigh but impossible, so it makes more sense to concentrate on those who need the minimum of state intervention to survive. Welfare is classed as the fulfillment of need. As the middle and upper classes require the least social provision to fulfil their needs, from a capitalist view it makes sense to allow them to prosper. By doing so, the lower classes will shrink, as most will be unable to survive, and the problem will solve itself. This argument is rather unethical, but conforms to the logic of unbalanced growth economic theory.

Fairness is another key issue in welfare provision. Assuming the current system of sliding taxation related to earnings, arguments are that those who pay more taxes are entitled to more than those who do pay less. While strong from a capitalist point of view however, it raises questions over pay itself. Under a contributory system of welfare questions are raised over pay itself. Are public sector workers like cleaners paid too little, and should be entitled to more? Are bankers paid too much? It's far too difficult to quantify. Instead selectivity based purely on the fact that a worker is contributing to the economy is often touted. By working, they are at least attempting to live off their own bat, rather than relying on the state, and this should be applauded.

By promoting the welfare of the economically active, the government minimizes cost, while ensuring that it will be able to adequately maintain its social welfare structure, with a healthy, contented work force. Benefits are no longer a means of benefiting the poor at the expense of the rich. Instead those who contribute receive returns on their contribution, leading to a greater desire to work, reducing benefit fraud, and ensuring an inherent fairness in the system, so that people realize they are working for their own benefit, rather than for others. The feeling spurring this on is not the government helping the poor, but rather the lack of help for the workers themselves.

By spending less on the poor, the government can instead invest in infrastructure and securing global trade, which improves the overall wealth of a country. Increased trade demands more workers, which gives a wage to the poor, and helps them achieve self sufficiency, while encouraging a work ethic beneficial to the entire of society, in contrast to the belief that the welfare state is "harmful to the moral fibre of the nation". There is a strong argument in favour of selective welfare available to economic contributors in that universal welfare gives no incentive for "self improvement", and is support for an endemic social problem rather than the prevention of it in the first place. Critics argue that this will replace the "can work, won't work" attitude, with nothing to fall back on.

An alternative to selectivity based on economic productivity is welfare allocated on the basis of need. This is an interesting alternative to selectivity based on economic contribution as it is based on humanitarian concepts, which suggests a form of ethical capitalism previously denounced by Marx as impossible, and was instead an attempt to placate the lower classes to stop their uprising. Society has recognized that fulfillment of the lower classes needs are necessary "to survive as an organic whole and to assist the survival of some individuals". The change in attitudes so that it is no longer though of as a means of benefiting the poor at the expense of the rich, and rather as improvement of society as a whole is crucial in the school of needs-based welfare. As welfare for the middle classes moves away from needs and more towards quality of life, there is a recognition that others in society are in need, and that society can afford to help them. Morally, this argument makes the most sense. A society that defines itself as Christian (BBC News) needs to pursue such a strategy in order to maintain its faith-based focus and credibility.

Help provided where it was need the most has many benefits. By providing benefits only to the poorest, more money can be spent per person, increasing the potential effectiveness of welfare itself. The system is self-regulating to a point. If any who do not qualify for social welfare fall below the required line for welfare, it becomes provided, quickly pushing them back out of the "need" category. Theoretically the welfare state would eventually be transformed into the middle class state. Outside of welfare, people could rely on the free market and increased choice, safe in the knowledge that the state can support them in crisis.

Needs-based provision avoids a fundamental flaw in contributory-based welfare-that some are physically incapable of work due to disability, illness and other reasons. There has been a growth in public concern and responsibility for states of dependency in society. There are people that require help to survive-this is need provision and therefore welfare in its purest state. It is inarguable. Universalism gains the benefits of both systems, but also the negatives. While it becomes easy to implement, as there are no criteria to qualify for benefits, it allows easy abuse of the benefits system, fuelling the "can work, wont work" culture. Universal benefits means "people can stop worrying about the basics", but needs based welfare provision provides equality in this sense. By providing welfare for all, the rich can use the state's provisions entirely, regardless of need, saving money otherwise spent on welfare provision in the market. This saving accelerates the gap between the rich and the poor, giving the rich far more purchasing power through their savings in welfare. The poor are having their needs met that would be otherwise unobtainable. The rich are not.

Universal state welfare provision harms the market, starving them of an audience, while the limitless funds provided for welfare by the state are also damaging for the market competitively, who must break even, whereas the state does not. Welfare is a black hole of public funds that could be better spent elsewhere on those in dire need of help for survival, or could fund tax cuts, helping stimulate the free market that liberal governments are so in love with, particularly in the current recession.

Welfare benefits are a controversial issue. The prevailing attitude in the media today is that welfare benefits are over provided, particularly in the UK, encouraging abuse of the system when given out universally, with no limitations as to who can get them. They appear over provided, and with for those facing the prospect of jobs on minimum wage, appear a viable alternative to working. This is the deterioration of "moral fibre" so worried about by Pahl that would be caused by benefits.

Selectivity is contentious. Critics argue it ignores endemic white privilege, social structure and disability causing some of these problems, and presents a reductionist view. Proponents of the scheme say it represents a fair result, based on a capitalist mode of thinking that those who don't work are a burden to society. Ethically this is shady.

Needs based welfare provision appears to me to be the best solution. If the initial problem of defining those in need can be overcome it truly can be the system that changes society. Welfare is the fulfillment of need. Self sufficiency is ultimately aimed at in needs based welfare, and can be seen as a stepping stone to better things, rather than the end of the road for welfare claimants. Looking after oneself is achievable to most, and this should be recognised in social policy.

The Right to Housing in Universal and Selective Housing Regimes

According to Article 25 of the UN Declaration of Human Rights, everyone has a right to a standard of living adequate for the health and well-being of himself and his family – including housing. Similar statements are found in corresponding European documents. And in many countries housing is in fact considered to be a right – or at least said to be. Nevertheless it is often unclear what should be meant more precisely by a right to housing.

Advocates of state intervention often use the idea of a 'right to housing' critically, either to insist that housing *should* be seen as a right or – if housing is already declared to be a right – to maintain that the right is *not fulfilled*. Critics of state intervention, on the other hand, often claim that the expression is an empty phrase. But if the expression is empty, why is it so often controversial?

Having a right is often seen as *being entitled to something without having to pay for it* – except perhaps a symbolic or small nominal sum. In a democracy this is true of the rights to political vote and to legal justice, and in many countries also of the rights to basic education and medical service. With such a definition, however, a right to housing would not exist in any country, since everywhere people are in principle expected to pay for a dwelling. Consequently it makes no sense to interpret a right to housing as an entitlement for free.

But what interpretation would make more sense? The reason why the right to housing is seldom clearly defined is not that the concept is empty, I will argue, but the opposite, that it embraces the whole set of principles that constitute a national housing regime. The right to housing is a *political marker of concern* pointing out housing as an area for welfare state policy. The more precise meaning of that marker can only be understood in terms of how the relation between state, citizens and housing provision is in fact perceived in a certain national housing discourse.

To understand what is meant by a right to housing we must scrutinise the national housing discourse and, more particularly, the dominant policy theory behind decision-making in housing. (A policy theory can be defined as 'the total of causal and other assumptions underlying a policy'.)

An Example from the Swedish Housing Discourse

One Swedish political document where the ideas behind a right to housing have been spelled out is a Cabinet Proposal from 1974. In his discussion of the goals of housing policy, then Minister of Housing Ingvar Carlsson (later to become Prime Minister of Sweden) describes it as 'out of date' to compare housing to other commodities supplied in the market. In 'modern thinking', he says, good housing and an acceptable local environment are instead seen as 'an indispensable asset in the life of human beings that cannot, unlike many other goods and services, be replaced by other commodities'. In consequence, Swedish housing policy is said to be based on the idea that good and commodious housing in a good environment is an 'indispensable social right', and it is the responsibility of the society to guarantee security in the housing field.

This, of course, may sound like one rather paternalistic minister's view of what citizens should have. However, Minister Carlsson has got more to say than that. Immediately after having laid down that housing is an indispensable social right he observes that this view does not imply that market mechanisms can be neglected. Housing must have a price, another arrangement is inconceivable, he declares. People who demand housing must also be able to choose between dwellings of different size and shape, and in different types of environment. 'It is in the nature of things that such differences must also be allowed to have an effect in terms of price differentials', points out the now rather market-friendly Minister of Housing.

It would be only too easy to brush aside Ingvar Carlsson's argument as the incoherent drivel of a politician who is doing his utmost to sit on two chairs at the same time. How could housing possibly be an indispensable right as long as its price is determined in the market? A reader who means that even politicians deserve to be taken seriously, on the other hand, sees Carlsson's argument as an attempt to sum up the particular policy theory of housing: Housing is a social right, but people should be able to exercise that right in the market.

Housing: Both Market Commodity and Public Good

In my experience, housing researchers seldom confront explicitly the fact that housing in all modern welfare societies is *at the same time* seen both as an individual market commodity and as a public good demanding state involvement. Since housing is always provided through markets, analogies with other welfare sectors, where state allocation is the main mechanism of distribution, are often misleading.

Housing policies in most Western countries are best perceived as *the state providing correctives to the housing market*. This means that market contracts serve as the main mechanism for distributing housing, while state intervention has the form of correctives, defining the economic and institutional setting of those market contracts. In principle housing is distributed by means of *voluntary contracts* between buyer and seller, between landlord and tenant, and so forth. Housing is perceived as an *individual good*, which, as far as possible, should be distributed in accordance with individual consumer preferences. Hence, and in contrast to other welfare commodities, the politically defined needs of housing should not be fulfilled by *direct state allocation* but only by state correctives to the market.

But how can state intervention be defended in a market for what is seen as an individual market good? The eternal debate on that point can be summarised in two conditions that must be fulfilled for state intervention to be justified. First, the commodity should be of great importance to the citizens. Second, the commodity would not be supplied to all citizens at acceptable price and quality in an unregulated market. Either of the two conditions is not enough, if that had been the case we would have state correctives to the markets for bread and for butlers.

Few would argue that housing is not of basic importance for people's well-being. But would it be possible to supply good housing in an unregulated market? Here, as we know, opinions differ. Those arguing in favour of state intervention often refer to the *peculiarities of housing as a commodity,* peculiarities that may cause market imperfections and other problems to housing provision. Since housing is complex and indivisible, heterogeneous and spatially fixed and characterised by high transaction costs, it is questionable whether buyers and sellers, tenants and landlords, can interact on equal terms in the housing market. At least, the notion of such inequalities between market parties has been used to defend state intervention.

A Non-Paternalist Interpretation of Housing Needs

The core rationale behind a policy theory based on market correctives is a *nonpaternalist conception of housing needs.* If we agree on political goals related to housing standards and costs, we may express these goals as housing needs. But if, at the same time, we see housing as an individual good, we may find direct state allocation too paternalistic. The only possible way to handle the dilemma would then be to make market transactions fulfil *both housing demand and housing needs.* That is precisely the logic behind a policy theory of state correctives to the market.

This may seem like a paradox rather than a logic, since needs and demand are often regarded as contradictory concepts. However, the political concept of housing needs, like housing demand, is based on preferences and willingness to pay. One might say that the aim of the state correctives is to make the outcome of transactions in the existing, non-perfect, housing market more similar to what it would have been in an imaginary perfect market. In economic terms this idea may be justified by the theory of 'second best'.

This is what makes housing policy unique. Correctives to the market are expected to contribute towards the simultaneous fulfilment of the households' demand and their housing needs. I have referred to Ingvar Carlsson's text because it illustrates both the logic and the dilemma of a policy theory of correctives to the market. I would, however, claim that Sweden is not special in this respect. The policy instruments that have been applied in most Western countries are based on the same general logic. State-regulated finance of housing production, housing allowances, tenure legislation, rent control and non-profit housing organisations are all examples idea of state correctives to the market.

Two Interpretations of a Right to Housing

If we accept that the market is seen as the main distributive mechanism, the state has two alternative options to help improve the housing conditions of its citizens. The difference between those two approaches corresponds roughly to the distinction between a *selective* and a *universal* housing regime.

One option is to allocate housing specifically to households that are unable to provide for themselves in the general market. In a selective regime the political 'marker of concern' about the right to housing would indicate that the state is expected to provide for households of lesser means beside the general housing market. The other option is to intervene in the functioning of the general market in order to make it fulfil better the housing needs of all households. In a universal regime such a right would indicate that the state is expected to correct the general housing market, so the market can provide for the housing of all types of households, regardless of their economic situation.

This means that a selective welfare logic indicates a more *legalistic* concept of rights, whereas a universal logic implies a more *social* concept.

Universal Housing Regimes and Housing as a Social Right

In a universal housing regime the right to housing is typically not codified in formal or legal rules. *E.g.* in Sweden there is no rights legislation in housing as there is in education, social care or medical service. The legal regulation concerning the distribution of housing is far less comprehensive than in the selective English system. Instead of providing legal guarantees, a universal housing policy has the aim of supporting the household in its position as market actor. In Sweden this has been done to a large extent through *tenure legislation,* above all concerning the rental and cooperative tenures. The normative logic behind this 'biased' legislation has been the individual tenant's allegedly weak position on a free housing market – due to the market peculiarities discussed above. Tenure legislation has been complemented by *general subsidies,* which in modern time have not been directed towards specific tenures or housing units, so both regulations and subsidies have functioned through the general market.

In a universal housing regime like Sweden's, the political marker of a right to housing can be related to T. H. Marshall's classical discussion on rights and citizenship. Marshall divides citizenship into three parts, each based on a particular set of rights: *civil* rights, *political* rights and *social* rights, the latter described as 'the right to share to the full in the social heritage and to live the life of a civilised being according to standards prevailing in the society'.

Interestingly enough, Marshall takes housing to illustrate the relation between civil and social rights. While civil rights are claims that must be met by the state *in each individual case,* social rights are obligations of the state *towards society as a whole.* In housing the individual legal rights that protect the tenure of existing dwellings must be distinguished from the citizens' legitimate expectation of a home fit for a family to live in.

'Housing as a social right', as used *e.g.* in the Swedish housing discourse, is best interpreted as a case of Marshall's third category of rights. The rights are part of a general programme of social advance and not necessarily expected to be fulfilled by the state at all time in every single case.

More precisely, 'housing as a social right' should be interpreted as meaning that all citizens should be able to solve their housing question *through voluntary transactions in the market.* If this is seen as the normal way of providing housing, 'the right to share to the full in the social heritage and to live the life of a civilised being according to standards prevailing in the society' would imply that citizens are in fact able to find decent housing in that market. Instead of granting citizens the formal right to go to court, the state is expected to care about their capacity to provide for themselves in the market.

Universal Versus Selective Welfare Regimes – The General Logic

The distinction between universal and selective is of great importance to our understanding of the role of the state in late capitalistic societies. In a policy field based on state allocation, like education, a universal education policy means that all children have the right to go to the publicly financed school, whereas a selective education policy grants such a right only to children of poor families.

The normative logic of a selective system is the charitable one of 'take care of thy neighbour' – though by means of the state. Better-off pay and worse-off receive. In this perspective the important thing is that state support really goes to the 'truly needy' and not to others.

The general idea behind a universal system was once expressed by Gustav Miller, Swedish Minister of Social Affairs in the thirties, as 'only the best is good enough for the people', indicating that no special services should be targeted on *e.g.* working class people. The moral logic here is one of solidarity, where all citizens are involved both as givers and receivers, though to a varying degree according to their needs and capacities.

In a universal system it is no problem if the state would give with one hand and take away with the other. Quite the contrary, 'bad precision' is part of the overall logic.

Universal systems of state intervention appear to be more acceptable to citizens in general than selective ones. According to Margaret Levi's 'theory of contingent consent', the reason would be that they do not draw a clear line between 'us' as givers and 'them' as takers, and that they do not rely to the same extent on monitoring, sometimes in stigmatising forms, the needs and means of prospective clients.

Universal or Selective – A Question of Width

To be applied to housing with its deviant policy theory of correctives to the market, the dichotomy universal–selective must be defined to embrace both state allocation and market correctives–without losing its basic reference to the difference between solidarity and charity.

My suggestion is to define universal and selective in terms of *the width of the policy field,* i.e. the share of the sector towards which the state policy is directed. In such terms a universal sector policy can be defined as having a *wide policy field,* in principle including the whole sector, while a selective sector policy would have a *narrow policy field,* including only a minor share of the sector reserved for citizens of lesser means.

A universal housing policy would then aim at making it possible for all citizens to find decent housing *in one and the same general housing market.* This, I argue, is what is regarded as universal *e.g.* in Swedish housing policy. In contrast, a selective housing policy would only aim at influencing the housing provision of citizens with a modest income.

What a universal housing policy has in common with a universal education policy is the wide policy field. Both policies are targeted on the majority of the citizens, directly in the school case and indirectly, via the market, in the housing case.

Applied to housing, Gustav Miller's motto would read: 'Only the best housing market is good enough for the people'. In a universal housing policy the role of the state then is to *adjust the general housing market*, so that the demands of *all types of households* could be met in that market. This would be a case of *universal market policy*.

A selective policy, on the other hand, divides housing provision into two parts, one 'open' market and one 'protected' sector, the latter aimed at less well off households. In the open market there is virtually no state intervention. Typically, the protected sector consists of a well defined housing stock with individual needs-testing, far-reaching regulation and selective subsidies.

This is what Jim Kemeny has called a dualistic rental system with a 'command economy in public renting'. If it is really a command economy it would even be a selective allocation policy. If less so it would be a selective market policy. The discussion is summed up in the figure, where the conceived distributive mechanism in a policy theory is combined with the width of the policy field.

Swedish Housing Policy – Some Recent Developments

What has made the Swedish housing regime universal is that the policy field is seen as wide. The political discourse embraces all tenure forms, all regions and all types of housing. Neither on national nor local level is housing policy considered to be a purely social matter, targeted only at households with low income.

A clear expression is the fact that municipal housing is available to all types of households. In selective systems, in contrast, the allocation of publicly owned housing is typically means-tested in some way. Another expression of the universalistic housing discourse is the Swedish use-value system of rent-setting, the function of which is to make private and public landlords compete in the same rental market.

During the last decade considerable change has taken place in Swedish housing policy, like in many other countries. Most remarkably the state financial support has been turned into its opposite. One may wonder what these changes mean to the idea of housing as a social right. Is the dominant policy theory still that all households should be able to get housing in the same market, or has the housing discourse moved in selective direction?

My answer is a guarded 'no'. Housing is still said to be a social right. And the universalistic municipal housing companies and the use-value system of rent-setting still have their old roles. So even if the *outcome* is probably more selective than before, the *discourse* is still largely universalistic.

The question is, of course, for how long Swedish housing policy can endure such contradiction between discourse and outcome. I believe this may in fact illustrate a more general dilemma of a universal housing policy in a context of welfare state retrenchment. Perhaps the idea of housing as a social right – in Marshall's terms – is really a fair-weather ideology that will run aground when segregation is mounting and homeless people begin to turn up in the streets.

Instruments, Measures, and Requirements for Universal Service

There are, of course, many complex relationships of exclusion and complementarity among these three and within them that the figure can make little attempt to illustrate without sacrificing even minimal clarity. The aim is simply to draw attention to broad relationships.

Sources of finance for universal service can broadly be divided into those that originate from within the telecommunications sector and those that are attracted there from outside. However, the investment goals of such finance (and especially whether it is devoted to network extension and affordability) will be determined by a number of different actors, and each source imposes certain constraints as well. Some fund-raising mechanisms by nature direct investment to very specific universal-service instruments and ends. Others are unconditional: the proceeds can be invested anywhere, even outside the telecommunications sector. Indeed, much of the investment raised within the sector will alone contribute nothing to universal service but will be drained from the sector.

Other mechanisms simply involve internal transfers and cross-subsidies in which the instrument and destination are inseparable. Special attention might also be given to the role of innovation as a dynamic factor that affects all other factors in universal service.

10

Sources of Finance and Investment Control

Sector-Internal Sources

Profit reinvestment : Telecommunications is virtually everywhere a profitable business (or at least potentially). The most common means of financing universal service is reinvested profits. Generally, deciding whether to reinvest profits (and where) or to distribute them will rest ultimately with the owner, whether private or public.

The amount of net profits for investment in universal service will depend on the amount taken out. Governments, as owners of monopoly providers, often extract dividends for the general exchequer, and there are often significant debts to be paid. The commercialization of publicly owned operators generally means that operators gain more say in whether profits are distributed or reinvested and especially in the focus for investment. The threat of competition (whether at some specified date in the future or as a general possibility) will tend to direct investment away from universal-service needs and toward areas in which there is most likely to be competition.

Privatized operators, on the other hand, are generally less burdened with debts, but dividend payments to shareholders are rising and can sometimes consume virtually the entire profit. Liberalized regimes are also less likely to invest in universal service per se and more likely to invest in profit maximization (in the case of privatized monopolies) and in areas of competitive pressure (in the case of competition). Although these types of investment increase penetration, they might not do so according to the broader principles of universal service that focus on development.

Tariff cross-subsidies, when they are aimed at enhancing universal service and not at maximizing revenues, are in a sense a form of profit reinvestment, but the profits are foregone. (Cross-subsidy is considered below in "Mechanisms for Universal Service.")

Telecommunications-sector taxation : A number of tax systems have been devised by governments to gather additional revenue from users and operators in the telecommunications sector. In principle, the destination of tax revenues will be determined by government, but methods have been developed to ensure that revenues are reinvested in universal service and the development aims of the sector.

A development tax on all users, as a percentage of the regular bill, can be imposed; this is being considered, for instance, in Kenya. There is then, of course, the problem of ensuring that funds raised in this way will in fact be dedicated to universal service and development needs (Muigua 1994). To the user, this is in effect simply an increase in tariffs, with the prospect of only a very generalized benefit in the form of increased calling opportunities in the future.

A turnover tax on service suppliers has been imposed, for instance, in Peru, which is a relatively liberalized context. The amount, 1% of turnover, is imposed on firms supplying communications services, including basic service, value-added services, and even cable television (CATV). The problem of ensuring that the funds collected will reach their intended destination (in this case, rural network extension and other areas of priority concern) is addressed by setting up a specific fund, Fondo de Inversion en Telecommunications (FITEL, Telecommunications investment fund), legally dedicated to the purpose.

Licence fees : Although governments occasionally collect licence fees from their own monopoly providers, licence fees come to the fore when private operators are offered licences in areas of large unite demand and great growth potential. These licences (often consortia of local and international firms) may be offered an exclusive monopoly in totally unserved areas, may be competing with an existing monopoly in poorly served areas, or may be facing several competitors but in very lucrative markets, such as international telephony or mobile services. (A licence fee may also constitute an element in a privatization package.)

In large underdeveloped markets, huge sums can be raised through licences. The current issue of licences for basic and mobile services in India will yield the government tens of billions of dollars, although it is experiencing great difficulties in completing the process.

However, licence fees are ultimately passed on to customers in tariffs, and they are thus usually accompanied by tariff regulations to ensure that universal-service goals are addressed, as in India. There is thus necessarily a trade-off between high fees and affordable tariffs. In India, some claim that the balance struck will be to the detriment of universal service.

High fees can be used to extend the network and services to areas beyond the reach of competitive new licence holders or may be redirected to general government expenditure, on the basis that the government is disposing of a general asset (as happened in the United Kingdom with both licence fees and privatization receipts and will probably happen to much of the fee yield in India).

Interconnection fees : Liberalization creates the need for network interconnection, that is, for various service providers to have access to the networks of others. Usually, the dominant network provider will be required to make the network available to other service suppliers at a tariff closely related to cost. At the same time, the dominant operator (and possibly others) can be obliged to fulfil universal-service obligations pertaining to network extension and tariffs. Adjusting the interconnection fee is a means of collecting the money to cover the cost of such obligations.

This operation is complex, and there are several ways to calibrate the system, each with its own effect on competitive forces and on universal service. This system is currently used in the United Kingdom but will be replaced with contributions to a universal-service fund in 1997. In the United States, a variation on interconnection fees is used to ensure transfers from long-distance carriers to local-access networks.

Obligatory contributions (universal-service fund) : Taking advantage of the suppliers' need to interconnect services, a regulatory authority can collect interconnection fees to help finance universal service, or it can choose simply to impose obligatory contributions from operators (or only the dominant operator). The amount and distribution of these are determined by a number of possible formulae. These contributions are in turn usually directed to a universal-service fund, which is thus not a mechanism for raising finance per se but rather a clearing house for funds raised by other means. (Universal-service funds are sometimes used freely to raise finance from several of the sources outlined in this section, and the regulatory authorities can redirect them with various degrees of flexibility, using a variety of mechanisms.)

Such obligatory contributions, coupled with a universal-service fund, are the favoured option of the EU in the context of imminent liberalization, and such funds exists in many parts of the world, including Peru, Hungary, and Chile. These funds are usually relatively free from government control, being either directed by the regulator or directed by an independent though government-appointed body.

Sector-external sources

Often there is a pressing need for finance from outside the telecommunications sector, especially where the need for network growth is huge. Again, issues have already been outlined. There are basically three ways to raise finance externally: direct government investment; loans and development assistance; and privatization.

Direct government investment : Government finance is scarce in a development context but can be directed specifically to universal service and long-term development. Usually, the vibrancy of the general economy, the extent of pent-up economically feasible demand, the government's recognition of the benefits of telecommunications, and the pressures of competing investment needs will be among factors that influence a government in directing investment. Special mechanisms can be set up to raise funds. For instance, bond issues for those on a waiting list (as used in Japan, Korea, and elsewhere) can be used to raise finance from outside the sector because they attract some general investors seeking the guaranteed rate of return.

Loans and development assistance : International loans from regional banks and the World Bank and bilateral and multilateral aid are often conditional on focusing investment on only the more lucrative sectors (at the expense of universal service) and on liberalizing the sector. In monopolies, sector restructuring and commercialization are usually prerequisites for loan agencies, and direct loans to operators may be even more stringently linked to commercial priorities and the payback periods. Together, these factors can severely constrain the extent to which governments and national operators can direct loans to universal-service and national-development priorities.

Privatization : Privatization is the sale of public operators through share issues or direct capital injections. Although this has been effective as a once-off means to raise finance, globally the level of finance is diminishing relative to demand. Sale under pressure can also lead to less than optimal results in terms of raising funds and focusing on universal service.

Share flotations can be very hazardous undertakings with uncertain outcomes. Getting to the point of sale often proves impossible or is a protracted process. Although direct sale to external operators reduces uncertainties, the shares are often undervalued. The sale of a controlling interest renders it necessary to impose universal-service goals by regulatory means or licences, rather than directly by internal operator transfers, but anything less than a controlling share is relatively unattractive for most investors, especially in least-developed networks.

Instruments for Universal Service

A variety of instruments have been used to support the different elements of universal service. Commonly, network extension is assured through a government policy to directly invest in it as part of a general modernization of development strategy. Mechanisms to ensure universal service are associated with the issue of licences to provide services, especially in the context of privatization and competition. Various options for these will be outlined. Tariffs controls, a mainstay of most universal-service policies no matter what the regime, greatly influence not just affordability but also network extension.

Technological, regulatory, and institutional innovations (the potential of which, as we have seen, is growing strongly in the context of universal service) and a number of other possibilities will be explored. This will be followed by a look at support instruments for the final user, aimed at more effective use of telecommunications services and going beyond what is traditionally regarded as the ambit of universal-service provision and anticipating the Information Society.

Direct Government Investment

Government-owned monopolies and operators are subject to various degrees of government control in their investment priorities. When the operator is part of a government department, which was until a decade or two ago the most common model, control is total. However, the trend toward corporatization of structures and commercialization of operations has led to the development of specific universal-service goals relating to network extension, agreed to by operators (who remain relatively autonomous in day-to-day commercial affairs) and often specified in contracts for a given period.

In these contexts, universal service in the form of network extension has been pursued by direct government investment or through the provision of loan guarantees. This instrument has been remarkably successful in increasing overall penetration and in improving universal service; it was employed in early stages in the most developed countries of Europe, Australia, and elsewhere but has also been used more recently in rapidly expanding economies, such as Korea, China, Indonesia, Taiwan, and Singapore.

The conditions for this instrument's success seem to have been a rapidly expanding economy leading to significant unite economically feasible demand and the availability of appropriate domestic or external sources of capital. Network extension into areas most relevant to universal service, that is, where revenues generated may not in the short term cover costs, is always balanced in such circumstances by providing high-grade and advanced services to the business sector and urban areas, which generates significant revenue in a short time. Approaches to this and the complex trade-offs with tariffs and other factors are numerous.

Licence Conditions

The use of licence conditions to achieve universal service is increasingly the norm, even in public monopolies as they gradually commercialize and their relationship to government and national economic objectives becomes more explicit and formalized. The variety of approaches is increasing as different countries experiment in the context of liberalization policies.

Requiring network extension with a licence zone : During privatization (or in cases where operators were always private) or the introduction of competition, the most frequently used instrument is to ensure network extension as a condition for obtaining a licence for a given zone (nationally or for a region) or service. In most developing countries, including Mexico, Peru, Argentina, and India, the licence conditions oblige the operators, whether in competitive or monopoly supply, to expand the network according to specified parameters. These obligations can include the following:

- Increasing the overall teledensity within the zone to an absolute level of lines or a cumulative percentage within a given period;
- Supplying a number of public phones in a certain proportion to the number of private lines;
- Improving the quality of services provided, including noise signal ratio and percentage of completed calls;
- Decreasing the waiting time for telephones and the size of the waiting list; and
- Supplying services (perhaps only a single line) to towns and villages of less than a certain size.

Within an area, such licence conditions ensure the concurrent growth of access for non-commercial and commercial users and are also usually combined with tariffs controls. As always, the ultimate limit is set by the size and value of the commercial segment. Various means are used to ensure that such targets are met, including escrow accounts (that is, funds retained by a third party until specified conditions are met), regular review points, and so forth. Splitting the country into several licence zones (which is done in most larger countries, such as India and the Philippines) can also help tap additional sources of funding from smaller investors inside and outside the industry. This approach allows the hedging of bets and permits experimentation. However, the zones must contain both attractive and less attractive subareas to ensure that all licences are taken up.

Twinning of lucrative and non-directive licences : One of the most innovative licence conditions has been developed in the Philippines. The government bought back the privately owned monopoly operator in preparation for issuing licences in a number of regions, more and less lucrative, into which it divided the country. Applicants for the lucrative international-service and mobile-service licences in developed regions had to agree to take a licence in the poorer, more remote rural areas and put in an agreed number of new local lines (as many as 400 000 per licence) there. Using these means, the government plans to increase teledensity from 2.1% (that is, 2.1 lines for every 100 people) in 1995 to 8.4% by 2000. Extension of universal service in this manner reflects the highly polarized nature of Philippine society regionally (somewhat like South Africa) and the existence of a much suppressed demand in certain regions under the privatized monopoly.

Issuing multiple licences : Issuing competing licences for similar transmission and switching technologies in the same region is the usual route to liberalization in mature markets. It can, of course, lead to significant investment in network extension, although most investment goes to developing parallel networks, rather than to extending the network to new potential users. Benefits to consumers are usually seen in tariff competition and service innovation. However, there are other ways to use multiple licences to further network extension.

Splitting basic-service licences : Noncompeting basic-service licences can be issued in a given region after the network is split into local, national, and international segments. This opens the possibility of using alternative networks (developed, for instance, by the railways or the army) to extend services, devolve local network development, and permit various possibilities for cross-subsidies based on licences. Many countries have taken this route. Columbia, for example, will in 1997 open both long-distance and international markets to competition while retaining government ownership of the current long-distance (and local) monopoly. However, as long-distance and international services are the most profitable, the government, like others before it, faces the task of instituting an effective regulatory regime to ensure that universal service at the local level will not lose out; that is, it must devise means to divert revenues from all long-distance and international service to local access.

A possible advantage of this over other approaches is that local networks might tap new local investment sources (including business, government, and the public), and national and international networks can attract the more usual finance mechanisms. Local network corporations can also relate more closely to real needs. Beyond the local level, licences can be competitive or monopoly based. Examples of this can be found in Central and Eastern Europe, and this approach served to expand universal service in Finland.

Issuing licences for additional non-telecommunications services : An approach that will become increasingly common is issuing telecommunications licences to transmission systems that previously carried different services. Some countries, including certain European countries and the United States, have significant potential for introducing competition from CATV suppliers. Although the effect in these countries will mainly be on tariffs and services, the possibility of combining telephone services with a wider range of services, including television and radio, may increase the feasibility of adding certain customer segments in developing countries where entirely new networks are being set up.

Sharing revenue as an investment incentive : To rapidly expand their networks in areas where they are very poor, Malaysia chose the BOT scheme and Thailand chose the BTO scheme. A private operator (perhaps a foreign or local consortium) builds the network with its own funds, sooner or later passing ownership to the government and getting a return on its investment through sharing revenue with the government for a set period that is often linked to an exclusive licence.

Although one advantage of such schemes is that control eventually reverts to government, effective control for a significant period must be with the investor because the main attraction is a steady stream of income. Licence conditions must also carefully balance the network extension and tariff sides of universal service.

Lowest-subsidy licence auction : An option pursued very recently in Peru and funded through FITEL (the universal-service fund) was to call a competitive tender for licences in non-commercial areas, with the winner being the bidder seeking the lowest subsidy. In addition, the basic-service licence was split because it was restricted to supplying villages with fewer than 500 inhabitants. The main operator is obliged to supply service to larger towns. Licence applications were to be assessed during January of 1996.

Tariff Policies and Controls

Tariff policies can be effected through a range of options:

- Direct tariff control over providers;
- Licence fees and conditions;
- Regulation of competition;
- Voluntary activity by operators, whether competing or monopoly;
- Telecommunications-sector taxation and expenditure; and
- General exchequer funding.

Tariff policy is more suitable than, for instance, licence conditions for addressing an evolving situation and for fine tuning. Tariff averaging and cross-subsidization are the most extensively used mechanisms, and these will be summarized below (however, because they are intertwined and complex, a more extensive account is given in Appendix B). Methods of targeting specific groups of users will also be discussed below.

Tariff Averaging

Tariff averaging is a used virtually everywhere to reduce tariff variations to a small number of tariff bands. Averaging is applied to connection charges, periodic rental fees, and usage tariffs. It is most commonly discussed as an instrument for cross-subsidization, but it need not be used for this. In fact, tariff averaging is applied to rental and call fees even in the most competitive markets.

Averaging, on its own, tends to favour rural over urban areas, especially for connection fees. Rapidly falling maintenance and operation (usage) costs overall mean that the marginal cost for all users is both falling and converging, affecting the cost basis of rentals and usage. In theory, this should reduce the benefits and losses of averaging to any particular group, but the existing small number of rental and usage tariff bands means that low-volume users currently tend to benefit the most. As a mechanism for universal service, averaging per se does not discriminate between different groups of users, but there is a general though not necessarily extreme bias toward high-cost users, such as rural and low-usage groups.

Cross-Subsidization

As a mechanism for cross-subsidization, averaging comes into its own. There are basically three forms of cross-subsidization: within tariff elements; between tariff elements; and between basic and advanced services. Each form has distinct and often complex effects.

For instance, many countries have a single national connection charge, one or two rental rates, and at most a few usage tariffs. Such a restricted number of tariffs (that is, extreme averaging) implies considerable cross-subsidy between customers in each tariff. The effects historically, but by no means everywhere, have been to subsidize the following:

- Connection cost for customers in rural areas;
- Rentals for low-volume, mainly domestic, users (although there is a countervailing tendency here) and high-maintenance rural users; and
- Local calls, favouring domestic users and small, local businesses.

Within these broad parameters, the effects are indiscriminate.

Cross-subsidization between tariff elements (specifically, between usage tariffs and connection and rental fees) — Again, historically, but for reasons that still obtain in many countries, the tendency is for usage tariffs to be used to cross-subsidize connection and rental fees. However, the costs of the different elements are difficult to disentangle, and the supply and demand economics are intertwined, discouraging over generalization. This type of cross-subsidization both favours network expansion over more intensive usage and encourages the retention of low-usage customers, in both cases reinforcing universal service.

Cross-subsidization between advanced and basic services — The final type of cross-subsidization occurs between different types of services, specifically between advanced services (such as leased lines, mobile services, and value-added services) and basic telephony. The experience here is complex and difficult to determine. In some cases, advanced services have been premium priced and have in effect subsidized basic services. However, the general trend may be in an opposite direction. Because advanced services are more recent, they tend to be introduced in a more liberalized environment. Where monopolies have been maintained on basic services (and even in cases of competition), basic services can be used to cross-subsidize more advanced services to make the latter more competitive in the lucrative and growing advanced-services market. The general trend in cross-subsidy between basic and advanced services may thus be damaging to universal service and may favour larger business users.

Cross-subsidies in general are being reduced as competition and liberalization policies force prices toward their underlying costs. However, the greater emphasis that service providers are placing on growing and more lucrative markets could easily push this tendency so far that the effects run counter to the traditional effects of cross-subsidization. Thus, with tariff re-balancing, safeguards may be necessary to ensure not only that the traditional bias in favour of rural and small users is maintained, but also that a bias against these users is not created.

Reduced Tariffs and Targeted-user Support : Targeted tariffs are tariff reductions for specific, often very narrow, user groups.

These targeted tariffs are usually implemented explicitly as part of universal-service policy. Many have been devised, including the following:

- Lower connection, rental, and usage tariffs for low-income groups and vulnerable groups, such as older people, for standard usage terms;
- Limited service provision, such as receive-only or emergency-call-only telephony for low-income and vulnerable groups (outgoing calls might be allowed only with advance payment to a special account or with charge cards);
- Low usage rates for a select set of destination users, such as low rates for migrants to phone family members; and
- Usage support for certain groups that face specific and costly obstacles to use, such as people with sensory or mobility disabilities.

The tariff rate is not the only significant factor affecting affordability – the means and terms of payment can also be important:

- Should payment be in advance, in arrears, or in instalments?
- How great is people's fear of debt (which is related to the security of income)?
- To what extent does the service offer a means for users to monitor and control costs?

Targeted tariffs have the benefit of being highly discriminating, offering support to targeted groups relating to their specific needs. However, some of these schemes require means testing or eligibility testing. Means testing, for instance, can reinforce tendencies toward a two-tier society (Cordell 1996). In general, tariff targeting is more relevant where universal service is close to being achieved, and it allows a fine tuning of service provision. As well as being imposed by a regulator, tariff targeting can be implemented voluntarily by operators, even in competition (such as by British Telecommunications plc in the United Kingdom). This instrument is also being used in EU policy to selectively compensate certain groups for some negative effects of liberalization.

Innovation

Innovation deserves specific mention because it can influence all parameters of universal service. The primary goal is to create an environment that attracts or stimulates innovation in technology, organizations, services, and usage and ensures that when innovation appears, it can be diffused quickly. As already mentioned, an appropriate regulatory structure can be developed in either monopoly or competitive industry structures, although clearly not all the mechanisms suggested below can be implemented in each.

Examples of such innovation, as mentioned earlier, are various fixed cellular, radio, and satellite technologies for rural areas. The new cost structures of such services also give rise to the possibility of innovations in tariffs, such as eliminating connection and usage charges for communal-use phones or heavily weighing certain elements over others. Beirut, for instance, where the fixed network was severely damaged, has rapidly introduced cellular service as a replacement while the wired network is being reconstructed. Two suppliers were licenced but with a strict regime that limits the tariff for local calls to 0.05 USD per minute. Although there are connection fees of 500 USD and monthly rental fees of 25 USD, users take advantage of credit schemes for these fees and have clearly in some instances banded together to cover them. The resulting explosive growth to about 100 000 users has forced the regulator to insist that the operators sign up no new users until they can handle the traffic. The regulator also gets 20% of revenue, which can go toward the development of the wired network.

Bibliography

A K Malkani : *Social Work for the Poor*, Mohit Pub, Delhi, 2008.

A K Rizwi : *Social Policy and Social Work*, Mohit Pub, Delhi, 2008.

A S Kohli : *Human Rights and Social Work, Issues, Challenges and Response*, Kanishka, Delhi, 2004.

Abha, Vijai and Prakash: *Voluntary Organisations and Social Welfare*, ABD, Delhi, 2000.

Agarwal, L.B.: *The Harijans in Rebellion*, Taraporewala, Bombay, 1934.

Ahir, D.C.: *Dr B.R. Ambedkar: Buddhist Revolution and Counter-Revolution in Ancient India*, B.R. Publishing, Delhi, 1996.

Ahmed, Akbar : *Pakistan : The Social Sciences' Perspective*, Oxford University Press, Karachi, 1990.

Akash Gulalia : *Social Work Practice : With Mobile Population Vulnerable to HIV/AIDS*, Mohit, Delhi 2008.

Anand, J. H. : *Dalit Literature is the Literature of Protest*, Delhi, ISPCK, 1995.

Ankit Prasad: *Social Welfare and Social Action : YMCA at Work*, Mittal, Delhi, 2005.

Atal, Yogesh: *The Changing Frontiers of Caste*, Delhi, National Publishing House, 1968.

B.T. Lawani and I.S. Subhedar : *Social Work Perspectives*, Om Pub, Delhi, 2006.

Bailey, F. G. : *Caste and the Economic Frontier: A Village in Highland Orissa*, Manchester, University of Manchester, 1957.

Bakshi, S. R.: *Gandhi and Hindu-Muslim Unity*, Deep & Deep Publications, New Delhi, 1987.

Baldwin, Peter: *The Politics of Social Solidarity: Class Bases of the European Welfare State, 1875–1975*, Cambridge, Cambridge University Press, 1990.

Barnes, Bob.: *Social Survey Division in the 1990s*, Population Trends, 1991.

Benjamin, Joseph: *Scheduled Castes in Indian Politics and Society*, New Delhi, Ess Ess Publications, 1989.

Berger, P. L. : *The Sacred Canopy, Elements of a Sociological Theory of Religion*, Garden City, Doubleday & Company, 1967.

Beteille, Andre.: *The Backward Classes and the New Social Order*, Oxford University Press, Delhi, 1981.

Bhagwat, Vidyut: *Dalit Women in India: Issues and Perspectives - Some Critical Reflections*, New Delhi, Gyan Publishing House, 1995.

Bhai, P. N.: *Harijan Women in Independent India*, B. R. Publishing, New Delhi, 1986.

Bhatt, Anil: *Caste, Class and Politics: An Emperical Profile of Social Stratification in Modern India*, Delhi, Manhohar Book Service, 1975.

Bose, N. K.: *The Scheduled Castes and Tribes and Their Present Conditions*, Calcutta, University of Calcutta, 1969.

Bose, Pradip Kumar: *Social Mobility and Caste Violence: A Study of the Gujarat Riots*, Delhi, Adjanta Publications, 1985.

Brijesh Mishra: *Glimpses of Social Welfare in India : Problems and Perspectives*, ABD Pub, Delhi, 2006.

Campolo, T. & Fraser, D. A. : *Sociology through the Eyes of Faith*, San Francisco, Harper & Row, Delhi, 1992.

Carsten, F. L. : *The Rise of Fascism*, London, Methuen and Co., 1967.

Chaklader, Snehamoy : *Sociolinguistics: A Guide to Language Problems in India*, New Delhi, Mittal, 1990.

Charles D Garvin; Lorraine M Gutierrez and Maeda J Galinsky: *Handbook of Social Work With Groups*, Rawat, Delhi, 2007.

Chhaya Patel: *Social Work Practice : Religio Philosophical Foundations : Essays in Honour of Professor Indira Patel*, Rawat, Delhi, 1999.

Cravens, Hamilton: *Before Head Start: The Iowa Station and America's Children*, Chapel Hill, University of North Carolina Press, 1993.

D K Lal Das and Vanila Bhaskaran : *Research Methods for Social Work* : Rawat, Delhi 2008.

D.K. Lal Das : *Practice of Social Research : Social Work* Perspective, Rawat, 2000.

David Lewis and N Ravichandran: *NGOs and Social Welfare : New Research Approaches*, Rawat, Delhi, 2008.

Debotosh Sinha : *Aspects of Industry and Occupational Social Work*, Abhijeet Pub, Delhi, 2007.

Dennis Shirley: *Community Organizing for Urban School Reform*, Austin, University of Texas Press, 1997.

Dietrich, Gabriele: *Dalit Movements and Women's Movement*, Horizons India Books, New Delhi, 1992.

Donaldson, Gordon A. : *Cultivating Leadership in Schools*, New York, College Press, 2001.

Dumont, Louis: *The Caste System and Its Implications*, London, Granada Pub. Ltd., 1970.

Edward Chambers: *Roots for Radicals*, New York, Continuum, 2003.

Elisabeth Relchert: *Social Work and Human Rights : A Foundation for Policy and Practice*, Rawat, Delhi, 2003.

Ellul, J. : *The Technological Society*, Grand Rapids, Eerdmans, 1990.

Fisher, Michael : *A Clash of Cultures: Awadh the British, and the Mughals*, New Delhi, Manohar, 1987.

Frederic G. Reamer : *Social Work Values and Ethics*, Rawat, Delhi, 2005.

Freeman, James M.: *Untouchable : An Indian Life History*, CA, Stanford University Press, 1979.

G.R. Madan : *An Eminent Scholar, Saint and Social Worker*, Radha Pub, Delhi, 2008.

Ghurye, G. S. : *Caste and Class in India*, Bombay, Popular Books, 1950.

Gibson, R. : *Critical Theory and Education*, London, Hodder & Stoughton, 1986.

Glass, Joseph W.: *The Pennsylvania Culture Region: A View From the Barn*, Ann Arbor, UMI Research Press, 1986.

Gorhe, Neelam: *Social Development and Dalit Women*, Gyan Pub. House, New Delhi, 1995.

Gorringe, H.: *Untouchable Citizens : Dalit Movements and Democratization in Tamil Nadu*, Delhi, Sage Publications, 2005.

Grunlan, Stephen A. and Milton Reimer : *Christian Perspectives on Sociology,* Grand Rapids, Mich., Zondervan, 1982.

Gurukal, Rajan: *The Formation of Caste Society in Kerala,* Rawat Publications, New Delhi, 1994.

Hajira Kumar : *Social Work, Social Development and Sustainable Development*, Regency, Delhi, 1997.

Hana Nagpaul : *Social Work in Urban India*, Rawat, Delhi, 1996.

Harry C. Boyte : *Commonwealth, A Return to Citizen Politics,* New York, The Free Press, 1989.

Heinsath, Charles : *Indian Nationalism and Hindu Social Reform,* Princeton, Princeton University Press, 1964.

Hopkins, Thomas J. : *The Hindu Religious Tradition*, Encino, California, Dickenson, 1971.

I. Sundar: *Social Work Practices in Health and Medical Profession*, Sarup Book Pub, Delhi, 2009.

I.S. Subheda : *Fieldwork Training in Social Work,* Rawat, Delhi, 2001.

Jaffrelot, Christopher: *Dr. Ambedkar and Untouchability: Fighting the Indian Caste System*, New York, Columbia University Press, 2005.

Jainendra Kumar Jha : *Social Welfare and Social Work*, Anmol, Delhi, 2002

Jogdand, P. G.: *Dalit Women in India: Issues and Perspectives,* New Delhi, Gyan Publishing House, 1995.

K. Chakraworthy: *Untouchable Social Work in India,* Sumit, Delhi, 2006.

K.D. Gangrade : *Gandhian Perspective on Global Interdepen-dence, Peace and Role of Professional Social Work,* Authorspress, Delhi, 2008.

K.K. Jacob: *Social Work Education in India*, Himanshu, Delhi, 1994.

Kamble, N. D.: *Deprived Castes and their Struggle for Equality*, Ashish Publishing House, New Delhi, 1983.

Lakshmanna, C.: *Caste Dynamics in Village India*, Nachiketa Publications, Bombay, 1973.

Lal, Shyam: *Caste and Political Mobilisation: The Bhangis*, Jaipur, Panchsheel Prakashan, 1981.

Lindburg, Donald: *Social Organization of the Kutenai.* Chicago: University of Chicago Press, 1962.

M A Khan : *Social Work and Social Policy, Concepts and Methods,* Book Enclave, Delhi, 2007.

M R Kamble : *Social Work With Children,* Aavishkar, Delhi, 2007.

M.N. Parmar and Jagdish Solanki : *Social Work Perspective on Depressed Class Population,* Anmol, Delhi, 2006.

M.S. Bedi : *Social Development and Social Work* , Himanshu, Delhi, 1994.

Mallik, Suneila: *Social Integration of the Scheduled Castes,* New Delhi, Abhinav, 1979.

Manju Gupta : *Child Abuse, A Social Work Perspective* , Mangal Deep Publications, Delhi, 2001.

Margaret Alston and Wendy Bowles : *Research for Social Workers : An Introduction to Methods,* Rawat, Delhi, 2003.

Marshall, P. & VanderVennen, R. : *Social Science in Christian Perspective,* Lanham, MD: University Press of America, 1988.

McGivney, V. : *Informal Learning in the Community, A Trigger for Change and Development,* Leicester, NIACE, 1999.

Moberg, D. : *Wholistic Christianity, An Appeal for a Dynamic Balanced Faith,* Brethren Press, 1985.

Moddie, A.D.: *The Brahmanical Culture and Modernity,* London, Asia, 1968.

Mohammad Naqi : *Social Work for Weaker Sections,* Anmol, Delhi, 2005.

Murli Desai : *Methodology of Progressive Social Work Education,* Rawat, Delhi, 2004.

Murli Desai and Siva Raju: *Gerontological Social Work in India : Some Issues and Perspectives,* B.R., Delhi, 2000.

N.C. Dobriyal : *Social Work for Older and Sick People,* Sumit Enterprises, Delhi, 2008.

Narain, A.K. & Ahir, D.C.: *Dr. Ambedkar, Buddhism and Social Change,* BR Publishing, Delhi, 1993.

Omvedt, Gail : *Reinventing Revolution: New Social Movements and the Socialist Tradition in India,* New York, Sharpe, 1993.

P Murugesan: *Social Welfare Programmes and Fertility Decline,* Abhijeet Publication, Delhi, 2009.

P.K. Bajpai : *Social Work Perspectives on Health,* Rawat, Delhi, 1998.

P.M. Parmar : *Social Work and Social Welfare in India,* Sublime, Delhi, 2002.

Pamela Trevithick: *Social Work Skills : A Practice Handbook,* Rawat, Delhi, 2009.

Patnaik, Nitayananda: *Caste and Social Change: An Anthropological Study of Three Orissa Villages,* National Institute of Community Development, Hyderabad, 1969.

Pekka Himanen: *The Information Society and the Welfare State: The Finnish Model,* Oxford UP, Oxford, 2002.

Perkins, S. & Rice, C. : *More than Equals: Racial Healing for the Sake of the Gospel,* Downers Grove, InterVarsity, 1993.

Prakash M Katare : *Social Work and Folk Culture,* Arise Pub, Delhi, 2006.

Prasanta K. Pattanaik: *Essays on Individual Decision-making and Social Welfare,* Oxford University Press, London, 2009.

Pratima Chaturvedi : *Social Work : Theories and Practices,* Book Enclave, Delhi, 2005.

Premanand Choudhary : *Child Survival, Health and Social Work Intervention,* ABD Pub, Delhi, 2008.

Profulla C Sarker : *Issues and Perspectives on Social Work and Social Development,* Serials Pub, Delhi, 2008.

R.B.S. Verma, H.S. Verma and Raj Kumar Singh: *Empowerment of the Weaker Sections in India : Interface of the Civil Society Organizations and Professional Social Work Institutions,* Serials, Delhi, 2006.

R.P. Arya : *Training for Social Work and Rural Development,* Manglam, Delhi, 2007.

Raj Bala Mathur : *Modernisation of Social Work, Planning and Administration,* Book Enclave, Delhi, 2007.

Raj Bhanti : *Field Work in Social Work Perspective,* Himanshu, Delhi, 1996.

Ramesh Chandra, *Government and Politics of India,* New York, St. Martin's Press, 1995.

Rameshwari Devi and Ravi Prakash: *Social Work : Methods, Practices and Perspectives,* Mangal Deep, Delhi, 2004.

Ranjna K. Devi : *Social Work, Philosophy, Concepts and Dimensions*, Omega, Delhi, 2009.

Rao, M. S. A.: *Social Movement and Social Transformation: A Study of Backward Class Movement*, New Delhi, Macmillian Press, 1978.

Ritter, Gerhard A.: *Social Welfare in Germany and Britain: Origins and Development*, Kim Traynor, New York, 1986.

Robert Fisher and Peter Romanofsky: *Community Organizing for Urban Social Change, A Historical Perspective*, Greenwood Press, Delhi, 1981.

Robert Fisher: *Let the People Decide, Neighborhood Organizing in America* 1984, Twayne Publishers, Delhi, 1997.

Roy Burman, B.K.: *Beyond Mandal and After Backward Classes in Perspective*, New Delhi, Mittal, 1992.

S K Sen : *Social Work Practices*, Book Enclave, Delhi, 2007.

S.K. Bhalla : *Social Work With Lawbreakers of Society*, MD Pub, Mumbai, 2008.

S.P. Ramachandran : *Social Work for Minorities*, Sumit Enterprises, Delhi, 2008.

Sandhya Joshi: *Child Survival Health and Social Work Intervention*, Concept, 1996.

Sangwan, Satpal : *Science, Technology, and Colonisation: An Indian Experience, 1757-1857*. New Delhi, Anmika Prakashan, 1991.

Sanjay Bhattacharya: *Social Work : An Integrated Approach*, Deep and Deep, Delhi, 2003.

Sarat C. Joshi : *Gandhian Social Work*, Akansha, Delhi, 2009.

Seerveld, C. : *On being human: Imaging God in the modern world*, Lanham, MD: University Press of America, 1989.

Shaikh Azhar Iqbal : *Principles and Practices of Social Work*, Sublime, Delhi, 2005.

Shaikh Azhar Iqbal: *Problems of Social Welfare and Social Work*, Sublime, Delhi, 2005.

Sherry Joseph : *Social Work Practice and Men Who Have Sex With Men*, Sage, Delhi, 2005

Shilaja Nagendra : *Social Work and Social Welfare in India*, ABD Pub, Delhi, 2005.

Silverberg, James: *Social Mobility in the Caste System in India,* Mouton Publishers, The Hague, 1968.

Simon, Robert Leopold: *Spiritual Aspects of Indian Music,* Delhi, Sundeep, 1984.

Singh, S. N.: *Reservation: Problems and Prospects,* New Delhi, Uppal Publishing House, 1987.

Skillen, James W. : *A Covenant to Keep : Meditations on the Biblical Theme of Justice,* Grand Rapids, MI: CRC Publications, Center for Public Justice, 2000.

Stephens, S. : *Children and the Politics of Culture,* Princeton, Princeton University Press, 1995.

Tejomayananda, Swami : *Hindu Culture: An Introduction,* Chinmaya Publications, Piercy, CA, 1993.

Tripathy, R. B.: *Dalits: A Sub-Human Society,* New Delhi, Ashish Publishing House, 1994.

V.V. Devasia and Ajit Kumar : *Social Work Concerns and Challenges in the 21 Century,* APH, Delhi, 2009.

Vijendra Kumar : *Problems and Perspectives on Social Work and Social Welfare,* ABD Pub, Delhi, 2002.

Whitley, O. R. : *Religious behavior: Where sociology and Religion Meet,* Engelwood Cliffs, Prentice-Hall, Inc, 1964.

Wolterstorff, N. : *Until Justice and Peace Embrace,* Grand Rapids: Eerdmans, 1983.

Wuthnow, R. : *God and Mammon in America,* New York: Free Press, 1994.

Yolton, J. W.: *John Locke: Problems and Perspectives,* Cambridge Uni. Press, 1969.

Zelliot, Eleanor: *From Untouchable to Dalit: Essays on the Ambedkar Movement,* New Delhi, Manohar, 1992.

Zimmer, Heinrich : *The Art of Indian Asia,* New York, Pantheon, 1955.

Index

T

U

V

W

□□□